Crafting

Transforming Materials
& the Maker

Crafting

Transforming Materials
& the Maker

Radically Redefining Learning

HANDS on PRESS

Transforming through Crafting

How traditional Crafts and practical skills can enhance Education

Bernard Graves & Co Authors
Editor – Jonathan Code

Produced by Hands on Press Association

Aboriginal Hand cave painting – Grampian Mountains. Australia

First published 2019

Published by Hands on Press Association and under licence by

www.selfpublishingpartnership.co.uk

ISBN printed book: 978-1-83952-026-6

Cover design by Kevin Rylands
Front cover illustration: *Transformation – Forged by Fire*
by Bernard Graves & Matthew Graves
Internal design by Jenny Watson Design
Illustrations & art work: Kamar Finn
Icons, diagrams & logo: Axel Keim, Jenny Smith, Matthew Graves
Hands on Press editor: Jonathan Code
Illustration & picture editor: Matthew Graves

This book is printed on FSC certified paper

Printed and bound in the UK

Crafting – Transforming Materials & the Maker

This book is a compilation of chapters written by a number of authors whose texts arise out of their professional practice and first-hand experience of teaching a variety of practical crafts. This book was the initiative of Bernard Graves, founder of Pyrites – Living & Learning with Nature, an educational initiative that promotes and facilitates Practical Skills Education in Schools & Practical Skills Teacher Training Courses throughout the UK and worldwide. Bernard is an experienced traditional craft practitioner and tutor, both with children and adults, facilitating workshops in practical skills and activities combining ancient and contemporary technologies as a means to access vital areas of experience and learning.

This book is co-authored by:
(ordered by chapter)

Bernard Graves – Craft Practitioner & Trainer
Johannes Steuck – Sculptor and Artist
Simon Gillman – Outdoor Educator
Frances Graves – Felting Craft Tutor
Jeannie Ireland – Leather Work Tutor
Lucy Meikle – Willow Basket Tutor
Richard Turley – Green Woodwork Tutor
Sue Harker – Potter and Ceramicist
Arian Leljak – Blacksmith Tutor
Jonathan Code – Adult Educator
Martin Levien – Craft Practitioner and Tutor
Jo Clark – Outdoor Education Practitioner and Tutor
Hattie Duke – Outdoor Education Tutor
John Lawry – Outdoor Education Tutor
Aonghus Gordon – Founder & Executive Chair Ruskin Mill Trust

Authors' biographies can be found at the end of the book

'Nimble fingers beget nimble minds'

Dedication

For all the makers – young and old

'The brain discovers what the fingers explore… if we don't use our fingers, if in childhood we become "finger blind", the rich network of nerves is impoverished – this represents a huge loss to the brain, and thwarts the individual's all round development… and their aesthetic and creative powers'
Matti Bergstrom[1]

'Strike whilst the iron is hot'

Crafting

Transforming Materials and the Maker

Book Sections

T his book is written by a number of different authors and, although edited carefully so as to have a coherent structure and content, the separate chapters stand on their own merit. Therefore a reader may wish to begin reading this book at any chapter. The use of 'she' in some chapters is intended to refer to either gender.

Bernard Graves

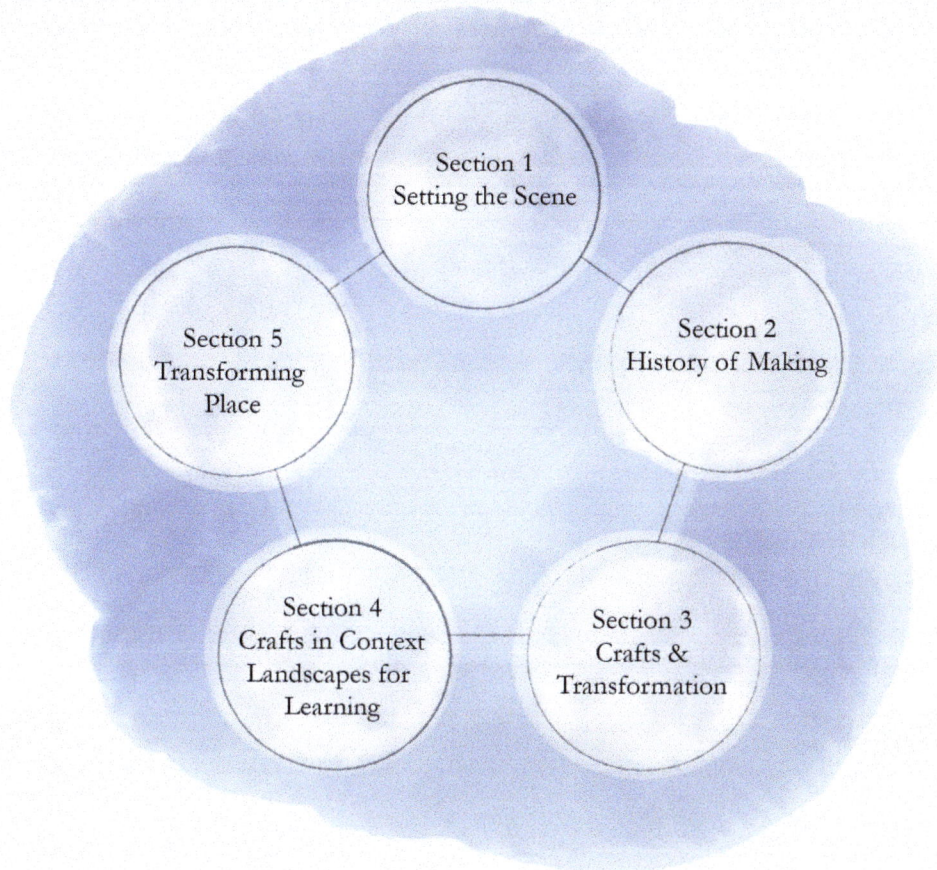

Section 1
Setting the Scene

Section 2
History of Making

Section 3
Crafts &
Transformation

Section 4
Crafts in Context
Landscapes for
Learning

Section 5
Transforming
Place

Contents

Foreword

It is a wonderful achievement to see this book in print. Congratulations to Bernard and his colleagues, the craftsmen and women who teach in schools and who have worked with such generosity and commitment in this endeavour.

The Hiram Trust is delighted to have supported the publication of *Crafting: Transforming Materials & the Maker*.

The original objective of The Hiram Trust in the early 1990s was to support teachers in Rudolf Steiner schools, in a renewal of practical work in their Upper Schools as an antidote to the increasing focus on exams and academic work. In this we were inspired by a similar movement unfolding in Holland, and especially helped by Wim Moleman, who was an Advisor working with the Rudolf Steiner schools in England.

Although handwork was always an essential aspect throughout the Waldorf curriculum, and Rudolf Steiner[2] had often indicated the importance of educating our hands[3] the need for a more practical application in science and handwork seemed to be needed in the Upper and Lower schools. This also meets the contemporary interest in environmentalism and care for the planet.

The support The Hiram Trust offered included visits to schools to do a Site Survey with pupils in their own school grounds, to see how these grounds could be used to get, or grow, the raw materials needed for craft work directly from nature: for example, digging a clay pit, or planting dye plants for dying fleece and wool and paper, or planting a hedgerow for harvesting materials for basketwork.

This approach was successfully innovated by Aonghus Gordon, a Trustee of The Hiram Trust, at Ruskin Mill College in Nailsworth. This unique approach was to take young people into the landscape to access the materials they needed, giving them thereby the opportunity to understand what nature provides and how their work with these materials can transform them into useful objects.

The work of The Hiram Trust continued, with an annual Summer Conference for Waldorf teachers, and with Bernard Graves as its Director, until 2006.

The Hiram Trust had also intended to publish a book under the title *The Outdoor Classroom*, as a last gift to teachers before it closed, but the project was never completed. Now, through the dedication of Bernard and the collaboration of his colleagues, *Crafting: Transforming Materials & the Maker* is published as a practical guide to inspire teachers to bring the wisdom of learning through working with materials sourced from the landscape, and make it available to all pupils in the school.

This gives me the opportunity to recognise the encouragement and support from many teachers, including Catherine Cardon, Martin Levien, Roy Allen, Martin Rawson, and the generosity of Ian Tomlin, who gave us funding to start the Trust. We are also indebted to Bernard and Francis and the Pyrites initiative – *Living & Learning with Nature* – for carrying this valuable work to all corners of the world.

I wish for all those who read and use this book to enjoy rewarding experiences with their students.

Sarah Brook
Trustee of The Hiram Trust

PROLOGUE

The Blacksmith
and The Acorn:
Life-changing events

Bernard Graves

The title of this book, *Crafting: Transforming Materials & the Maker,* says it all. Its contents are the fruits of a unique collaboration between craftsmen and craftswomen who share a passion for teaching a variety of practical skills activities in an equally varied range of educational settings. We have worked together to create this book as a celebration of the transformative potential of engaging with materials and with making.

Transformational

As co-authors of this book, we have not set out to suggest an alternative school curriculum, or another recipe for teaching, but rather to illustrate how a variety of *practical skills* and *craft activities* can be incorporated into existing curricula. We strongly believe that once the basic principles and values of what constitutes practical skills, or *hands-on learning*, are absorbed, courage should be taken to develop your own practical skills activities. Essentially, any curriculum that we develop should be suited to – and situated in – specific environments and available resources.

This book sets out to make the case for *crafting* in both the practical sense of '*making craft*' as well as by drawing attention to those often overlooked, but extremely important, aspects of making which involve the '*transformation of the maker*'.

Throughout history humankind has created objects to help make sense of the world – this was the origin of all craft objects. By teaching crafts in schools, young people can be reconnected to these vital resources, at a time when the busy modern world increasingly distances them from experience as '*makers*' – creators with materials sourced from nature, but also makers of *meaning*. This book gives detailed support for the value of craft teaching and shares the experiences of teachers who have spent their lives dedicated to understanding and developing the teaching of craft.

Indications are given, in *Section One* of the book, as to how to think about hands-on learning in the context of educational theory and contemporary discussions about the aims of education. A history of art and craft, and their place in human development (*cultural and individual*), is the focus of *Section Two*. The transformative nature of craft – both for the materials that are transformed and for the individual engaged in *crafting* is addressed in *Section Three*. Finally, as the *context* for learning is brought to the fore when practical skills education is put into practice, several chapters of the book are dedicated to *landscapes for learning* in *Section Four* and *Transforming Place* in *Section Five*.

As this book arises from insights and experiences gained over many years of hands-on teaching and learning, the perspectives presented by its authors are often of a very personal nature. And this is, in fact, where the book starts. As the convener of this book on *crafting* I would like to begin with a window into my own biography and what led me to devote my educational work to practical and hands-on learning.

My 'acorn' moments

I have come to refer to two significant, life-changing experiences as my 'acorn' moments – instances of profound personal awakening. The first of these 'acorn' or 'eureka' moments occurred when I was a child watching the village blacksmith at work. The second occurred much later in my life – during a period in my career when I was working as a conventional class teacher. Both of these experiences warrant an explanation at the outset of this book, as they will hopefully help to make clear what has inspired its creation and what are its aims.

Schoolboy days

I can still remember growing up in the 1950s and 60s in a world that was a very different place from the one we now live in. Society had yet to enter the digital age and to be confronted with, as we are today, our carbon footprint.

My childhood experiences of school and provincial rural life in and around the south-east English counties provided me with a rich tapestry of memories that I could call upon in later life when contemplating the relevance of traditional practical skills and craft practices. I had the good fortune to witness, and be part of, a number of these in my formative primary school years.

I attended the Catholic primary school of St Augustine in the town of Tunbridge Wells, Kent. Although my childhood memories of school are few and far between, I do recall quite vividly arriving in the school playground for my first day in school. Being in the first class, all

My two acorn moments

of us new and anxious children were somewhat overwhelmed by the formality and regimented style of this occasion. The headmaster, though he was my uncle, gave me no special recognition or accommodation on that day, nor on any of the schooldays to follow. It was his custom to give a welcoming homily to all of the classes and teachers, dutifully lined up in class rows.

The new class of children had no idea, of course, how to form an orderly line. The smallest child was meant to stand at the front of the row, and all the rest of us were meant to line up in order of height. We were constantly shuffled around by an elderly spinster teacher called Miss Sweetman – though I have to say that for us children she was far from sweet and was rather more 'bittersweet' in our experience.

Once we had been formally lined up to Miss Sweetman's satisfaction, we were expected to introduce ourselves one by one, by saying out loud our name and date of birth. It was the smallest child at the front of the queue that had to begin, followed by the child behind and so on. How lucky it was for me that there were half a dozen children in front of me! Although I knew my name, I can still recall the anguish and trepidation of having to call it out loudly and to say – correctly! – my date of birth. When it came to my turn, I blurted out (for fear of embarrassment), 'Bernard Graves the tooth of May'. More than a few chuckles and laughter ensued from children in the neighbouring rows. This ordeal was my initiation into the schoolboy phase of my childhood.

Our classroom was a square box, dimly lit and sparsely furnished, with simple writing desks all lined up in neat, narrow rows. Up-and-down these rows Miss Sweetman would sometimes march to get to a particular child quickly. At other times she would meander up and down between the desks, looking over our shoulders as we tried to complete the tasks she had given us.

The teacher's desk was set squarely at the front of the classroom. In the centre of the wall space behind the desk was a well-used blackboard and easel with a ruler hanging off of it by a piece of string. Later we were to experience that this ruler was not used so much for drawing lines on the blackboard but as an instrument to 'rule and correct' those children that she judged needed 'bringing back into line'. Or it was used to threaten us when we stumbled on some recall task that she had demanded of us. Much of our learning was by repetition and what we came to refer to as 'learning by Rot'.

Classes at the school were divided into four groups: A, B, C & D. The A group consisted of the brightest children in the class, while the D Group was reserved for those sometimes labelled as 'dunces'. I soon found myself placed in the D group.

Miss Sweetman ascertained which group we would be placed in by subjecting us all to various tests in numbers and letters. As I recall, every day started with either reciting the times tables or spelling and grammar – none of which I was good at. Letters and words on a page were as alien to me as the script of Arabic or Chinese is today. I had no choice but to attempt to learn everything we were expected to know by heart, a habit that persisted throughout my schooldays. There were limits to this approach, however, and so I gradually fell increasingly far behind the others. Schools, at that time, were not familiar with what educational psychologists came in time to recognise as dyslexia – a difficulty processing words and text, and a condition unrelated to levels of intelligence. Instead, my academic challenges and learning difficulties went unacknowledged – and I was allocated to the D group.

Later in my professional career as a teacher, I realised that it is just those children who suffer from learning difficulties that respond particularly well, and even show great aptitude, skill and creativity when engaged in practical skills activities.

Village smithy – the first 'acorn' event

As it happened, my grandfather was a retired school headmaster living not far away in the village of Wadhurst, Sussex. As soon as I was old enough to travel unaccompanied on the bus, arrangements were made for me to make my way to my grandparents' house for a weekly extra lesson and coaching in reading from *Janet and John* readers.

Although I found the lessons tedious, I lived for the freedom that I had after lessons to play and explore the local village, with its working village blacksmith and granary. The anticipation of these visits sustained me throughout the school week. As the blacksmith workshop was on the way to my grandparents' house, I would come to it first as I made my way through the village. I can still vividly recall my first encounters with the burly blacksmith.

For several weeks, I passed the workshop with its large barn doors always closed. I would warily pass by the big workhorses standing outside waiting patiently to be shod. I smelled the pungent smell of burning hoof and heard the rhythmic beating on the anvil of the master as he worked the new set of shoes. All these impressions and experiences engendered in me excitement and a longing to know what was happening behind those large, closed doors. I sometimes stood secretively outside the workshop for considerable lengths of time, trying to guess what was going on inside – for I had never seen a blacksmith at work.

One day, when making my usual stop outside the smithy, I found that the barn doors were slightly ajar, just enough for me to look inside. I plucked up my courage and poked my head through the gap between the two doors. There I saw a sight like nothing I had seen before. Amidst the glow of the fiery hearth and the wafting smoke, the blacksmith stood with his back to me, stripped to his waist and running with beads of sweat. To my childish imagination (I was only nine at the time) the blacksmith performed a kind of dance between the hearth and the anvil. A musical accompaniment was provided by the rhythmic tapping of the horseshoe he was fashioning and the secondary taps on the anvil between the shaping strokes. I was to learn

The village Smithy – a mighty and strong man was he…

later that these secondary taps are necessary to help sustain a protracted rhythm over hours of hammering.

The symphony of sounds and smells and the dervish dancing of the blacksmith had a dramatic effect upon me. My childish consciousness was altered. I became mesmerised by the blacksmith's art. I do not know how long these spells of enchantment lasted but I know that I was deeply fascinated and even captivated by the skilful movements of the blacksmith.

Later in life, these childhood experiences and memories would be there for me to draw on while teaching blacksmithing to children. I have never stopped striving to understand the powerful effect that repetitive craft movements have on those engaged with them, as well as on those looking on – as they did for me in that village smithy when I was nine.

I mention these fond childhood memories not only for their being indicative of a very different era – the tail end of which I was fortunate to be part – but because I am deeply interested and concerned about where children today can have such real-life, valuable experiences.

Although I did not take up a life of craft and making until after my second most informative experience, my childhood experiences of the blacksmith's workshop were to prove to be powerfully formative, and they changed my life direction and career.

Teaching – The second 'acorn' event

My second life changing, 'acorn' moment occurred in my mid-thirties, and it was very sudden and dramatic.

By this time, I was pursuing a career as a teacher in a special education school. Like most classroom teachers, I relied upon life's experiences for my lesson preparations, topped up by facts and information gleaned from books – there was no Wikipedia back then.

It was during a botany lesson that the second 'acorn' moment happened. I was holding between my right forefinger and thumb an acorn. I was using the acorn as an example of nature's potentiality and the miracle of nature's ability to produce (albeit in many years) a magnificent, giant oak tree from a relatively small seed. As I spoke, the class of children before me receded into the distance and the acorn between my fingers appeared to grow large. In that moment I became poignantly aware of my 'not-knowing', for I had never planted an acorn, never watered and nurtured one or watched one grow. How could I know anything about the miracles and science of nature's unfolding?

This moment was one of self-realisation and a feeling of how inadequate I been, not only as a teacher but as a human being. This moment proved to be cathartic, and it was a turning point in my life and career. I stopped teaching immediately, and after a time of complete disillusionment as to what I wanted to do, I found myself working on a neighbouring farm mucking out the cattle stalls. This proved to be very beneficial and helped me realise a new direction in my life and work.

It took some years before I had the confidence to return to classroom teaching, and I was only able to do so after pursuing a career in various practical skills and traditional crafts. Having tried my hand at various materials and processes, I found that working with willow was my favourite. I embarked on developing and teaching traditional willow basket-making to senior pupils and adults. It was during these years of coaching a variety of people, some with special

The Oak tree – Still bearing fruit in old age…

Modern and traditional tools – the mouse and the hammer

educational requirements, that I began to realise the potential therapeutic and educational value that traditional crafts could provide.

During the years that followed I began to develop crafts and educational programmes as an alternative to the conventional and largely sedentary-based learning that occurred in the confines of the indoor classroom. I also encouraged a growing number of colleagues in this approach to education, and gradually the idea for the *outdoor classroom* and an integrated practical skill curriculum started to emerge.

Along with our work in developing and imparting practical skills, I realised that we would have to put forward valid and persuasive arguments for this approach to education if we were to be successful in getting schools to agree to incorporate a variety of practical skills activities into their curricula.

This work started to develop and deepen at the same time that various publications began to appear by a number of educationalists who were, from their own perspectives, giving validation to an experiential and practical approach to learning. These included the works of authors such as Prof Frank Wilson MD[4], Dr Matti Bergstrom[5], and writer, activist and environmental educator David Orr[6]. The fundamental premise of these authors for adopting an experiential approach to learning is based on the following:

'Basic education is a process of learning through doing. It recognises the organic connection between the fingers, the senses, and the mind, and the greater vitality and retentiveness of knowledge that is gained by doing and making things than by merely reading books or listening to lectures.' Wilfred Wellock[7] – Ghandi as a Social revolutionary

After all, it could be argued that an experiential approach to learning is the oldest and most tried approach known to humankind, and it has served us well.

In the field of education today, we are required to be highly accountable, to demonstrate and measure the smallest increments of learning and progress possible – but this approach is questionable, particularly if it seen as the *only* valid approach. It is a system that far too often fails to generate enthusiasm and inspirational teaching. In the United Kingdom it is a fact that we live in what has been described as an increasingly *de-skilled* society, and there are concerns that our school curricula should include a balance of practical subjects and activities that have fallen off the curriculum in recent years due to political and educational directives.

> *'85% of primary school children can use a computer keyboard. Only half that number can chop carrots and peel potatoes.' Suzi Leather, 'RSA Focus on Food Campaign'*[8]

It is through doing the simplest of domestic tasks – such as knitting, sawing and splitting wood, and forging a poker – that children can develop dexterous manual skills as well as a practical intelligence that neurological science informs us is necessary for developing *creative* intelligence.

Through industrialisation the hand tool has been replaced with the keyboard, mouse and computer screen. Crafting for a livelihood may, in some regards, belong to the past but due to a variety of challenges facing educators today we may well be coming round to realising that making is an essential human capacity and spiritual necessity, and it needs to be part of our schooling. In the moment of making we can have a full sense of who we are and where we are going – it affords us confirmation of ourselves as part of the continuum of civilisation.

The inspiration for this book

As stated at the outset, this book is co-authored by a group of professional, practical skills educators who are active in a variety of settings and who have come together to pool their experiences, knowledge and teaching insights. We have crafted this book to be both inspirational and informative, and to be a resource for practical skill teachers and potential craft practitioners. We are all acutely aware of the need for information and ideas to support those wishing to provide a hands-on learning approach to education – be that in a formal school or among the increasing numbers of parents who have elected to home-school their children.

The initiative for this book is also a response to the often unspoken voice of children who yearn for practical skills and knowledge, and who wish to experience through their own engagement 'where things come from and how they are made'.

Many of us also had this type of question, and remember that our childhood education often failed in practically satisfying and answering every child's inherent inquisitiveness and potential creativity. *Crafting: Transforming Materials & the Maker* recognises and endorses the quality and the values of learning fostered through hands-on activities, and hopefully inspires you with the insights and the means – in whatever field of education you are currently engaged – to give it a go!

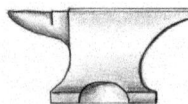

SECTION ONE

SETTING THE SCENE

I n this section we explore the meaning of education – 'what is education for?'
We asked ourselves this question at the outset of the project and each of the authors
suggested an answer from their own point of view and experience as an educator.

Johannes Steuck has compiled our responses into an opening chapter – and added
some tales to capture and creatively share our musings on this crucial question.

Simon Gilman follows this opening chapter with an overview of some of the challenges we
see in how education is approached today and what educators might consider to bring a more
hands-on and human centred approach to teaching and learning.

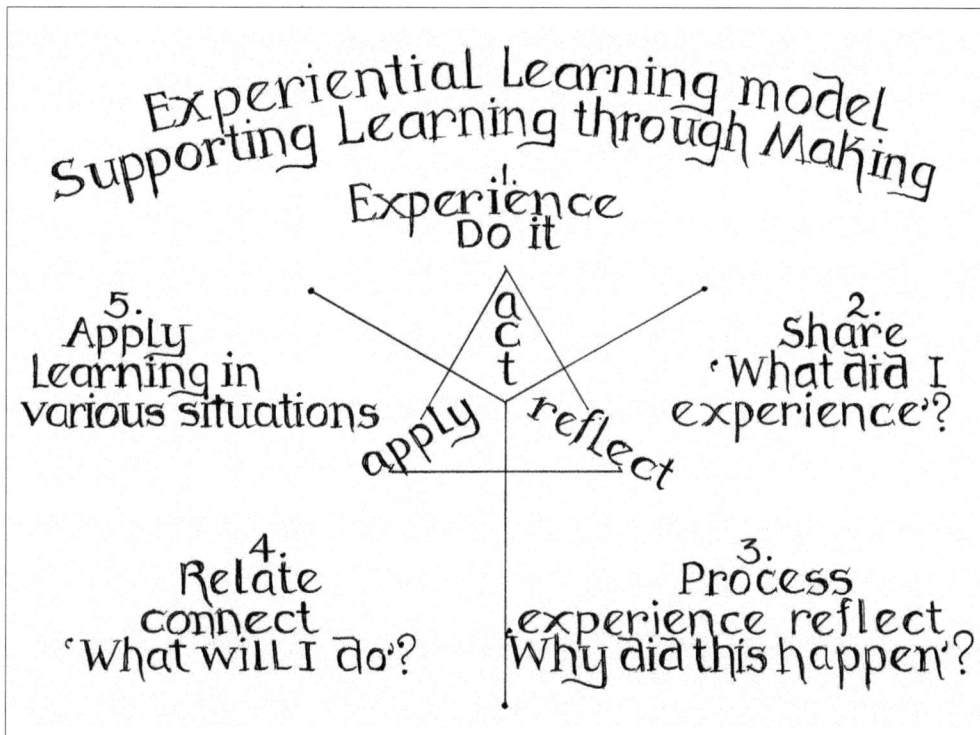

Experiential learning model

CHAPTER 1

Meaning & Making

Johannes Steuck

This is a book about education and the making of meaning. It is about creating respect for each other, about deepening our connection with – and understanding for – the natural world. It approaches education as a process of restoring and fostering health, balance and well-being in children, in adolescents and in our adult years. The authors of this book invite you to see nature as an integral part of ourselves, and do so by inviting you to discover what is possible by working with natural materials and processes. We are dedicated to supporting learners both young and old to discover their role and responsibility as stewards and guardians of the future, to nurture a sense of purpose, and to feel empowered to find solutions to the challenges that face our Earth at this time.

In the pages that follow we want to re-kindle questions of the 'why', 'what', 'how' and 'who' of the process of learning. Rather than merely asking about 'what' we should teach, we see a much more fundamental question in asking: what is learning *for*?

Where can we turn to for some insight into this question?

Much wisdom is transmitted through traditional tales. They exist as a kind of underground stream, flowing beneath the 'stone and concrete' of contemporary culture. Transmitted aurally to children, they are understood intuitively rather than rationally. Many stories unfold in a threefold manner; three tasks, three brothers, three skills. In the '*Three Brothers Stories*' the third and youngest brother is often neglected, left behind. He's the simpleton, the Ivan Ashblower, eating crusts that are flung to him and snoozing by the stove while his two clever, elder brothers toil and sweat. The Gypsy story *Dilino and the Devil* is a classic tale of this kind[9].

Dilino and the Devil

Somewhere in the remote wildernesses of Eastern Europe there live a family of gypsies. They scratch a miserable living by making charcoal and selling it to the town-dwellers nearby. Hard times come for the charcoal-burners and Dilino, the not-so-clever one, is forced to leave his cosy corner in the hut and do his bit in the forest. Dilino wanders about cluelessly, swinging his axe and sack, and towards evening starts hacking away at an old hollow tree. As chance would have it, this very hollow tree is the temporary residence of a devil who has been booted out of hell for doing something good. The devil has to remain holed up in the tree for seven years and, if he can do that, he will be pardoned and allowed to return to hell. Dilino's axe strokes terrify the devil. Time's not up yet and if his tree is destroyed, he stands no chance of ever going home. The devil immediately strikes a deal with Dilino, and the boy goes home with lumps of charcoal that are half solid gold. Now at last the gypsies are 'in the clover' and build themselves slick mansions. The helter-skelter process of life begins and Dilino can no longer doze away his time. Forced to consider wedlock, he reluctantly opts for the highest prize – a princess. Dilino's father is sent to broker the marriage, but is first rendered invulnerable by a little magic water supplied by the intimidated devil in the hollow tree. It is a good thing too, as they don't think much of Dilino's father at the palace. They set the dogs on the ragged, dirty old man. Canines have a healthy instinct for what's right and wrong, however, and they soon slink away, whining, with their tails between their legs. The king then tries blasting the old man with canon. Even the 12-pounder doesn't seem to ruffle the old charcoal burner's hair. Terrified and deeply impressed, the king agrees to the match. Meanwhile, Dilino receives his third and final 'gift' from the devil, a golden acorn that, when placed in the mouth, will magically procure everything that Dilino could not possibly have thought out, or indeed provided himself: sumptuous clothes, exquisite food, a carriage and coal black, dashing horses. The princess is suitably besotted and all goes well until, on the way home, Dilino chokes on the acorn. The princess thumps his back vigorously and the golden acorn pops out of the carriage window and rolls into the dust. In that instant the devil appears in a swirl of sulphur, scoops up the acorn and, laughing, hotfoots it back to hell. His seven years of exile are up. Something extraordinary has happened to Dilino; he is no longer a nitwit and becomes instead a successful shoemaker. And what of his wife the princess? She loves him, even though he ends up not being the super-rich foreign potentate she thought him to be at first.

Now, what is it that Dilino has that his two able-bodied and clever brothers don't? He's got luck, but perhaps there's something else too. *Potential.* His brothers are skilled charcoal burners, that's all they are and that's probably all they'll ever be. Dilino can't do anything to begin with, but with the devil's help, anything is possible.

If we consider this story from an archetypal perspective, we could say that the clever brothers, Dilino, and indeed all the characters in the story are in fact one. From this point of view, what is being imagined in this tale is the *realisation of the potential* within each and every one of us: that which has been set-aside, neglected, perhaps even derided or forgotten. Dilino receives three 'gifts'; let's take a closer look at them and perhaps 'crack' their significance.

The first is the charcoal that is half gold. One could say that this solves the 'material question' – Dilino, and indeed his entire family, have no further worries. What does that mean? It means that they are 'well anchored in the world', the basis for all that might follow has been laid down. The invulnerable water that the father is anointed with saves him from annihilation, but is perhaps also something else: a self-sufficient 'emotional completeness' that is ready to acquire a

Dilino the charcoal maker at work

Dilino – the charcoal maker

princess on his son's behalf. As for the acorn which completes the triad, this is the capacity of thought, which gives self-awareness and independence.

This book seeks to address the hidden potential of the human being. A potential that, all too often, is left snoozing behind the stove, a potential that needs above all else to be developed, given the chance to grow and expand.

Hands-on learning

Educating through the hands offers an opportunity to unfold potential. Tools and making handcrafted items are not merely the means of changing the world, they also change the relationship of the maker with that world, the relationship she has with others and, significantly, the relationship she has to herself.

Modern archaeology seeks for early evidence of humanity in three areas of activity: i) artistic expression, ii) religious practice and iii) tool making. These areas, it could be argued, take equal precedence in defining our humanity. The pierced shell, pollen in the grave of Neanderthal man and the chipped flint all testify to something uniquely human – the ability to shape, modify and affect the surrounding world.

Unlike animals, whose bodies are highly specialised, humans are born naked, vulnerable and at the beginning of a long road of learning. We exist as creative and destructive *beings-in-potential*, and in order to survive and make our home on earth, we need to develop tools and technology.

A study of so-called primitive cultures has revealed that tools originally had an artistic, ritualistic and functional dimension. They separated humans from the great 'other', the cosmos and nature, but were also a means of tapping into it. So powerful was this sense of the appropriate ritualistic function of a tool, that taboos were laid down to limit new invention and inappropriate use. Here, too, we can turn to the wisdom of stories to understand this important aspect of tool making, and tool use.

There is a wonderful story in Credo Mutwa's, *Indaba my Children*[10], a kind of alternative shaman's history of Africa. A young man called Malinge has invented a deadly and efficient new snare for catching antelope. He is very pleased with himself.

The tribal leader, a goddess called Marimba, is not. Malinge has broken out of the mode of permitted archetypes and forfeited his life. This is highly significant, for what has been broken – interrupted – by Malinge's new invention is the 'blessing of the ancestors', a magical current that flows from the remote past into the present, imbuing it with power and integrity.

Mere mortals cannot simply invent things; their task is to follow the old time-hallowed forms faithfully and without deviation. The goddess then does something extraordinary – she transforms the lethal new snare into a musical instrument, into a Marimba or thumb harp. The transgressive energy poured into the new snare is redeemed through music.

Two other transformations are credited to Marimba: an old mortar is made into the first drum and a deadly Masai bow into a *makweyana* or bow-harp.

What can these stories tell us? They can tell us that everything has its own momentum, an energy that cannot simply be stopped but that somehow needs to fulfil itself. The snare, the broken mortar and the bow cannot just be un-made, they are transfigured; their 'intention' is cleansed, re-aligned.

We take it very much for granted that each new invention or technical development is, if not benign, then at the very least inevitable. Progress strides ahead. To question or indeed resist innovation carries the risk of being left behind, or at worst being branded a luddite. Inventiveness is a limitless resource and unless we can truly develop some sense of our human potential, humanise our potential, we will give rise to conditions and states of being that are not compatible with being human. If the wise 'inner Marimba' does not intervene, we may easily soon find ourselves in a place we had no intention of ever reaching.

Our civilisation could be said to be in a state of crisis: we face environmental degradation, pollution, species extinction, poverty, starvation, continual warfare and climate change, to name

African 'makweyana' – bow harp

but a few. Perhaps these are the outer manifestations of an ailing culture. It is as if we have left ourselves behind.

Our civilisation has lost touch with the potential synergies of the three great pillars of culture: Science, Art and Religion. Already drifting apart in the Renaissance, these have further separated and fragmented in modern times. Has Science, natural spawn of philosophy and whose watchword should perhaps be 'Truth', become ever more susceptible to commercial interests? Has Art, which should perhaps weave experience into 'Beauty', become self-obsessed, lost in a hall of mirrors? And has Religion, whose business should perhaps be to nurture 'Goodness' become an ineffectual club or a platform for prejudice?

There are elements in our society that tend towards a kind of reductive fundamentalism, which denigrates the human being to the status of a 'machine' and consciousness to that of a 'computer'. There is no purpose or meaning to life except the egotistical striving for the three Ps – Power, Pleasure and Plenty.

The only way out of this dangerous quagmire is to search for *meaning*. Meaning is intimately bound up with purpose and identity. Is it because we have forgotten who we are, that we cannot evolve into what we might become?

> *'I believe that our central problem is that we do not know what or who a human being really is'*
> *Georg Kuhlewind, From Normal to Healthy*[11]

There's a great little Sufi riddle that defines the challenge of our contemporary predicament perfectly. A man has to take a wolf, a goat and a cabbage across a stream by boat. He can only take

The ferryman's dilemma

one at a time. If he ferries the wolf and leaves the goat and the cabbage, the former will consume the latter. If he takes the goat and leaves the wolf and the cabbage, his next trip will inevitably lead to disaster. What is he to do? It seems to be an impossible task! The answer of course is always to have one or other in the boat with him, and to make four, rather than three trips. We must not be lazy; we must protect the three things from each other. And what are these three things that we must preserve and nurture? They are intelligence, emotion and motivation. In our one-sided world, the wolf of our intelligence is forever voraciously consuming the goat of our emotions, and our feeling goat is nibbling away at the deeply asleep, self-enclosed cabbage of our will.

There are many hopeful signs of change, green shoots are springing up everywhere. Yet the voracious wolf of a one-sided intellect still holds sway, and our outmoded western style classroom-based education seems to be in an ongoing state of crisis. In spite of good intentions, increasing numbers of children are being left behind.

The vast reservoir of human potential is only dipped into with a runcible spoon. If we are honest, we need to revise education completely. Education needs to be freed from the vested interests of politics and economics and address the needs of the 'whole human being'. The challenges we face to *re-think* and *re-do* education – to fundamentally *re-found* schools to meet the pedagogical needs of children today and of society tomorrow – have already been expressed by such enlightened educationalists as Prof David Orr from America. Orr wrote at the end of the twentieth century:

> *'Students in the next century will need to know how to create a civilisation that runs on sunlight, conserves energy, preserves biodiversity, protects soils and forests, develops sustainable local economies and restores the damage inflicted on the earth. In order to achieve such ecological education, we need to transform schools and universities'*[12]

This book advocates the urgent need to transform education. It invites us to renew our attention to the unique capacities of our hands, hands that engage in rhythmic craft processes, hands that become skilled and transfer their instinctive knowing to the totality of our being. Consciously re-discovering the craft gestures, which are as old as mankind, will re-establish our humanity and reconnect us to living nature. A *hands-on* approach to education can contribute to the rediscovery of *meaning* in education and in modern life. Meaning is not something that can be taught or formulated. Meaning-making is a science, an art and a sacred practice. It is the work of the hand, the head and the heart.

On reading the following chapters, we invite you to consider the 'meaning of making' as described by the different craft makers and the transformative journey to be had at the hand of Crafting.

'Charcoal that is half gold…'

CHAPTER 2

Pedagogical Approaches

Simon Gillman

Hands-on Learning – historical and contemporary attitudes to education

In this chapter we will examine some historical and contemporary attitudes to education and offer a point of view on what school is *for*. We also consider what role there might be for hands-on learning in education today, as this is a vast subject worthy of a great deal more research and discussion than it usually receives. This focus will lead us into some of the conflicts that can arise between different educational objectives. The main aim of this short chapter is, however, to provide a rationale for practical and experiential learning – it does not attempt a comprehensive review of this theme but will rather serve to set the scene for the various contributions that follow.

All of the authors of this book are educators and craftspeople/practitioners in their own right, many with intimate experience and connections with Steiner Waldorf education. We do not

Victorian school model

intend to use this space to advocate exclusively this approach to education, however, but rather wish to celebrate any colleagues pursuing *hands-on learning* with children in whatever context they are working. Steiner Waldorf education does, nonetheless, take crafts and outdoor work seriously, and in this spirit a few comments on Waldorf pedagogy will be offered to give context for the fostering of hands-on learning in education, where many of us have had direct experience.

School league tables and targets

In the current educational landscape of the United Kingdom it is very difficult to step back from the abstractions of school *league tables*, competitive exam results and the narrow approach of holding teachers *accountable* for the success (or otherwise) of their pupils so as to see what education is actually about. Similar issues confront concerned educators in many parts of the globe.

We feel strongly that a good deal of current educational debate focuses too narrowly on exam results as a selection tool for higher education and the path to a 'good' career. Too often the 'losers' and dropouts of this educational paradigm have to struggle to find their way at each stage. We have witnessed this competitive dynamic extending into relationships between pupils, between schools, in national and international comparisons, usually accompanied by the fear of falling behind in the race to produce 'world class' students who will drive the economy forwards. This dynamic has tended to support a goal of academic excellence, epitomised perhaps by the university professor as the quintessence of 'achieved' learning and wisdom, but it has failed to acknowledge the great diversity of learning styles, approaches and opportunities available when academic success is not taken as the sole or dominant focus of education.

We are acutely aware that schools have historically found the integration of practical activities difficult, and have tended to reserve them for those students who are not the winners in the academic races. However, we have seen time and again that it is often *craft* or *land-based learning* which creates meaning and values for many learners, and highlights the potential role for artistic, social and creative learning in contemporary education.

Hands-on learning

Hands-on learning can strongly support the acquisition of life-long skills, in contrast to some aspects of academic work, where information is solely learned for an assessment and is often rapidly forgotten after the test or exam has been taken. An educational approach that embraces the practical and artistic spheres of life is, therefore, orientated towards the aim of enabling a more rounded development of the individual as a 'whole' person, rather than on an assessment of the sum of their knowledge and its perceived economic usefulness in the marketplace. This approach already creates a certain tension between specialism and a broad-based approach to learning, between finding the new elite to drive research and economic competition forwards and creating conditions for people to develop as creative individuals.

The rise of schooling that emphasises academic achievement arose historically with the goal of making pupils sufficiently literate and numerate to participate in an industrialising democratic society. Children needed to be equipped, it was decided, with the knowledge and information that society deemed to be necessary to share in its values and participate in its norms. Often determined by the government of the day, this 'official knowledge' has been (and is) open to abuse and the subject of much debate about what should be included or excluded from school curricula. This has had the result that curricula have a marked tendency to expand as time goes on and that there is a permanent climate of tinkering and change to content and approach.

It is easy to see some of the conflicts this goal of learning may have with academic work aimed at research for the future, or with the personal development aspects where a certain level of individual freedom has to be created for the young person to find his or her own values.

Standardisation

The model adopted for schools in the 19th and early 20th centuries can be described as an industrial one, akin to the factories that were transforming the social and economic landscapes at that time. One can see the factory model in the creation of special purpose-made buildings, often lacking in aesthetic value. These structures are functional (at best), often somewhat separate from the community, in which children are taught in rigidly age-determined cohorts. Alongside this industrialisation of education came the development of standardised curricula, designed to meet the perceived needs of society, with standardised outcomes for learning measured by competitive testing.

The top-down management systems employed in these schools also reflected the business forms of the time. They ascribed standards for behaviour that were demanded of the pupils and emphasised the importance of obedience backed by disciplinary sanctions. These elements of education epitomise industrialisation: standardised materials subject to a production process with standardised outcomes 'delivered' at the end. This system has affirmed the importance of academic-learning-as-education.

It established, as Ken Robinson pointed out in his famous TED talk:

'...the hierarchy of subjects that now reigns in every school system in the world, where maths, sciences and languages are at the top, passing through the humanities and down to the arts and crafts at the bottom. And in spite of the fact that pretty well all schools claiming to offer a broad-based curriculum, and the modern understanding of different needs or ways that children learn, this hierarchy continues unchanged'[13].

In spite of all the social and political changes that have swept the world in the last 150 years, this industrial model of the school-as-factory remains the dominant one in many countries around the world. In the present time, there is possibly an even tighter grip on education exercised by the academic stream than at any point since the early part of the 20th century.

Dissatisfaction and consequences

The degree of dissatisfaction with current educational approaches in the UK is reflected in the extraordinary numbers of teachers leaving the profession[14] with the recent declaration by education minister (2018) stating that there would be NO changes to curricula and testing, etc. for the remainder of that term of office, and the lamentable increase in mental health issues amongst children. There is increasing evidence that English children are amongst the least happy in the developed countries and that the inspection regime is one major cause of this.

Contemporary education is still predominantly head-based learning, done mainly sitting at desks or in front of screens, and retains a strong emphasis on finding the 'right' answers. Anyone who seriously questions this might like to look at the guidelines for marking the placement of colons and commas in recent tests for 10- to 11-year-olds.[15]

What price does this form of learning pay? The drivers for the system are 'standards'. It is notoriously difficult to generate any statistics or 'hard data' in education that allow pupils, schools and teachers to be compared in terms of their performance, except through standardised, graded testing. This creates the danger of the tail wagging the dog, with the need to create comparative statistics impacting on the learning process.

The Cambridge Review (the largest enquiry into Primary Education in the UK) suggested that

'...the pursuit of a very limited concept of standards has compromised children's legal entitlement to a broad and balanced education'[16]

and we suspect this situation has become worse since the report was published in 2010.

The obedience and discipline of the early mass schools have morphed into compliance with the key idea, both in terms of learning content and process. But passing tests is not equivalent to learning, holding a quantity of information is not knowledge, and the ability to manipulate that knowledge is not wisdom. Test and inspection regimes will tend naturally to over-emphasise a very narrow approach even to academic subjects, so where does that leave the arts and crafts?

Hands-on research

A growing body of research suggests that skilful hands are a prerequisite for an agile mind capable of engaging with complex information and able to construct meaning. In his fascinating book *The Hand,* Frank Wilson[17] examines this theme in the following way:

> *'Self-generated movement is the foundation of thought and willed action, the underlying mechanisms by which the physical and psychological coordinates of the self come into being' (1998 p.291)*

There is such a lot in this short quote, and our experience of the contribution of hands-on learning in education is very much in agreement with this statement. Increasingly, the work of neurologists is suggesting the same theme, i.e. that movement develops and strengthens connections between the brain and the nerve pathways around the whole body, and lays the foundations for intellectual work. The acquisition of the intentional gestures of the different crafts (explored at length by Bernard Graves in the next section), the exposure to experiences, activity and work in nature create lifelong links that fundamentally evoke human values in the young person. These include some that are in high demand in modern society: creativity, perseverance/resilience, grounded thinking, problem-solving capacities, social and moral qualities.

Key educational reformers – Pestalozzi, Rudolf Steiner and John Dewey

It is interesting to note that many early educators concerned with the philosophy that informed schooling tried to keep the *head, hands and heart* tri-unity integrated in the learning process. Johan Heinrich Pestalozzi (1746–1827), the Swiss reformer and educator, is one of the best known and most influential of these, and can serve as a good example. He was very concerned with the plight of the poor, who were often not educated at the time, and believed in the ability of every child to learn and their right to be educated. His work helped to establish education as an area of knowledge in its own right, but his concern was to develop a unified theory of education to enable people to live fulfilled lives. We could call this aim holistic:

> *The Johann Heinrich Pestalozzi approach to education aims to develop children into well-balanced and responsible adults by fostering their "Head, Heart and Hands" – that is, academic knowledge, moral and social awareness, and vocational skills.*[18]

There is an act of rebellion in his work, a response to existing schools' focus on texts and rote learning, which does not touch the whole person. In advocating this approach Pestalozzi was himself a fine role model, with his background as a clergyman, farmer and entrepreneur.

Pestalozzi's work inspired the German educator Friedrich Froebel, remembered mainly for the creation of kindergartens. Froebel also sought to encourage the creation of educational environments that involved practical work and the direct experience of working with materials. In France there is the more recent example of Celestin Freinet[19], whose work gave rise to a network of schools working with his methods. Amongst these principles we find the *pedagogy of work,* where pupils are encouraged to learn by making products, often in cooperative groups pursuing enquiry-based learning. There is also '*la method naturelle*' which emphasises the child's need to make her own authentic experiences as a basis for learning about life.

From America, the highly regarded work of John Dewey, whose theories gave rise to the concept of experiential education, where '*knowledge comes from the impressions made upon us by natural objects*' is well known. According to Dewey, the child needs to connect his learning to his personal experiences in order to create value and understand content. Art also has a major role to play for Dewey, as a process of enquiry and finding meaning in its own right.[20]

A full list of aspiring reformers would be lengthy and would need to include Krishnamurti and an increasing number of Montessori schools that have connections to land-based learning (see also *La Ferme des Enfants*, the influential work of Sophie Rabhi in France)[21].

So we can see that there have been many attempts, both theoretical and practical, to bring together the practical, artistic and intellectual streams of learning – streams that exist in every human being. We are also aware of many individual schools that have developed an identity connected with practical work, often in the private sector, but sometimes within the state system as well. These initiatives are often linked to insightful individuals with leadership roles in their schools; many wish to acknowledge the changing needs of society by providing individualised programmes or prioritising digital learning, or integrating bush craft or gardening.

Perhaps at this point we can insert a few comments about Steiner Waldorf education.

Instigated by Rudolf Steiner[22] in Stuttgart in 1919 with the founding of the original school, Steiner Waldorf education has grown into a worldwide network of over 1,000 schools. As with many of the other reformers previously mentioned, Steiner was concerned to educate the whole person, to unite the experience of learning with the heart, head and hands by putting the learning process in an artistic context. He differed from the other

Johann Heinrich Pestalozzi (1746–1827)

John Dewey (1859–1952)

Rudolf Steiner (1861–1925)

educators cited above in being highly specific about ways in which this unified approach can support the development of thinking, feeling and willing in the individual child.

Steiner developed a comprehensive picture of child development and a curriculum, activities and content centred on the idea of *age appropriateness*. The craft practitioners and contributors to this book acknowledge this pedagogical consideration in their work, though recognising that varying ability depends on the child's hitherto practical experience.

A crude, thumbnail sketch of Steiner's insights into basing education on a thorough understanding of child development can be seen in his recommendations for fostering free and imitative play as a key feature of learning in the first period of the child's life. There are parallels between Steiner and Piaget in these insights. For Steiner, *learning through doing* should predominate in the early years – the child making primary experiences of the real world by being physically active in maintaining indoor and outdoor spaces and by making them as beautiful as possible. Imitation is the creative self-activity of the child – one cannot force imitation! – and play is the springboard for activity, creativity and socialisation.

Between roughly the age of seven (or when physiologically the child is going through the change of teeth) and puberty, Steiner gives emphasis to a more teacher-led approach to the educational process. During this phase a strong emphasis on physical activity remains, and an artistic and social context is created for the introduction of literacy and numeracy. This allows learning to unfold more through the child's *feeling life* than through their intellect and abstract thought processes. The use of painting, colour, drawing, recitation, singing, music and craftwork gives depth and meaning to the learning process of each child, and the care and quality that can be brought to the learning process again represents the child's self-activity. The outcomes are not standard but are imprinted with the child's emerging individuality.

It is only after puberty (roughly 14 years of age) that a more intellectual, head-dominant approach is used in Steiner Waldorf education, but this sits alongside the active and artistic elements rather than replacing them. The aim at this phase remains that of uniting the three different domains for learning by the end of school. The intention is that this approach allows the child to have strong personal links with content so that her imagination, creativity and ability to work with others can express itself.

The Steiner Waldorf curriculum, which has developed further since Steiner's time, both guides and supports this process by being recapitulatory of human development, from oral traditions of storytelling, through Greece and Rome, and down to modern, digital times. The curious reader is directed to *Waldorf Education* by Martyn Rawson and Christopher Clouder for more – but very accessible – insights into this pedagogical approach[23].

Waldorf education – key pedagogical principles

It is the intention that manual skill and academic achievement are equally prized in Steiner Waldorf schools. Indeed it can be seen that crafts and practical projects have a strong and important place in the school, from the early years right through to school leaving age – they are taken seriously as front-line learning at school.

The teachers are fortunate to be offered curriculum time – though it is frequently under pressure with current inspection regimes – to develop a wide range of practical, outdoor and craft work, and related activities. The contribution of the crafts – *learning through making for human development* – as eloquently expressed by the authors of this book – is as valid now as it was in the 20th century. We recognise that crafts may not be an obvious or direct route into the world of work. However, the gestures and activity they engender have an enhanced meaning in our era, where so much time is spent looking at screens or in sedentary work or leisure.

In our age the disconnect between head and heart is reflected in the dizzying array of social problems that confront our society, and the disconnect between head and hands is mirrored by our knowledge of climate change and impending environmental collapse, and our collective refusal to take any real action to address it. Perhaps it is time to move consciously away from the industrial model for education; to teach *cooperation* rather than *competition*; to allow children to *reconnect with nature*, even if the majority of them are living in cities; to develop a new sense of *wonder and respect;* to allow *joy* back into learning and to push back the elements which bring *fear;* to allow pupils to construct meaning rather than drowning in information overload; to develop values rather than theories; to value consciousness rather than abstraction; and to have the right to try things out even at the cost of not getting it right first time round.

We believe that the land, craft and practical work contribute to all these areas and give rise to essential tools for modern people and modern living:

- clever hands, open hearts and grounded, flexible thinking;
- creativity, imagination and an aesthetic eye;
- respect and appreciation of the environment;
- co-operation, social inclusivity and responsibility.

We invite you to get your hands on!

SECTION TWO

A HISTORY OF MAKING:
Craft in the Light of Human Development

In the following chapters we consider the history of crafting and its significance for human development.

Johannes Steuck provides an overview – a 'big picture' account – of the relationship between art, craft and the religious or spiritual life, and how 'making' has informed this over several millennia.

Bernard Graves follows this chapter with an overview of the cultural significance of hand crafting, development of movement in humans and animals, and the craft Gestures as archetypal movements that contribute to healthy human development.

Spiral Stained Glass window Dallas, Texas, USA, 19 May 2008
The spiralling stained glass-windowed ceiling of the Thanksgiving Chapel recreates the Fibonacci sequence in Dallas

CHAPTER 3

Art and Craft: Origins

Johannes Steuck

I will say from the outset of this chapter that the overview of art and craft I will present will be far from complete and can only ever consist of fairly subjective and selected 'vignettes'. I have focused on European developments, not because I think them more important than those in other parts of the world but because they are particularly relevant to the considerations addressed in this book.

Until very recently the main criteria for assessing the evolution of humans and of culture seemed to focus on technical developments. Developments in brain-power (from this perspective) gave rise to technological innovation, which in turn made further increases in brain-power possible. There have been, however, some radical rethinks of this approach of late, not least the discovery of 'Neanderthal art' thought to be some 65,000 years old. Discovered in three locations in Spain – in La Pasiega, in Maltravieso and in Ardales – these sites pre-date the arrival of modern humans in Europe by about 20,000 years.

Art was long thought of as being a distinguishing feature of the more technically superior Homo Sapiens, whilst poor old Neanderthal was seen as a somewhat cloddish dead-end: big-boned, strong and hairy, and – although equipped with a slightly larger brain-pan than us – definitely on the slow side. What these recent discoveries seem to imply, however, is that art was there right from earliest times. It did not necessarily arise out of increased leisure time won through more efficient hunting techniques and the products of a superior technology, but out of an inner compulsion and probably one as focused as the need to make tools.

Evident also in those few ancient artistic remnants is another significant dimension, that of religion. Religion in this sense does not mean some kind of formalised institution but the intent of making sense of the mysterious universe and establishing a reciprocal relationship with it. It is my premise that we should unite all early forms of human innovation, be they technological, artistic or religious, as primary expressions of humanity. The difference between us and animals is not just that we make tools, but also that we paint, draw, make ornaments and bury our dead.

Technology, art and religion

We can therefore identify three 'strands' of human creativity that were at one time united; Technology, Art and Religion. Tools were functional (they had to be), artistic (they were well and beautifully made), and cultic – they had some ritual significance. One could argue that the act of tool-making itself, which separates the human from nature and other mammals, was an artistic and religious statement. Gradually, in the course of time, these three strands of human creative activity separated. This was probably due to the evolution of more complex and sophisticated forms of human culture, which entailed greater specialisation.

In Hans van der Stock's article 'The Spiritual Origin of Everyday Things'[24] he describes a process of secularisation; something starts by being an embodiment of an archetype, an altar or a

Cave painting – Vezere Valley, France

throne, and finishes as a table and a chair. According to this scheme of things, the primary table was an altar, and the food-stuffs offered upon it were sacrifices to the gods. A horizontal plane, a piece of 'earth', at first elevated above the ground to honour the gods, eventually is put to practical use and becomes a table. Even though there was this inevitable trend towards the functional, a direct link with the archetype had to be maintained. Thus, we have the creation of objects that are purely 'ceremonial' rather than useful.

The creation of the religious or ceremonial object entailed extra effort, time and ingenuity and was rewarded with high honours and status. In Aztec times the sculptor[25], commissioned to work on the holy images, was considered sacred. He left his family and lived a simple, austere life; food and drink were rationed, his entire purpose was dedicated to the service of the divine. On completion of his project he was loaded with gifts, feather ornaments and fine food. The space for making the sacred objects for the worship of the gods was a separate space, one isolated from the everyday, and the cultic objects themselves were the highest fruits of skill and achievement – extra-ordinary. What was true for the Aztecs was probably true for all ancient cultures. From these vignettes we could infer that the beginnings of art were entirely separate from craft, having its roots in the ability to evoke the realm of the gods.

Definition

Perhaps it's time to grope towards some kind of definition. What is the essential difference between craft and art? This is not easy, as mankind has had thousands of years when this distinction was more or less irrelevant. As I have posited above, every human activity whether it be tool-making – artistic or ceremonial – is at heart 'creative'. Yes, craft has a strongly functional element, a jug, a basket or a cloak have to 'work'. It is this functional element that defines crafts' purpose. Art has a separate function from the purely utilitarian, perhaps just as rigorously defined by its context and culture, but essentially non-practical. The elaborate, truncated and pictorial flint axes found in the Mayan settlement of Copan were definitely ceremonial rather than functional. One could turn the argument around and say: both craft and art are art; craft is art whose purpose is defined by practical function, and art is art that, certainly in ancient times, was defined by its ceremonial or religious function.

Art and identity

The entire Egyptian Epoch of 3,000 or so years was marked by a relative lack of significance given to the individual, to individuality. It was not until the 6th century in Greece that this phase was accomplished – the mark of the individual in art, the imprinting of the identity of an individual maker who rises up out of the vast anonymous ocean of human creativity. Greece in the 6th century BC provides us with the first examples of signed work in the painted pottery of Sophilos, Exekias and Kleitias. Sculpture is not far behind, though most of it exists only in Roman copy. Examples include Myron of Eleuthera, famous for his bronze discus thrower from the 5th century, and of course Phidias of Athens (493 to 430BC), who is forever immortalised by his work in the Parthenon, the great temple of Athene. These two examples of pottery and sculpture form a kind of polarity. Pottery arose around 9,000BC[26], and in the case of Greek civilisation, reached its final figurative, high-art phase in the 7th century BC. The pottery vessel (often a commemorative urn) became the canvas for artistic genius. Sculpture, in the form of small portable fetishes, had been around far longer. The oldest undisputed representation of a human figure, of Venus carved in mammoth ivory, was found in the Hohle Fels Cave in Germany, and was made around about 40000–35000BC[27].

Some individual Roman painters achieved fame in their lifetime, but little remains of their work. With the birth of Christianity and the fall of the Roman Empire, the artist/craftsman once again sank into anonymity. The art of the Catacombs and of the so-called Dark Ages is primitive compared to the sophistication of classical times. Yet it carries elements of religious 'expression' arguably more potent than the realism of Rome.

Detail from the Francois Vase: Ajax carrying the body of Achilles, c.6th century BC. Artists: Ergotimos, Kleitias

Craft into art

Let us have an 'intermezzo' in our considerations of the rise of the individual artist in the development of European art and look at something else – the birth of two artforms out of 'crafts'. Literacy was preserved in the Dark Ages by monastic scribes, both nuns and monks. In the Celtic- inspired illuminations such as the Book of Kells (c.AD800) and the Lindisfarne Gospels (AD715 to 720), pattern and ornamentation predominate. One has the feeling that this patterning has some profound significance that one is as yet unable to comprehend, that the relationship between so-called decoration and image is not random but has meaning. In fact, it is likely that 'meaning' existed on three different tiers of understanding: the scribed words, the narrative pictures and the ornamentation.

Book of Kells – AD800: symbol of St John

The Carolingian (AD780–900) and Ottonian (AD919–1024) illuminated works seem to lay stress on 'writing' and 'picturing'; decoration has less significance. The laborious and painstaking creation of illuminated books did not only preserve literacy, it can also be seen as the seed bed of European painting. The troubled and bloody years of the Dark Ages did not give rise to large-scale altar or mural painting but transmitted, in miniature form – firmly welded to the craft of bookmaking and the text – the art of painting.

Sculpture was 'liberated' from its block by the Greek sculptors. Egyptian art was monumental and static by comparison. As an independent art form it more-or-less vanishes from the European scene until the Romanesque and the Gothic era. The Romanesque era (AD1000 – 1200), which really saw an extraordinary revival of artistic and cultural activity in Europe, 'synthesized' a medley of influences; Roman, Byzantine, Germanic and Celtic. Sculpture, certainly on any significant scale, had died with the collapse of the Roman Empire. In the Romanesque era it was reborn, the child of architecture, the patterning motifs of illuminated manuscripts, and small-scale carvings in ivory. This process reached its fulfilment in the Gothic, where the sculptures seem to step out of the architectural framework (the pillars) into a more independent state of existence. In both these examples, illumination into painting and architecture/ornamentation into sculpture, there is a shift from an activity that could be described as 'craft' to one that could be defined as 'art'.

The Renaissance

In the Renaissance, which can be seen as the dawning of our era, craft and art are sundered from each other, seemingly absolutely. The visual arts jostle for recognition and glorification in a hitherto unprecedented manner. Neither painting nor sculpture were included in the elite list of 'Liberal Arts' taught in the late Medieval School of Chartres. They now became the substance and framework of civilisation.

The fragments of past cultures bear within them the genius of a people. They were created by individual artist-craftsmen, but the overriding inspiration was greater and far more potent than the individual. They worked out of a totality of integrity, out of an instinctive service for the divine. Each cultural epoch brought something new, a form entirely suited to itself, but the people striving to manifest it did not innovate or invent out of themselves.

The Renaissance brought something entirely new into the world. It was possible for the first time in human history for an individual to represent a whole culture in themselves. Leonardo da Vinci (1452–1519), Raphael (1483–1520) and Michelangelo (1475–1564) were geniuses in the fullest sense of the word. They attained a new pinnacle of human achievement hitherto undreamt of – a status and influence on a par with princes and potentates.

Art into craft, the Baroque

Where did developments in art go from there? At first, there was the development of mannerism, which was an attempt to win some quirky individual recognition outside the glorious aura of the great. The religious unity of Europe was sundered forever through the Reformation, and the Baroque style started in the early 17th century as a form of religious/artistic propaganda to counter its austerity. It can be noted for two seemingly contradictory elements: an attempt at absolute realism seen, for example, in the pithy and deeply human paintings of Caravaggio (1583–1610) and the creation of fantastical florid environments. And perhaps because art had been drawn into the service of power it became somehow compromised by gold and glitz. This is not to say that there were not great artists in this period, there were many, but certainly what one can observe in the extravagant palaces and churches of the time is a kind of blending and melding of art and craft. The emphasis was on 'show' rather than 'inwardness'. Craft, certainly within the context of architecture, became more 'arty' and art more of a craft. Great stress was laid on 'effect', less on truth and honesty to materials.

Bernini's St Teresa 1647–1652

Secularisation

An inevitable trend in art is what my History of Art tutor in Cheltenham, Peter Gorge, would have called *secularisation*. Something that starts off as a high and noble ideal, such as the Sphinx in Gezeh – that great desert guardian – ends up as a merely decorative, kitschy motive on a 19th-century chamber pot. With the development of the 'individual' on the Western European scene, and the loss of Church power and authority, there came the inevitable separation of art and religion. The glorification of God became the glorification of the human and of nature. Small beginnings had been made before but a whole plethora of secular art was created, particularly during the Reformation in northern and western Europe. Portraiture (prominent in ancient Rome) came into its own, as did an interest in landscape, historical scenes and still life. In the 17th, 18th and 19th centuries, art concerned itself with the world and with the worldly.

The Industrial Revolution and the death of crafts

A direct consequence of the 'freeing up' of the human spirit, seen in the development of humanism from about 1413 onwards, was the Reformation instigated by Martin Luther (1483–

1546). The great scholastic thinkers of the Middle Age such as St Thomas Aquinas (1227–1274) had taught that thinking could be a tool for the understanding of God. For Luther, thinking – like most other human capacities – had been corrupted through the Fall and could not be relied upon to provide a reliable pathway to the Divine. The only legitimate means of reaching God was through piety and devotion. This 'de-coupling' of thinking as a godly-gift in the service of God, freed it up, directed it downwards to the material world. Nature became objectified, the raw material of industry: the Industrial Revolution could happen.

By the mid-19th century the Industrial Revolution had gathered huge momentum. Steam trains and ships made travel fast, easy and convenient. The factory had replaced the skilled craftsman's workshop. Skilled tasks formerly performed by one person could be contracted out in what was called the 'division of labour'. Some people got very rich indeed, but many more lived in the most appalling squalor and poverty. Child labour was still the norm; where children had formally acquired the skills of their parents by degrees, in a rural or craft setting, they were ruthlessly exploited for their labour. Children worked in all conditions: mining, industry and of course chimney sweeping.

Mass-production and the 'division of labour' led, inevitably, to the death of crafts. The 'Fine-Arts,' catering for a wealthy elite, still had their place, but their sister the Crafts, became redundant and began to fade away. This book is very much about the consequences of this death, so I will not say much about it, except that many of the ills that beset our world are due to this disconnect with making things and with nature.

William Morris and the Arts and Crafts movement

In the 1800s the time was ripe for a radical rethink of all the forces that were pushing civilisation forward in an uncompromising and one-sided manner. The 'counter-movement' came with William Morris (1834–1889) in the form of the Arts and Crafts movement and its associated group of Pre-Raphaelite artists. The Pre-Raphaelite Brotherhood (founded in 1848) saw its inspiration as definitely pre-Industrial and pre-Renaissance. It was a looking back at the 'glory-days' of the Middle Ages, a time of Romance, Chivalry, King Arthur, a simpler life.

Morris was much influenced by the writer, art critic, social thinker and philanthropist John Ruskin (1819–1900). Ruskin was a 'champion' of the Pre-Raphaelite movement, giving substance and an intellectual framework to the ideals of pre-industrialisation. He emphasised the connection between Nature, Art and Society.

After his marriage to Jane Burden – a great beauty of humble origins and the muse of the Pre-Raphaelite movement – Morris built 'The Red House'. This was a sumptuous palace of art with oak staircases, painted furniture, embroidered tapestries and stained glass. It was here that the 'Firm' started.

William Morris (1834–1889)

The ideal of the 'Firm' was to create an integrated world of craftsmanship in which the artist was the designer and the executer, creatively engaged in the whole process from start to finish. The artist called the shots – not the capitalist demanding quick returns for cheap, shoddy goods. In Morris's view all arts were equal: there should be no distinction between artist and artisan; artists and craftsmen should work together and share their income. Thus, the Arts and Crafts Movement, like the Baroque (but in an utterly different manner), was a coming together of art and craft. Morris said, 'Have nothing in your houses that you do not know to be useful or believe to be beautiful'. Craft was indeed ennobled, shone through with a robust decorative glory, but perhaps painting became a little pale and insipid by comparison.

Morris led an astonishing, busy and productive life, and although rejecting the fruits of the Renaissance, he himself fulfilled at least some of the ideals of the 'Renaissance Man'. He was a writer of prose-poetry, a researcher into ancient methods of manufacture, a lecturer, designer, translator and traveller. The work of the Firm created mural painting, wall paper design, tiles, furniture, metalwork, jewellery, architectural carving and stained glass. Later, after a change of premises and expansion of the Firm, dying wool and

William Morris Tapestry, The Woodpecker 1885

carpet weaving were added to the list. When Morris died in 1896, aged 62, one doctor declared the cause of death as, 'Simply being William Morris and having done more work than most 10 men'. Morris had strong socialist leanings, believing in evolution rather than revolution, and young orphaned boys from underprivileged backgrounds were apprenticed by the Firm. Inevitably, the success and fame of the Firm rode on a wave of bourgeois interest and commission; affordable artefacts went to those who could well afford them.

Needless-to-say, the overpowering force of Empire and Capitalism could not be checked, and the Arts and Crafts movement, although leaving a lasting legacy, lacked the influence to bring about lasting change.

Antoni Gaudi – I Cornet

Arguably the most total and complete synthesis of art and craft was created by the Catalan architect Antoni Gaudi (1852–1926). A quote from John Ruskin, whose writings enjoyed

immense popularity in Spain is entirely appropriate here: 'Ornament is the origin of architecture.'

Gaudi, best known for his monumental work the Sagrada Familia, was not so much an imitator as a 'vehicle' of styles bursting out in the most cohesive, original and contemporary way. To Gaudi's total synthesis of art and craft were added two other dimensions, a working with nature and the use of highly evolved architectural and engineering skills. Gaudi took longer and longer to create his masterpieces and worked much of them out as he went along. This gives an incredible organic cohesion to the structures; they were not just rolled out from the drawing board. Things were studied and contemplated as they unfolded and spontaneous decisions were made.

Gaudi's Güell Park is an extraordinary convergence of the natural and man-made environment. It was conceived as a settlement by Güell, the wealthy Catalan businessman, who was Gaudi's staunch patron. Not quite social housing but certainly a place in which ordinary people could be placed into a beautiful and aesthetic environment. It never became a settlement, only two houses were ever built. Gaudi moved into one of them where he looked after his 93-year-old father.

The park was a barren wasteland almost entirely without vegetation. Gaudi devised ingenious methods of trapping water and irrigating the park. The natural organic environment developed or grew at the same time as the manmade one. Gaudi did not level or change the contours of the landscape; staircases, viaducts and cavernous half tunnels were created to lead the visitor up and through the park. His starting point was respect for what *is*, a very different attitude from most building projects, where everything is radically bulldozed according to some concept. Nature is *not* overcome – Gaudi saw himself as a collaborator with Nature.

Güell Park (1852–1926)

The park is surrounded by an almost unclimbable wall, topped with rounded mouldings and mosaics. As one enters the gate, past the two pavilions, the visitor encounters an enormous stairwell. Double stairs are divided by strange organic sculpture. Near the top is a gigantic dragon covered in mosaic and a snake's head. These act like totemic guardians but also conceal cisterns for water storage. They are both functional and symbolic.

At the top of the double staircase is a temple-like structure. A veritable forest of Doric-type pillars mosaiced around their bases. The outer ones taper but the inner ones are all of the same size. The pillars support a mosaiced, undulating roof. This temple is also a floor as it forms part of a gigantic auditorium, half built on solid ground the other half resting on the columns.

The columns look solid but are in fact hollow. The floor of the above square is not concreted: water is absorbed into it and then gathers in specially designed drainage pipes. These have slits at the top and perforations at the base. The water trickles down through the hollow columns and into the cisterns; the one concealed by the dragon can hold 2,600 gallons of water.

The most famous features of the park are the extraordinary meandering benches which ring the auditorium. They are covered in mosaic tiles (the ancestor of collage) and are a unifying principle in the space while also providing little intimate nooks for people to sit and chat in.

The other important feature of Gaudi's projects is that they are dependent on the work of countless highly skilled craftsmen. Hundreds of people came together to realise Gaudi's projects; one could say he was the instigator of an entire culture. A culture which – like the Arts and Crafts Movement – was to have a lasting ripple effect but which could not turn the tide towards a more organic, sustainable, hand-crafted and nature-friendly building scheme.

On the 5th of June 1926 Gaudi was hit by a tram and dragged along by it. Nobody recognised the shabby old man, and taxi drivers refused to take him to hospital. Passers-by carried the unconscious Gaudi to hospital where he died on the 12th of June. Despite the conditions of his death, Gaudi's funeral procession was two-and-a-half miles long and consisted of thousands of mourners.

Separation

In the Western world in the 1970s, while I was at art college, all elements of 'craft' had been ruthlessly eradicated from art. Skill was positively discouraged as were any notions of aesthetics or 'usefulness' in a broader societal context. Art had gone the path of greater and greater reductionism – from minimalism, where something still existed by implication, to conceptualism where (ultimately) the work of art exists only in the head of the artist. When I wanted to learn stone carving at college there was no one on the staff who could teach me. A mason from Gloucester Cathedral had to come in and show me the basics.

Art had not only separated absolutely from craft, it had also parted with most people's understanding of what art should be. It was spinning off into a void, propelled by an inevitable trajectory of necessity and forced into a corner. Just as the Industrial Revolution had sounded the death knell to the crafts, an increasingly technological society killed off the necessity for *living* art. All former aspects of the artist's work were usurped by the clever inventions of science. Photography largely negated the need for painted portraits; huge advertisements for mundane products became contemporary paintings. Recorded music reduced the numbers of music makers, musicians and composers. Television and screen culture made obsolete home-entertainment as well as visits to the opera, theatre and ballet. The artist, in a traditional sense anyway, lived and worked in a culture which had made him redundant and impotent.

The artist-craftsman

As a counter movement to the above, the mid 20th-century saw the rise of the artist-craftsman, men and women who did not come from a craft tradition but who through deliberate choice and conscious endeavour became artists in their craft. One such individual was the potter Bernard Leach (1887–1979). Born in Hong Kong and inspired by Japanese ceramics, Leach promoted pottery as a synthesis of Western and Eastern philosophy and art. His work centred around traditional Korean, Japanese and Chinese pottery and combined with traditional English and German techniques, such as salt glaze and slipware. For Leach, pottery was a combination of philosophy, art design and craft – even a total way of life. Leach's pottery was exhibited as art.

The present condition

To save itself from oblivion art has 'bled out' into two seemingly contradictory spheres; technology and craft. Many artists have channelled their creative energy into new forms of expression, using video installations, lighting and sound techniques, computer graphics and sophisticated engineering. The great divide between art and craft has also largely disappeared, and 'making things' has become a legitimate art again.

Grayson Perry

Grayson Perry (b.1960) embodies the fluid modern universal man: not compressed into a 'gender', cross-dressing, acknowledging his feminine 'alter-ego' and expanding his creative interests into many different spheres. He is a writer, lecturer, film maker, tapestry designer and ceramic artist.

Perry's ceramics reference several traditions which include folk art and Greek pottery. He has said,

> *'I like the whole iconography of pottery. It hasn't got any big pretensions to being great public works of art, and no matter how brash a statement I make, on a pot it will always have certain humility ... [F]or me the shape has to be classical invisible: then you've got a base that people can understand.'*

Grayson Perry Vase

He uses the coiling technique, allowing for larger more organic shapes. Very complex surface techniques are employed, which include embossing, incision, photographic transfers and glazing. They are works of great ingenuity, requiring several firings.

Sometimes Perry will add sprigs and little relief sculptures will be stuck to the surface. Perry's work demands enormous skill and involves layers of complexity and meaning. The high degree of skill required by his ceramics and their levels of meaning distance them from craft pottery. Like the Greek pots of ancient times, they are not merely functional or decorative but express ideas.

Many autobiographical elements are expressed in his work. Perry reflects on his stepfather's rejection, the lack of boyhood guidance in proper male conduct, the family and class.

This coming together of art and craft really represents the only possible future for the creative survival of human beings. The two sisters of art and craft should support each other – nay, become almost interchangeable. Craft needs to be imbued with individual intelligence and innovation, and art needs to take on board the acquisition of skill, knowledge of materials and a relationship to place and people.

Just do it!

What is of overwhelming and pressing urgency today (and this is the purpose of this book) is to see art and craft as a *process*. Yes, of course it's good to saturate this dreary grey planet with works of meaning, beauty and skill (there's not enough of it), but all this is secondary to *doing*. To find our true identity, to function as human beings, and have a positive rather than a destructive relationship with the world, we need to be *makers*. This is our birth right, which – sadly and for all-to-long – has been neglected and denied. But to *making* should be added another dimension – *meaning*. Not that the products of our *doing* should necessarily be profound; it's not so much message as meaningful *process* that matters. And here we have the rub of things; art and craft should unite, but so should the separated strands of technology and religion. By religion is not meant anything churchy or denominational but religion as spirituality: a font of moral, spiritual, humanising and ethical ideals.

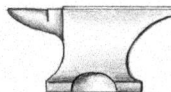

CHAPTER 4

The Cultural Significance of Handcraft Gestures

Bernard Graves

---

i) Handcrafts: Historical Perspectives

In preceding chapters, Simon Gilman and Johannes Steuck strongly advocate that 'making' should take a more prominent role in education today. We are aware, however, that many teachers, parents and even policy makers will still have the question: Is there really a place for learning the skills of the potter, the smith or the weaver, in this increasingly technological age of the 21ˢᵗ century? It is easy to think, perhaps, that learning artisan crafts was once justified but that these skills now belong to a bygone era. Learning to throw pots or forge knives is surely not – from this point of view – going to provide the necessary skills needed to gain employment in the digital age...is it?

Artisan Potter at work

As a step towards addressing the above questions let us look a bit more deeply into the historical context for craft and the value of craft practices worldwide for human development – both individually and culturally. We will do this by looking back briefly over the ways in which handcraft practices have developed over time. We will follow these considerations with detailed descriptions of handcrafts (Section Three) and their transformative potential.

Handcrafts through time

Historically, crafts have played an important part in human and cultural development worldwide. As Johannes touches upon in the previous chapter, their origin and function was not initially purely utilitarian, but was rather a part of lives lived in connection with a deity-filled world. Handcrafting, in other words, furthered the act of creation. For our ancestors, craft belonged at first to religious life and practice and only gradually did the developing utilitarian mind separate out pragmatic ends for crafts from their spiritual and cultural context.

The baskets, figurines, pots and textile crafts of Indigenous peoples – the native American Indians, the Polynesians, the Maori for instance – were and still are decorated with metaphysical representative designs, depicting spiritual history and living culture. Each pot or piece of textile can be thought of as a page in a great book where all-important cultural lore is scripted for succeeding generations to read.

Handcrafts, in these examples, literally served as the repositories of a culture's core beliefs.

The relevance of handwork and craft: for child, adolescent and adult

What is the role of handwork and crafting in the unfolding of human and social development? Human development is indeed a long, rhythmic process that continues from early childhood into adulthood and on throughout life – human beings are never complete, finished, as it were, with their development. We are continuously in the process of becoming.

When such an attitude survives among educators in daily life and work, only then, I believe, can there be a fertile foundation present for the potential creativity of each individual.

For those of us involved in handwork, craft or manual skills education, whatever the age of the pupil, we can bear witness to an area of activity that is uniquely human, namely creativity of the *human spirit* which is carried out by our hand, perhaps the one organ that most differentiates us from all of the animal world.

First fires

'The alchemist, like the smith, and like the potter before him, is a "master of fire". It is with fire that he controls the passage of matter from one state to another' Mircea Eliade[29]

Among the earliest of man's craft activities, one of his first technological achievements was the discovery of fire making. Fire had, of course, been integral to man's early experiences prior to the mastery of its making, but this was experienced as natural phenomena or occurrences of nature. These 'given' fires were those sparked by a lightning strike or the spontaneous combustion of certain trees such as the eucalyptus, which is known to ignite in arid areas. Other natural fires were those caused by natural emergences of magma in volcanic eruptions. We have little or no evidence of the use of this naturally occurring fire, but can imagine that early human beings stood in awe of it, rather as we might do today. In any case, it is likely that such natural fire was taken advantage of when it occurred – the storing of embers of these fires would have been very difficult. Storage of embers, as with the horseshoe fungus (*Fomes fomentarius*) in northern temperate zones, was probably only discovered after human beings were able to generate fire by means of various methods of friction (see Jonathan Code's chapter on fire lighting in Section Three).

In the history of the emergence of civilisation and early technologies, the use and control of fire is said by archaeological scholars to have begun circa 800,000 years ago by Homo erectus.

Fire lighting – generating fire by friction – is thought to be one of the earliest steps in our early mastery over nature and probably preceded other early domestic skills. Intentional shelter building using natural materials, as opposed to the use of cave dwellings, is thought to have begun 400,000 years ago; that is, long after the mastery of fire-making[30].

Whenever it was first learned, there is no doubt that the new skill of fire-lighting-on-demand gave human beings unheard of freedom and the potential for altering prevailing life conditions. Not only could they make fire to provide warmth and to prepare food, but they could start to transform the materials in their environment[31].

Baked earth: pottery

Pottery is recognised as one of the most ancient of crafts. The fire-hardening of shaped clay follows the early mastery of fire and continues right up to the present day, both as a creative leisure activity and in the production of industrialised ceramics[32].

Ceramics is the art of fashioning an artefact in clay and then fixing its shape by subjecting it to intense heat – around 1100°C – in a kiln. In this process, the clay body undergoes a substantial change, with the fire transforming clay to a new substance called ceramic. The process is irreversible: it is not possible to obtain the original clay back again. The oldest ceramic artefact found to date is a small figurine statue of Venus Dolni Vestonice in modern day Czech Republic said to be dated 29,000BC[33].

Molten earth

How, when and where the methods were discovered to extract metals from

Venus of Dolni Vestonice 29000–25000BC

mother ore is not known concretely. We do know, however, that human triumph in this respect underpins every civilisation worldwide – and it, too, was founded upon the mastery of fire.

So important was the discovery of a new metal, the means of working it, and its impact on human life, that the metals have given rise to the very name we use to classify whole ages of human civilisation.

Prior to the manipulation of metals, our Stone Age forebears used natural materials such as stone, sticks, and animal bone to help do more than was possible with bare hands. The step from using natural materials to using metals was, therefore, a huge one, but it could only become reality when human imagination and creative capacities were directed to unlocking the secrets of *interestingly coloured stones* – metal-bearing ores.

Metalsmiths – Copper, Bronze and Iron ages

Metal ores only gave up their secrets gradually, and smelting them required that progressive steps be mastered in the use of fire and in the means of manipulating both the ores and the metals that are separated out from them. The Copper Age began c. 5000BC. It was followed by the Bronze Age, c. 3000BC, and more recently the Iron Age dawned across Europe c. 1000BC (early evidence of iron ore smelting in the Middle East reaches as far back as 1400 years ago). The industrial use of iron, forming the basis for our modern industries, machines, bridges railways etc. was at its height during the Industrial revolution circa AD1750.

Crafts and the Guilds

Pouring molten metals

Craft practices enjoyed their heyday in Europe during the Middle Ages, where they were eventually organised into guilds[34]. Guilds were strictly guarded and guided institutions that were set up to preserve the specific crafts in their techniques and vital processes. Each craft guild was set up having an earthly as well as a saintly patron. St Antony is, for instance, the patron saint of the Basket Makers Guild with St Joseph traditionally adopted by carpenters. The earthly patron would be some local noble or dignitary who was the Guild's chief benefactor.

The status of *Master Craftsman* was awarded to one who had thoroughly practised and embodied all the skills and knowledge of his craft. He was also the master teacher and would have apprentices training under him. The guilds were instituted to safeguard the treasured secrets of each specific craft's techniques, as well as to help maintain standardisation and quality of work. They were also the institutions that set the financial remunerations for its workers and the prices of the work produced.

Before the advent of formal education for those less well off in society, a young boy would be expected to enter into his father's workshop as an *apprentice*. Crafts, with the exception of certain aspects of the textile industries, were primarily a male prerogative. After a period of strict training and guidance by the master, the older teenage boy would be sent off as a *journeyman* into the world to continue his training under another master in another village or town. In this manner the boy would have his skills honed and improved. He could then return later to bide his time while waiting to take over his father's workshop, and so continue the tradition.

In this fashion craft practice provided a valuable part of a boy's education. He may not have been able to read letters but he would have become highly skilled, and would be a highly rated artisan, providing a valuable contribution to the life and well-being of his community.

The master craftsman in return, accomplished in his skill, was satisfied that he had worked in response to the needs of his community. In this manner, craft practices were in part responsible for maintaining the moral and social well-being of the local community. Traditionally, good honest work formed the foundation for a personal sense of vocation and provided the basis for a moral work ethic.

St Joseph adopted guild patron for carpenters

The Craftsmen of old had a strong sense of vocation and were highly valued among their communities. This all changed, however, with the Industrial Revolution, which unfolded from approximately 1760 onwards. The Industrial Revolution focused attention on *economy* of production and output, and industrial, mechanized processes replaced hand-crafting. This trend has continued to this day and has resulted in ever more automation of all aspects of what were once handcrafted processes.

The craftwork which, up until the Industrial Revolution, was organised within small cottage industries throughout England, eventually succumbed to the rapidly developing mechanisation of industrial production. With the advancement of technologies such as the Spinning Jenny (1764), water-powered and steam-powered machines eventually replaced the hand spinners along with many other traditional handcraft activities that could be mechanised and industrialised.

With the industrialisation of craftwork, the hitherto direct link between the maker, say the cobbler, and his customer was also lost. What had been a sense of vocation around traditional crafts was replaced with exceedingly hard, and often very poorly remunerated labour. The history of the industrialisation of the craft process as witnessed in the West has been repeated again and again around the world.

Craft Guilds, along with notable exponents for handcrafts and the arts such as John Ruskin (1890–1900) and William Morris (1834–1896) made concerted attempts to preserve the handcrafting traditions. However, the guilds eventually weakened and slowly disappeared, with only a very few surviving to this day. These include the Worshipful Company of Basket Makers, which preserves its *Honourable statutes.*

Craft in the United Kingdom: 20th century

For a time, some craft apprenticeships continued into the late 1950s and 1960s, with a host of technical Colleges up and down the United Kingdom offering training and potential careers for young men and women in a variety of crafts and industries. However, these were eventually axed for reasons of political expediency.

Up until the late 1980s, what was offered in the way of practical skills education in schools, such as woodwork, engineering and domestic science, were also phased out and were replaced with what is now called *IT & Design Technologies*. It seems more important in today's world that children learn the skills to design pizza packaging, and how best to market the pizza, than it is to have the opportunity of learning how to make and cook a pizza.

From a case study and petition by the UK Craft Council (published 1998), endorsed by several universities and sent to the education department of the day to bring back 'Learning through making', we are informed that:

> *'85% of primary school children can use a keyboard but only half that number can cut carrots and peel potatoes…' Wendy Titman*[35]

With technological gadgetry and 'ready meals' providing for our everyday needs, the necessity for our practical involvement in life has been severely curtailed. This degree of deprivation of practical experience and knowledge is alarming and only serves to negate further every child's right to experience and wonder at what nature can provide.

In most schools, at primary and secondary years, the implementation of any traditional craft or other practical activities is left up to the choice and discretion of the head teacher. As Simon Gilman has noted previously, the emphasis more than ever for schools in the United Kingdom is to achieve their league table targets and raise their standing in international comparative metrics, and this means a focus on raising literacy and numeracy skills above what would otherwise be considered extra-curricular activities such as handwork and crafts.

A crisis at hand

There is no doubt in my mind that the practice of crafts and handwork has been devalued and they currently lack due recognition in many school settings. In this trend, schools not only reflect the poor regard held by many for traditional craft practices but consequently also negate the educational opportunities that they can provide.

Since the 1980s, with the increased amount of disposable income available to spend on ourselves, some people can choose to attend any number of the many traditional craft workshop weekends that are on offer. Attending such activities can satisfy a deep need for creativity and provide a welcome balance to the tedium of a desk-based job, but the true value and substance that any honestly practised handcraft can provide can nonetheless elude us.

If we return now to the question posed at the outset of this book: Is there a place for traditional handcrafts in education today?, the authors of this book offer a resounding '*Yes*' in response. It is the firm conviction of the practitioners and authors who have contributed to this book that handcrafts have an essential role to play in education and human development today. This book addresses itself specifically to the educational and pedagogical opportunities that crafting offers for a contemporary, integrated practical skills curriculum.

To grasp the opportunities that are afforded by processes of making, attention must be placed not merely on how handcrafts developed in a historical context, but rather on how the individual, growing human being, whether school student or adult learner, can take up the crafts and access the transformative *craft gestures*. For it is these gestures, the skilfully executed economic movements of *hands and body*, that can contribute effectively to a healthy development of *hand, heart and head*, with skills, aesthetic appreciation and practical knowledge. These are all areas of experience and learning that require attention and engagement in what could be called holistic education.

Traditional basket maker at work

ii) Handcrafts: Movement and Human Development

Human beings share with animals the ability to move. Whereas animals acquire and adopt the movements they need for life more or less at birth, human beings – in contrast – require several years of practice to develop even the fundamentals for a life of moving about in the world.

Many creatures display remarkable abilities to manipulate materials to functional ends. The weaverbirds, for instance, stitch grasses together to fashion their nests. Spiders generate an intricate, geometrically designed web with which to entrap their prey. The puffer fish constructs an elaborate sand mandala nest to attract a mate. However, none of these creatures can choose to do anything different in shape, design and use of materials than its species dictates. Neither does it appear that these creatures have had to practise their specialised form of making. There are no apprenticeships for weaver birds or puffer fish!

Where Nature's creations can provide inspiration for us as potential creators, human creativity is *not* instinctive but rather stems from latent capacities of imitation and ingenuity. These human qualities need to be fostered and refined as they are *undeveloped* imitative capacities in the younger child.

A spider's web – by nature's design

Child, finger knitting – by human design

Human making

Most animals have developed highly specialised limbs where their movements and actions have evolved around a singular purpose of survival. This is not so with the human being. The hands with which we come into the world are *non-specialised*, at first even clumsy and uncoordinated. Unlike with animals, it seems that we have the potential to evolve as a free and independent being not restricted by specialised movement capacities and skills. The human being can, with innovation in tool making, potentially turn a hand to anything!

When making a candle, for instance, taking the raw materials provided by nature, in this case beeswax and the cotton for the wick, we start a host of creative processes that culminate in the single act of lighting the candle. What was previously held within the raw materials is released, through human activity in creativity, in the light and warmth of the burning candle. Such an image, I hope, helps serve to show the purpose of a human being's creative power. There should moreover be no boundaries in a human being's creativity for, unlike the instinct of the honey bee out of which a honeycomb is built, human actions are not meant to be actions in response to given situations but free actions that transcend the limitations imposed on the animal, actions that serve the well-being of one's neighbour, for instance.

We know that practically every artefact used today can be made from oil-derived plastics, in factories somewhere, by machine-minders who are challenged to survive a life of intense boredom. This is manifest where machine operators who can only respond in a mechanistic way to the commands of the machine by repetitive motor movements (actions), not lifted to the realm of skill, tire easily and cannot take real interest in their work. The basic need for meaningful work by which the individual can find expression and be of meaningful service to others, is scarcely met.

Toys and other artefacts produced in this way, and not as a result of the labour and love of the worker, take on a cold and uninviting appearance. Those who are surrounded by such a world of dead objects have little to please the eye or, in the case of the child's toy, little to stimulate fantasy and develop imagination.

In such a situation, where the truly creative process of the maker or receiver is obstructed, how can willpower be transformed to beautiful shape? For beauty in an artefact or a toy depends on the nature and texture of the materials, combined with the skill and love with which it was created.

As a further and far-reaching consequence, to which we are all subject with the increasing proliferation of all manner of artefacts intended for the home, for use in school etc., we have almost no need any more to do anything ourselves, except be consumers of goods. There is very little incentive to be practical, let alone artistic in daily life, since someone, somewhere has thought of relieving me of my practical involvement by offering me, at competitive prices, just that product that would do the job with ease and more efficiency. With each step down this road of a purely material response to meeting human needs, the sense for the artistic, that which is uplifting to the human mind and the ability to be creative, are in great danger of being lost.

The hand: tool of the mind

Though non-specialised, the human hand is vital in all that we do. When human beings adopted an upright posture, walking on two legs and feet, our hands became freely available for tool-making and use. With our *free hands*, we could work, create, control and effectively change our environments[36].

Of all man's limbs – and I include the head here as a kind of limb (a perhaps contentious suggestion) – the hand could be considered in evolutionary terms as our *primary tool* for enabling human development, specifically in terms of intelligence(s) and cultural development.

Without the development of human hands and their use in the exploration and manipulation of the material world, personal development, intelligence, and social values would not have arisen as they have.

Immanuel Kant, the German philosopher, was among the first writers on the human disposition to refer to the hand as 'the window to the mind'[37]. Indeed, several modern scientists go as far as to propose that human intelligence, particularly in the manner in which we *think*, is a direct consequence of the first manipulations and experiences made by the hand, and in particular the fingers, as they grapple with the material world.

It is now well documented that these *hands-on,* manipulative experiences, coupled with the *sensorial* experiences of the material world (touch), convey information to the brain which is then confined to memory.

It is a remarkable thought to consider that from the earliest hand-hewn flint tools to the numerous specialised and mechanised robotic machines found in today's workshops, not only have we given shape to the materials we have manipulated but also, the creative processes and subtle movements plied by hand and tool have helped shape the human brain.

Every child, through her first experiences of touching the material world, explores the nature of her surroundings, discovering whether something is hot or cold, rough or smooth, round or square. This first exploratory phase of *touching* the material world is then followed by the *naming* of our experiences.

In this tactile manner we get to 'grasp' the material world, we get to 'grips with it' and attain its meaning and significance for us. Our varied cumulative sensory experiences aid and add to our understanding of the world.

In child development, 'making and creating' first takes place within the domain of the hands, with the mind continually acting as a kind of mirror: mapping, naming and cognising our every action.

'The more we take into account ... that intellect develops from the movements of the limbs, from dexterity and skills, the better it will be.' Rudolf Steiner[38]

Close up of working skilfully on a pole lathe

As makers, however, we do not merely remain with *naming things*. With fingers and hand, we start to manipulate the material world. We take, for instance, an amorphous lump of clay and change its shape and give it a new form. We are able to bring to our manipulation of matter something new, something from out of our imagination. By doing so, we rise above our creature (and 'created') state to become a co-creator. In this manner man's theomorphic potential engages where nature's creative activity left off.

The human hand and its potential

The hands are indeed a complex, yet versatile structure, an 'organism' having distinct parts. Thumb and opposing fingers surround the central palm, all of which have to work in *sympathy and antipathy* with each other. In the action of *gripping* a tool, for instance, some muscles contract whilst others have to relax in order to enable a smooth and coordinated action or continuous motion to be achieved.

Some anthropologists and evolutionists suggest[39] that it has been through the use of our hands that the *free human condition* has developed. With our hands we may well become specialists, displaying high levels of skill like that of the juggler or glassblower, skills which we are not born with but which have to be practised and learned.

This process of learning skills can only take place, however, following the integration of the primal reflexes: for instance, once the instinctual gripping reflex has been forgotten. Certain motoric conditions (such as dyspraxia), which causes difficulty in acquiring *voluntary hand movements,* can occur where these natural reflexes are not integrated. These initial reflexes are thought to be hangovers from instinctual reflexes linked to 'fight and flight'[40].

At first our ancient ancestors were manually unskilled, as is every new-born infant. Both are at first *non-specialist* in the use of their hands. In the case of developing traditional handcrafting skills, it can take many 1000s of hours of diligent practice before we can say that we have mastered a particular series of techniques. This has been shown to be the same as the average time for an apprentice to be adequately trained; in most crafts and industry this equates to about 5 to 7 years of training.

In the hand, particularly within the finger tips, the neurological network of nerve endings is as complex, finely packed and tuned as with the brain nerve receptors.

Without the use of our hands, either by chance, accident or design, the creative form-building capacities that our hands have afforded us would be thwarted. This would represent a huge personal and cultural loss. Matti Bergström[41] states that this loss of tactile ability and dialogue with the material world would in effect result in what he calls 'finger blindness'. This condition is conceivably even worse, and has more severe consequences for us, than eye (sight) blindness. The blind person can compensate in a variety of ways for physical blindness, whereas the 'finger blind' will not be able to attain a deeper sense of *meaning and value* that we gain from our tactile handling of the material world[42].

Human Hands 'freed from resting on the earth

I have myself been personally inspired by the writings of Arthur Auer (1949–2015), an arts Teacher and educator in the USA. In his book *Learning about the world through Modelling: Sculptural ideas for School*[43] he cites a poetic description of the hand, written by Arvia MacKaye Ege (1932–1989) – a former Waldorf School handwork teacher. I include it here and trust that it also offers some insight and inspiration:

> 'Through the fact that man is an upright being and his hands are thus freed from resting on the earth, they have become, down through the ages, the most marvellous instruments. The shape of the hand with its five delicate, mobile fingers surrounding the quiet centre of the palm, intimates

its connection with the rays and impulses of the five-pointed star, the pentagram – that special creative form found, for instance, in the rose family and also basic to man himself!

'An organ of the sense of touch, it can be used to feel, to grasp, to move, mould, intertwine, or to relate other objects to one another, but also to make free gestures expressive of the inner dictates of the soul. Through infinite variations of all these, it has become one of man's most creative and, at the same time, selfless organs. Rudolf Steiner has spoken of the hands as, "the eyes of the rhythmic system". And one who works much with his hands may well feel how an essential part of his being would be blind without them.

'The rhythmical use of the hands works in a mobile, living way upon the development of brain cells, so that [the child's] physical brain will become a far more pliant and sensitive instrument for "living thought" and for clear, strong, mobile knitting of thoughts when he has grown to full adulthood.' Arvia MacKaye Ege[44]

The increased use and development of the hand is considered a key by evolutionists for determining the point at which *Homo Sapiens* (meaning *Wise Man*) emerged from his predecessors some 200,000 years ago[45]. This point, during which early man started to make use of the opposing *thumb and forefingers* for the handling of items – to grip and use simple tools more efficiently – is considered the defining moment in time in which our ancestors started to develop an array of more complex hand skills and intelligences.

Initially, the skills and knowledge acquired through increased hand use and dexterity served the needs of daily life. But given the passage of time, the initial survival skills were put to use in developing more efficient hand tools that could be used for 'pre-craft' activities. With modification, a stone cutting tool could be given a more curved edge and point, and could be made into a scraping tool for cleaning skins. These could then be simply sewn together with sinews using a shaped splinter of bone for a needle. In this manner it is quite possible for simple tailoring to have begun far back in the Stone Age. These so-called *primitive technologies* can be rightly considered the *cradle* for all our later sophisticated Crafts and Craftsmanship skills – see *Stone Age Skills for the 21st Century* by Bart Blankenship[46].

Physically opposing thumb and forefingers

Over the course of time, through generations of practice and ever-increasing capacities for ingenuity, the physically opposing thumb and forefingers have enabled us to develop and refine finger and hand skills to the point required for wedging large lumps of clay, for kneading bread and eventually for lacemaking and writing.

Tracing the development of hand skills reveals the story of mankind's increasing ability to forge an independent and autonomous life[47]. The *intelligent hand* afforded us the means to acquire the skill to become masters of our crafts, and at the same time to develop the knowledge of *where things come from and how they are made.*

This knowledge, derived from the hand-brain connection, is there to be seen in the artefacts of our craftsmanship, originating in the deceptively simple flint arrow tips of stone age times and developing right up to the sophisticated materials and technologies required to manufacture the modern silicon chip. However, with the rapid advancement of today's technologies the question remains, I believe: are we really *more intelligent and wiser* than stone age man, *more independent and freer,* or have we become *more subservient* to our own creations, increasingly unable to provide for our everyday needs?

I recently had the opportunity to view some ancient Bushman cave paintings in South Africa, scenes depicting their domestic livelihoods. The somewhat ironic question posed above arose in

Man's first art work – painted hands cave paintings

me in juxtaposition to the recollection that I was only there at the foot of the escarpment by virtue of the fact that I had been transported half way round the world by sophisticated means of transport. The same question arose for me later while I committed my experiences to virtual paper on an i-pad.

We cannot say with absolute certainly why the early painters who created those first cave paintings depicted scenes of hunting antelope with spears, or why a print of a hand or hands[48] frequently appears on the scene. Was this just the maker's mark, a signature, or was this considered an iconic symbol depicting a degree of emerging self-consciousness and awareness of the hands as the tools of the makers? Perhaps it was just the painter's way of letting us know he or she was also there.

Even with scholarly accounts to hand, which are continually being updated with new evidence on the value and importance of the usage of the hand for neurological development, those who leave out *hands-on learning* in the development and delivery of school curricula seem to be *finger blind* to the evidence put before them.

There is no doubt in my mind that an increasing majority of children today would do well to be given the opportunity to develop their potentially *nimble fingers* and to acquire the means to explore and shape the material world. In doing so they will stimulate their imaginative faculties and hone their independent thinking about the world and themselves.

The Hand and 'I' – development of movement skills

The new-born infant expresses a multitude of movements of which it is not yet master. Control comes from above to below, from eyes to legs and then lastly to the feet. Movement takes hold of the child from the *outside* to begin with, and controlled limb movements are only gradually mastered by the child through much playful interaction with her surroundings.

At first the new-born child displays a series of primitive reflex movements – the ability to suck, to grip a finger placed into the hand, and even to mimic the as yet undeveloped ability to walk when suspended in the air with the soles of the feet just touching a flat surface. In the normal course of events these reflex movements will fade away to be replaced with more conscious intent and self-willed activity. These early reflex movements are referred to as *autonomic primitive reflexes.*

The young child's ultimate goal and achievement comes in attaining uprightness and then in those first tentative steps, in walking. This is however only the beginning – and it will have taken roughly a year to achieve! The expression of movement in the child leads on to the development of other faculties. Crawling, walking and all manner of bodily movements lay the foundation for the acquisition of many finer skills: speech and, ultimately, thinking processes are realised as a result of the internalisation of outer movement[49].

The capacities for movement, for gross and fine motor skills in the human being, are no doubt complex and are the study of much neurological research. Most science points to the origin of our movement impulses as being brain-centred; in other words, our movement impulses, according to this point of view, are initiated, determined and directed by a complex brain and physical neurological activity. This brain-centred origin for our impulses to move is not the only view, however. We can have the experience that our intention, our impulse to move to do something, has its origin not internally but enigmatically from the *outside*[50].

This can be experienced for instance in reaching out for a glass of water, we first form our intent and motivation to quench our thirst and inwardly reach an invisible hand to the glass. It just takes a split second for the actual mechanics of the arm and hand to follow at the command of the secondary impulse, which indeed stems from the brain. Similarly, we can consider a variety of sports. The archer, for instance, speaks of being able to hit the target by having his attention and intention already in the mark before releasing the bowstring[51].

This idea is further explored by Rudolf Steiner in his series of Educational lectures titled *The Foundations of Human Experience* (1918) where he suggests a possible explanation for the different orientation to *self-movements.* He puts forward the idea that *movement impulses* enter us from *outside,* which we *internalise* and make our own. Further, he suggests that in our limbs and the unconscious motoric system we not only embrace the movements we experience in the world but, unconsciously through our limbs, we connect to the whole universe[52].

When our *sense of movement* becomes embedded in our muscular system we refer to *muscle memory*[53]. Muscle memory originates in the capacity for imitation that we witness in the child, evident, for instance, when a toddler imitates with a stick the actions of the mother when she sweeps the floor. It can also be experienced by a practising craftsperson, who knows full well that learning new

Man in the Universe – Sensing Universal Movement

THE TWO STREAMS OF MOVEMENT

FIRST STREAM of movement
a lot of uncontrolled movement from below

SECOND STREAM of movement
– control & co-ordination starts here

Legs
arms
head
eyes
Least movement above

eyes
mouth
head
finger
Legs
feet-first steps in standing up

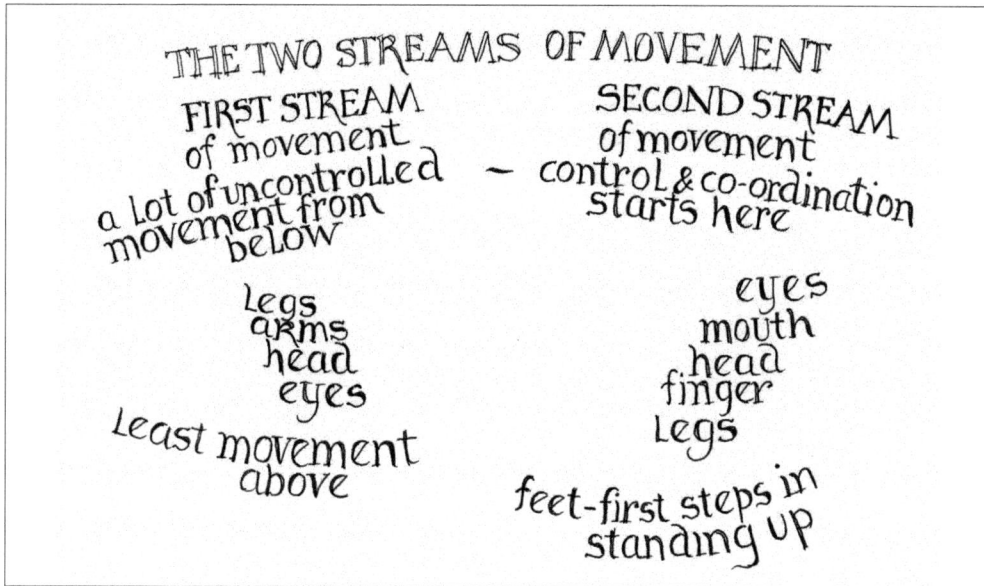

With every new achievement & physical skills attained there is an expression of 'joyful emotion'
Following the mastery of preliminary physical/ bodily and dexterous skills –
Movement impulses work subtly inwards to develop higher faculties

Thinking
Talking
Walking
Crawling

Development of unique human capacities, from Crawling to Thinking

hand skills and techniques is best demonstrated and acquired by observation first, only later to be followed by practice. This approach is more effective than trying to work from directions given in a manual.

Looking at the evolution and development of movement capacities in the growing child and young person, we can observe the following two streams of Movement development:

From play to work – the younger child

For the young child, we can observe the importance and formative effect that adult movements, habits and work can have for them to imitate. The working habits of the adults in a child's environment stimulate and inform the play and playing of children. The copying of adult work by young children generates a healthy playful imitation compared to that of a child who is only surrounded by machines and digital images.

As the child grows and enters its teens, the initial playful movement capacities undergo a change of character. From about the age of 12, the formative or growth forces that have helped to sculpt the child's organism from within are released and are available to the child to start to form and transform the outside material world. The older child starts more consciously to take hold of and re-fashion materials to suit her own intentions. These latent creative capacities become available and are utilised when taking up any form of handwork and craft practice.

The early years of childhood and middle school years could be said to have to do with the transformation of 'Play into the capacities required for work':

From Play and Learning to Working in the World

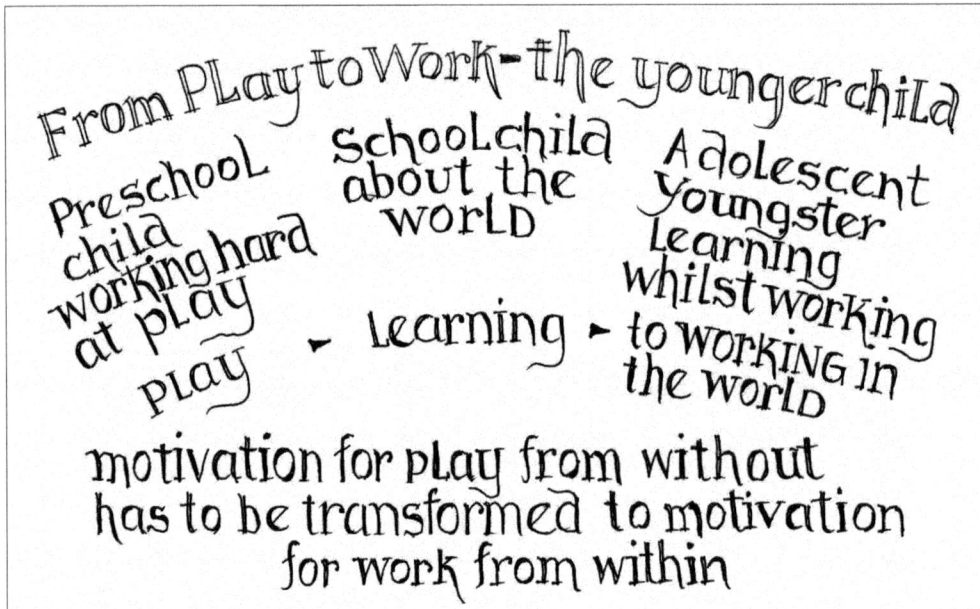

From Play to Work - the younger child

Preschool child working hard at play

School child about the world

Adolescent youngster learning whilst working

play - Learning - to working in the world

motivation for play from without has to be transformed to motivation for work from within

Growing 'From Play to Work'

Adolescence: transforming the self

I will now address the use and effect of movement in young people post-puberty. Movement for the adolescent takes on more significance and impresses itself into the soul of the young person in a different way from that of a younger child.

Puberty marks the distinct close of a certain chapter of human biography. The emerging human being leaves the joys and charms of childhood and enters the somewhat turbulent seas of adolescence – a time of ripening and maturing. The maturing child now steps – metaphorically speaking – out of paradise and onto the earth, for the first time coming up against its density, its material resistance. Inwardly this often manifests in a period of inward brooding (descent) – the adolescent's inner tendency towards densification. In response to the feeling of dropping under the weight of gravity, both physically and emotionally, there can be desperate attempts by the adolescent to gain levity – *freedom of spirit*.

Often just at this time, there is a crisis of will. The youngster, being a fledgling, is unable to fly gracefully at this time, is unable to exercise intellectual capabilities and is clumsy in the application of physical energies and movements. Often at sea, yet longing and seeking for a reunification and confirmation of identity, the burgeoning individual is above all seeking recognition of her/his attempts to become her/himself. We are, as teachers, parents or friends of adolescents, their spiritual midwives – helping them to be re-born out of themselves.

What seems very important in this phase of life is to give adolescents the possibility to find their individuality and afford them the opportunity to enter into a relationship with the world and their fellow human beings directly and practically. It is possible at this time to give the young people opportunities to exercise their *doing* – so that they can literally take hold of the world and its substances. In this very process the adolescents will not only mould, fashion and transform materials into useful objects – but they will be impressed, fashioned, influenced by the different elements and processes involved in the various crafts. Given the opportunity to become immersed in creative craft activities, the disciplines and innate *craft gesture*, will have a reciprocal movement, experienced inwardly, which helps give self-confidence and build self-esteem. There are some who can grasp the world intellectually. However, I believe for the majority, intellectual awakening and real understanding is attained via a more experienceable, 'hands-on approach'[54].

A certain wisdom is, perhaps, encapsulated in this ancient Chinese proverb:

'I hear and I forget' (essential to the process of all learning)
'I see and I remember' (middle school years)
'I do it and I understand' (senior school years)

Development of movement skills – Uncontrolled – practised – mastered

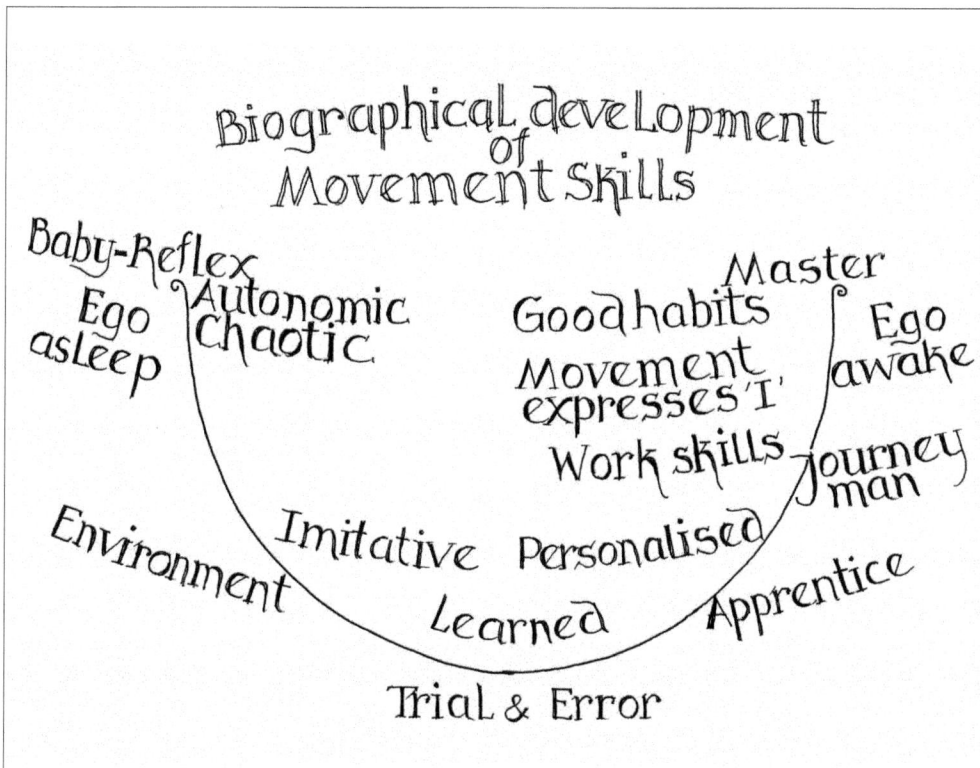

Development of Movement skills – Uncontrolled, – practised – mastered

Proud students with their wares – Class from Aquila Project 2008

Biographical development of movement skills

In many ways, the practising of handcraft invites the young person to explore their own creativity and at the same time temper their natural exuberance and flair with a healthy measure of pragmatism and realism. At the age when young people become most physically aware of their bodily nature, a healthy diversion in exploring nature's materials and crafting processes can provide a positive balance.

It has been our experience, working with young people, that immersion in a whole range of traditional crafts activities can be very beneficial, providing challenges and rewards similar to those that can be had in, say, white-water rafting or climbing a rock face.

Individual crafts have something unique to offer (these are explored in some depth in Section 3 of this book) yet all have in common the challenge to meet different materials, allowing the process to guide experience and creativity. This can prove to be a challenge for even the most pliant of youngsters who, at this age, naturally shy away from serious work and demanding challenges. Throughout my years of teaching, however, I have repeatedly witnessed how students that put in the effort are personally rewarded on completion of a well-crafted artefact.

iii) Craft Gestures: Visible Archetypes

It is claimed by educational psychologists that there are many different styles of learning[55] and that children learn best according to their natural dispositions – with some accessing learning more through the visual or auditory means or again others through more kinaesthetic routes.

Though the variant routes for accessing learning are described by educational psychologists, it is somewhat paradoxical that the preferred method of delivery in the classroom is usually via the spoken word and visual aids, with children mostly sedentary at their desks. Movement education is often restricted to the gym or outdoor playing field, with craft activities, sadly, seldom getting a look-in.

Throughout history, different civilisations have had different goals and expectations in education.

The Greeks, some 2500 years ago, had very different intentions and aspirations. Central to their understanding of what constituted a wholesome education for the body and the mind was the training of the physical body. They believed that in directing one's attention to training the body, the mind would be taken care of. The Greek art of gymnastics was primarily a training for the mind and the soul.

Along with teachers of other eastern *movement arts,* the Greeks understood that *bodily work is spiritual and spiritual work bodily* – both in the human being and in its effects on the human being. We could say metaphysically, 'Spirit is flooding around us when we do bodily work and matter is active within us when we do spiritual work.'

Greek statue – Discus thrower, c.460–450BC, depicting grace and harmony in movement

'Crafted movements' in pedagogical development and education.

As described in the preface, I first became aware of the powerful effect of a well-mastered craft gesture when as a young boy I watched the local blacksmith and was captivated by the movements he made as he forged the shoes for the workhorses.

Watching him at work, I experienced the ease with which he moved, the almost musical element sounding from his actions. There was a grace and lightness in his limbs, and though the work was hard, he performed a kind of effortless dance. When the music was over and the activity ceased, something emerged that had not been there before. Through human mastery of movement and physical skill, an idea is transformed, given shape and material expression, in the products we make with our hands.

The craft gesture and the complementary gesture

Each craft has its own symphony of working gestures. As important to the acquisition of the actual skills, such as hammering in blacksmithing or sawing a piece of wood in woodwork, is the point of rest and of counter-movement, which I call the *complementary* gesture. The arm hammers while the body moves away freely. In contrast consider that this degree of separation cannot be achieved by the animal in its movements. With a woodpecker, the whole body pecks – it follows the pecking limb and its entire body can but peck. In the human being this is different: we are meant to be free human beings and not stereotypical in our movements.

The point around which the working gesture and the complementary or counter-gesture move is an inner quiet space – a place where I am centred. It can be perceived as the place where I experience human ego-hood:

Blacksmith hammering

'I hammer' not 'it hammers'.

The schooling for the apprentice

How are work gestures acquired such that they become second nature for the hand? I believe this is done through a process of 'enhanced imitation', diligent practice and repetition – *Play is transformed into Work.*

Schooling of the will – the time of the apprentice

The first step in the process of acquiring the craft gesture is chiefly directed to the sphere of our will. At first the student has to perform and practise a series of movements till they become a habit, unconsciously absorbed by muscle memory or our habit body. Traditionally it was the job of the master to demonstrate, insisting at first that the apprentice follows his movements exactly. Over time, and with continued practice, the hands of the apprentice could execute the given movements independently and without thinking about them.

Only when the craft movements become independent in this way can the maker have a sense of freedom of movement, at which point one can adapt the almost archetypal 'given' movement to one that the craftsperson can call their own.

To the extent that we subject our will to that of the master we learn essential skills and techniques which would otherwise take us much longer to discover. I can remember how often I was impatient and attempted things for which I was not yet ready. Likewise, in my teaching,

I come across students who attempt to run before they have learned to walk. Practising a craft can indeed offer a student an exercise in patience and perseverance as well as in the mastery of craft gestures.

Here are what I call the three virtues of 'Will potential', three elements, if you like, of personal Will transformed through the crafting process:

- The undirected motor activity of the apprentice becomes skill when his individual will impulses become subject to the materials, tools and prerequisite processes.
- The creative impulses lying in the will can undergo a transformation into beautiful forms when one works artistically, bearing in mind function and form.
- A relatively insignificant activity can become a virtue when one can work in response to a need.

Journeyman: establishing our rhythm in the way we work

There is clearly an element to all craft movements that is more than the sheer effort of will – that of acquiring the right rhythm of work. When I adapt the working rhythm of the master to suit my own disposition and temperament I start to personalise my will activity in accordance with *my own* sense of rhythm. Traditionally this was the time of the Journeyman.

If we listen to the beating of the blacksmith as he hammers his iron we become aware that there are secondary taps on the anvil. His established sense of rhythm brings the two elements, first, of his own will, and second, the given archetypal or universal movement learnt from his teacher. It is for this reason that, as an onlooker, we can see how students personalise all that they are taught.

It is interesting to note that the different rhythms of craft work are revealed in the many kinds of work songs.

Mastery: the aspect of 'thought in the will' lives in the 'form element'

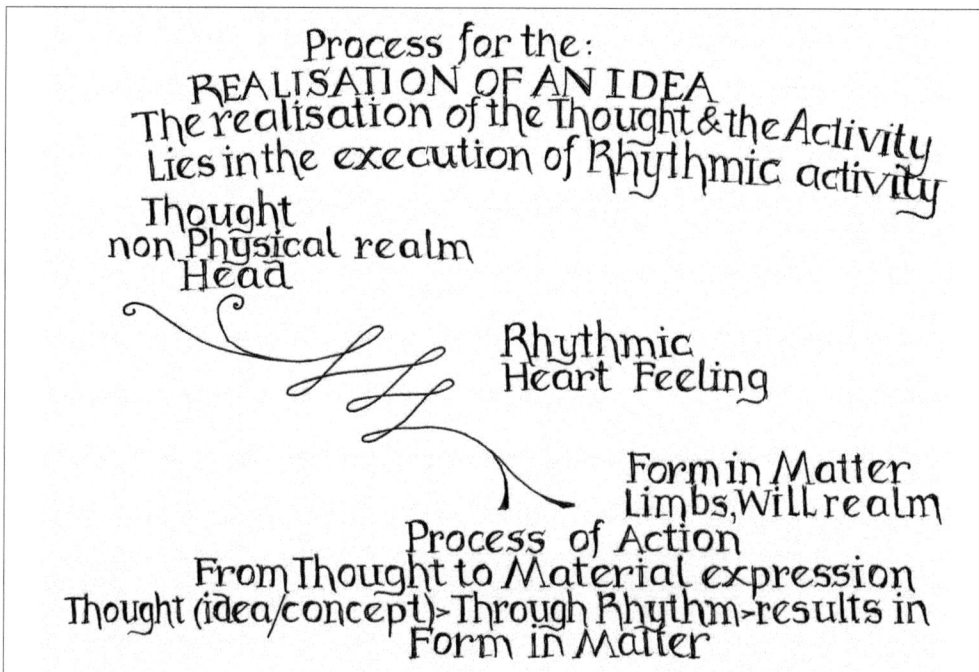

The crafting of an idea – Process

Finally, the aspect of thought that lives in the will is manifested in the form element of what is made. For although it is the hands and the limbs that execute the actions through which our will activity engages with different materials, the *form* that emerges as a result of this work came from our head nature, as the idea held in mind!

This is truly the time of the Master who has achieved the ability to replicate or intuit a given form and realise it time and again.

THOUGHT (idea) > Through RHYTHM > results in FORM IN MATTER

Although all the *three aspects* of movement *(idea, right rhythm & action)* are required and mostly happen simultaneously, the realisation of the *idea* we have of a particular shaped pot depends foremost on the *right rhythm* of work being achieved: for the experienced craftsperson, the form of a handmade artefact that emerges is intuitively sensed through the feeling nature, rather than the eyes alone.

Craft activities and their effect on those in the environment

The craft gestures that inform the making of craft items do not only impact on the individual who is doing the making. When mastered, craft gestures can in fact have a profound effect on the one who observes them being performed. Research on the physiognomy of sight has shown that whilst a person observes work, subtle changes can be detected in the tone of the observer's muscles – in the same set of muscles as those active in the one doing the work[56].

This phenomenon is related to the activity of imitation in the young child. The young child is open and impressionable and is deeply responsive to movement activities in its immediate environment. For instance, while Mummy or Daddy hammers in a nail, the child follows suit, knocking in a pretend nail, using perhaps a stick for a hammer.

Though the potential for inspiration and healthy play for children arising out of experiencing craft activities in their immediate village environment may not as yet have been documented, I am convinced by my own childhood experiences and those of others, that traditional artisan activities were beneficial in generating a healthy social environment and work ethos.

How wonderful it would be for the modern child to witness the blacksmith or the bodger at work – not that that would be as an intended vocation, but rather for the experience of wholesomeness and the opportunity for playful imitation and imaginations.

Therapeutic value of craft working gestures

We have come to see that each craft activity carries with it a specific *wisdom* and that it is this wisdom that makes a significant impression on the maker. It may well be argued that the practising of crafts can work in a therapeutic manner for all of us, especially in enhancing our sense of well-being, and more specifically, informing in subtle ways our inner capacities for actions and feeling, qualities and ways of thinking.

For instance, one can have the experience that elements of pottery particularly demand physical strength and strong *will for action*. Textile work such as weaving has an altogether a different gesture. In textile work the aspect of *rhythm* in working is in the foreground, with materials and designs stimulating our feeling life. Then there are those crafts, like knitting and crochet, that demand precise mechanistic movements and the grasp of complex patterns – in particular it is these dexterous movements that have been demonstrated to have the potential to affect our *cognitive capacities* and quality of *thinking*.

I have chosen three specific craft activities: ceramic work, weaving and knitting to illustrate these three basic archetypes of movement gesturing.

1. Pottery: particularly in the preparation of clays – digging, pugging and wedging – and in the modelling and sculptural aspect of clay work

Spiral kneading clay

Clay is constituted from dead matter: hard, solid, weathered rock (*granites*) which has been through a long process of decay and transformation. Once processed it is ready to receive form through the movements of the hands of the potter.

In preparing clay bodies and in modelling it is the realm of pure limb movement, say, rather than rhythm, that comes to the fore; pushing, putting, pulling responding to the clay, and allowing the form to appear. Only later, when the student has learnt to respond to the materials, does the actual will element recede into the background and thinking appears, reflected in the design aspect with an expression of feeling through the artistic elements. Yet these elements,

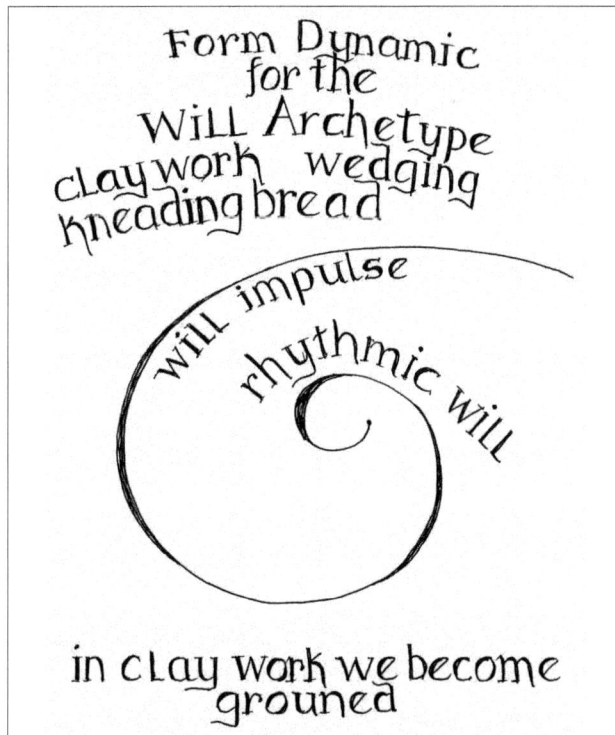

Form Dynamic
for the
Will Archetype
clay work wedging
kneading bread

will impulse

rhythmic will

in clay work we become grouned

Two-dimension Form Gesture for the 'Will dynamic'

too, have to flow through actual movements of the hand. Sue Harker describes in some depth in Chapter 10 the many transformative processes and potentials that are intrinsic to working with clay.

Archetypal movement gestures are of course in reality delivered and experienced *three dimensionally*. For the purposes of illustration, they are here expressed in *two dimensional* line forms for the three craft activities described. The reader should note, however, that although only the

Woman using a back strap loom

chief movement gesture is depicted in the following, there are a host of other refined movements that support and complement the suggested principle of arrested movement.

2. Textile weaving and weaving the sides of a traditional willow basket

In weaving on a loom, the most apparent gesture is initially the repeated and rhythmic up-and-down movement of the feet-controlled heddles and the in-and-out of the shuttle. Here we can witness that a kind of breathing process is imitated.

Straightforward weaving needs little conscious thinking. The limb movements of hand and foot are carried along by the rhythm, which is acquired. These repetitive rhythmic movements, in turn, can induce a kind of dreamy mood and atmosphere.

When at work, the weaver is neither lying down nor standing up, but is seated, indicating a bodily position indicative of a dream-like consciousness. Standing upright is indicative of being awake, whereas lying down suggests a disposition towards sleep-like consciousness.

The activity of weaving could be described as having a harmonising effect and can be seen as potentially therapeutic in generating inner harmony.

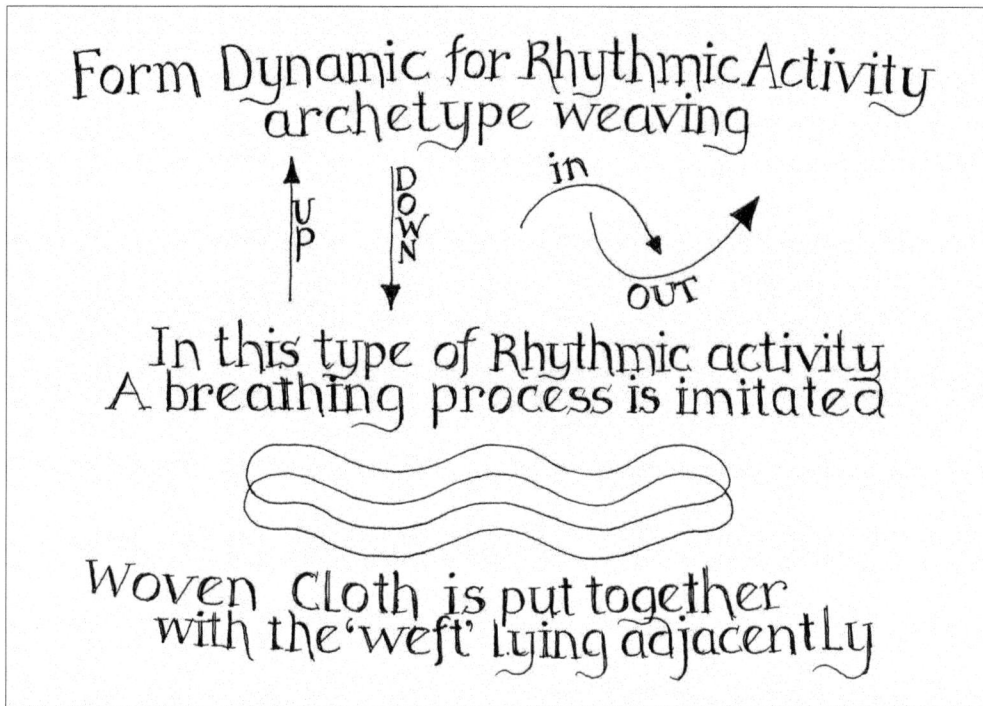

Form Dynamic for Rhythmic Activity
archetype weaving

UP DOWN in
out

In this type of Rhythmic activity
A breathing process is imitated

Woven Cloth is put together
with the 'weft' lying adjacently

Gesture for: Rhythmic – Feeling dynamic

With the master weaver, the purely rhythmic element is balanced with the knowledge, grasped through sequential thinking, of how different threads are picked up by the heddles and shafts. This enables complex weave patterns to be obtained.

It is similar with the basket maker, who is also seated for the siding of a basket, engaging in the rhythmic weaving of rows and rows of rods, to fill the side of the basket.

3. Hand knitting

In contrast to the weaver's wide sweeping movements coming from shoulder to shoulder, the knitter is circumscribed by more precise and confined movements, more so than in either weaving or modelling. They are more exactly determined by the in and out movements of two needles. The experience of movement passes here down the arms to the fingertips.

What raises the knitting movements to the point of consciousness is that the threads, and therefore needles, have to cross at every stitch. To execute left-hand and right-hand movements together, for instance in tying a shoe lace in the human being, means having the ability for a self-reflective, waking up consciousness and the beginning of the ability to form concepts.

Knitting, in particular, has the potential to activate thinking processes[57]. For this reason, Rudolf Steiner encouraged the practice of knitting in the early school years for both boys and girls[58]. Today we have neurological research that supports this observation made by Steiner. More recently elderly patients and those suffering from various brain neurological conditions have been helped by encouraging them to knit.

The following extract was taken from an article that appeared in Das Goetheanum Jan 14 1996:

Hand knitting – dexterous fingers

Form Dynamic for Thinking
Archetype- Knitting

To bring the right & Left hand
into movement and cross them
means for the human being
(or: person/child) an awakening of
consciousness - 'to wake up'

Gesture for Cognitive Faculty – Conscious Thinking dynamic

'Recent research at Muenster and Constance have shown that the often repeated and subtle finger exercises of violinists and guitarists enlarge the centre of movement in the brain.' Hella Krause-Zimmer, The Brain and Finger Dexterity[59]

iv) Craft Wisdom in Fairy Tales

As Johannes alluded in the chapter *Making & Meaning,* ancient myths and legends can be seen to contain an imaginative history of civilisation's development. Fairy tales, such as those of the Grimm brothers (1812), also contain many layers of meaning. There are a few fairy tales in which I believe the wisdom of traditional artisan crafts, and the hidden knowledge that they can elucidate, is illustrated imaginatively. For instance, the spinning of straw into gold in Grimm's *Rumpelstiltskin,* or the more elaborate crafting challenges given to the *haughty princess* told within the fairy tale of *King Thrushbeard*[60] are examples of archetypal human trials and ordeals.

In the story of *King Thrushbeard* we hear of the King's daughter – the 'haughty princess' – who refuses her father's wishes for a marriage of his choosing and is thus married off to a stranger instead. This stranger is a 'minstrel singer' who sets out to teach her a lesson in humility by subjecting her to three trials by three craft activities.

The Trials of the 'haughty Princess' from Grimm's Fairy Tale 'King Thrushbeard'

The haughty princess, daughter to the king, in the story of King Thrushbeard, is visited by various suitors, all of whom she rejects, dismissing them outright and calling them somewhat mocking names. Her father is exceedingly disappointed with her and informs her that she is to be married to the next visiting suitor, whoever that may be. As it happens, the castle is visited by a travelling minstrel singer all dressed in rags and tatters. The king carries out his promise and arranges a marriage for her with

The trials of the haughty Princess

this visiting minstrel. The bedraggled minstrel, seizing the opportunity, takes the reluctant princess from the castle and journeys towards his own land.

Unbeknown to the princess, the minstrel singer is a prince of high repute, and one of the suitors that she had rejected. Now in disguise, he took it upon himself to educate and teach the haughty princess a lesson. Rather than take her directly to his castle he takes her to a hovel in the woods where he gives the princess tasks to perform in the form of three traditional crafts – basketry, spinning flax and selling pots in the marketplace. Initially she fails miserably at the three challenges but, eventually, she overcomes her haughty behaviour, tempers her ways and manner, and is wedded to the Minstrel King, following which, they live happily ever after.

The fairy tale's metaphor

To elucidate on the trials undertaken by the princess we can ask: *What did she learn by making and using baskets?*

Essentially, by making a basket I enlarge the carrying capacity of my hands and bring something into containment. With a basket for instance, I can carry far more than in the palms of my hands.

Anatomically speaking, one could say that the arms and hands belong to the trunk, the middle realm of the human organism, along with the chest, heart and lungs. From a soulful and emotional perspective, this middle realm of the human being can be seen as the seat of my emotions, my life of feelings. From observations made by those that weave both baskets and textiles, the very rhythmic action of weaving has a calming effect on one's breathing and indeed with long-term practice, it can calm the nerves and stabilise the emotions.

In the process of making, a basket acquires its own centre, an enclosed space. It mirrors very much the middle trunk realm of the basket maker, where the ribs and chest cavity form a basket-like space, containing the rhythmical system, the unceasing beat of heart and lung. In the basket, the heartbeat is transferred to the rhythm of the weaving in and out, followed by moving the left hand between the upright rods.

The basket maker, in the changing body positions whilst working on various stages of the work, goes from a sitting, semi-prone position – indicative of a more dreamlike consciousness – into a more upright, perhaps even standing position, when we could say he has a more wakeful, alert consciousness.

The very characteristics of the willow work on those employing the material, being hard, tough, tense yet flexible, warm, wet and feeling somewhat alive. One has to meet and work with the very tenacious resistance of the willow rods, imposing one's own will and intent consciously or else the withies will have their own way. Could it be that the *haughty princess* was made to start with basketry to bring into balance her rather unrestrained emotional and self-centred behaviour?

Then the *haughty princess* is challenged to find her inner balance before she is asked to spin the flax. Spinning yarn can be seen as indicative of spinning thoughts and useful ideas.

Finally, she is asked to sell pottery wares in the marketplace – in other words, to have her wits about her and stand with her feet firmly on the ground.

All craft activities have varying degrees of what could be called transferable personal skills. In some instances, a specific action or demand of the craft gives rise to a number of social metaphors. Many will be familiar with the saying – 'strike whilst the iron is hot' meaning when something requires to be done, best get on with it – don't wait for the iron to cool or the moment to pass.

Moral aspect of making

As a maker, I ask myself on conclusion of my work: has it worked, is my work piece balanced? I then draw my conclusions. If I am honest, it is in the nature of anything I make that it will always fall short of the ideal! The question is, does this give me the motivation to try again and do better? Perhaps this could be called the *moral* aspect of creating and making.

In my experience, it is these embedded qualities and working gestures that present appropriate challenges and rewards to all of us. Crafting needs not only physical strength, for example in basketry to work with willows, but also the will to want to do something with the material, to make it obey one's own will.

Crafting is essentially concerned with *the schooling of the will*, the expression of an *idea in the material*, and in so doing, help to bring to birth an aspect of the *self* within. Perhaps because of these subtle informative and transformative qualities that crafts can convey, we can conjecture that the practising worldwide of craft activities through the course of time has been instrumental in, and contributed to, the 'civilising' of societies.

In the following Section of this book, different practitioners describe their unique approach to crafting and the transformative potentials that lie within a variety of materials and processes that are available to us as makers.

SECTION THREE

CRAFTING:
Transforming Materials
and the Maker

I n the following chapters, different craft practitioners tell us how they transform, and are transformed by, their craft materials and processes. Their accounts give us an insight into the educational value of the various crafts and the life-enhancing experiences that their craft has given them and their students.

This section is a richly woven tapestry – its warp provided by Bernard Graves, who introduces each craft with some leading thoughts and images, its weft emerging through the very personal and professional accounts of crafters working in wool, leather, willow, wood, clay, iron and glass. The section concludes with some considerations of the role of fire lighting – the root of all crafting – in making as well as in education.

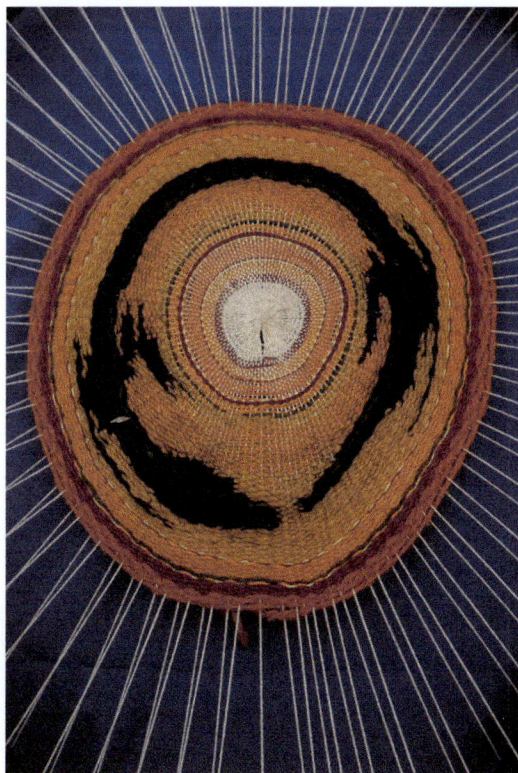

Life's rich tapestry

The Animal Kingdom
– from fleece to felt and skin to leather

Bernard Graves

The first material we will meet as we now delve deeper into specific examples of crafting is wool. Wool is eminently suited to felting, spinning and weaving. It starts, however, as a 'raw' fleece. The modern child will often react at first to this material with a certain amount of disgust exclaiming, 'Ugh! I'm not going to touch that!' Unwashed, natural fleece has quite a pungent smell. However, by beginning with a whole fleece we inform the children about the origins of wool. Better still is to have the children witness sheep being sheared in a farm environment. This really provides the opportunity for children to connect with the natural environment of the sheep. The raw fleece, once brought back from the farm, can be washed and dried carefully in preparation for use in felting or dyeing.

Wool is a material that is very easily accessible for the younger children, as it is not dense, hard or cold like iron – or brittle like glass. Wool appeals immediately to the young one's imaginative and creative aptitudes. A teacher who has given the children a bundle of wetted, soapy wool to work into a felted ball would do well to start by telling a simple story. Consider, for example, the following story: One day, a shepherd climbed a great mountain and with his crook reached up into the sky and plucked one of the clouds out of the heavens. On his way home, he gently massaged the cloud with his hands, compressing it into a ball. He continued to work the ball more rigorously until it became firm and beautifully round.

Throughout the storytelling, the teacher works the bundle of wool, and the children do the same. In no time at all they have a small felted ball and, with the addition of a gold ribbon sewn on, a playful throwing ball. In this manner the children work enthusiastically out of an imaginative picture.

CHAPTER 5

From Fleece to Felt

Frances Graves

I consider myself very lucky to have been brought up on a mixed cattle and sheep farm on the island of Mull, off the west coast of Scotland. I am not sure when I began to appreciate this but as a teenager I certainly did not – we lived three miles from the nearest hamlet and five miles from the nearest village.

When we were children, my two older brothers and I roamed all over the farm and woodlands; climbing trees, making dens, playing with imaginary friends, crawling along pathways we made in the tall grass, exploring the natural world – all the while being vaguely aware of nature beings. Our imaginations and problem-solving skills grew and blossomed. As Richard Louv says in his book Last Child in the Woods, Saving our children from Nature-Deficit Disorder: 'nature inspires creativity in a child by demanding visualisation and the full use of the senses.' This was certainly true for us as we were constantly creative by visualising what we wanted from the natural world and using all our senses to find our way in experimenting and exploring our ability to interact with, and take command of, the four elements: earth, water, fire and air. We modelled imaginary creatures out of sticky earth, dammed streams, played with the mill sluice gates, made waves and rivulets, broke up ice on the river and polled ourselves around on it. We made bonfires and burnt tracts of grass, swayed in treetops in the wind, made and flew kites and used our coats as sails. In our games a large old pair of bellows from a disused smithy became the 'Bellow Boys' who made the wind on the hilltop. We were often in trouble with our parents when we dared too far.

Black Face sheep

In my youth, tenant farmers like my father did not have much money. Everyone came together for haymaking, for gathering sheep from the hills, and for shearing and dipping. Neighbouring farmers did the rounds of the local farms to help each other out. These were great social events in the annual calendar to which we all looked forward. I particularly loved working with sheep and well remember shearing times when there were shearers working at their benches or boards and a sheep catcher to keep them provided with unshorn animals.

It was truly a feast for the senses; sheep bleating, the *clack clack* of the hand shears, the *twang* of the self-shutting spring gate as it closed behind the catcher and the shearers talking, shouting and occasionally swearing. The *clank* of dried up sheep faeces attached to the fleece hitting the shearing boards and the occasional *bang bang* of sheep's feet and legs hitting the boards as they kicked and struggled. The strong smell of sheep's urine and grease – and human sweat! – permeated the air.

I would watch, fascinated, as the shearers deftly turned the sheep into different postures to enable them to clip off the fleece. As the shears slid along between the fleece and the sheep's skin, opening and closing rhythmically with a *clack...clack...clack*, the fleece came off in yellowy-white billows. The fresh inside of the fleece was so much cleaner than the greyishness of the outside part. When the fleece had finally fallen away it would be snatched up quickly and bundled off. The white, naked sheep – released at last – would jump up and run off and then, in great surprise, bounce high in the air once or twice before joining the rest of the flock.

The fleece roller would roll the fleeces up after turning in the edges and then pull out a long strand and twist it with a deft movement of the arms. This would be wound round the fleece with the end tucked in firmly. Each time these activities were carried out in almost the exact same way, which I found somehow comforting.

It was then our turn as children. Massive hessian sacks were suspended from the rafters of the barn, the tops being about 7 ft off the floor. We would be helped up onto the rim of one of these sacks and would sit perched, holding onto the ropes with one hand and catching the fleeces with the other as they were tossed up one after another. We would stuff the fleeces down into the sack. After the bottom was covered, one of us would jump down inside and another would sit at the rim and throw the fleece down into the sack for the packer at the bottom to tramp them in firmly, filling up gaps, but at the same time being careful not to undo the fleeces. Gradually we moved up higher and higher inside the sack until at last we could see out the top. Now we had a clear view of all that was going on below. By the end of the day we were covered in sheep grease from head to toe with pieces of wool sticking to us and our clothes. We were totally immersed in the processes; we loved it and argued about whose turn it was next.

By the time I was a teenager the shearers had switched to using electric shears and one or two men could do the work of a whole team. It became my job to be the fleece roller. This was a real honour and needed special instruction from my father as to how to make a fleece look better quality than it actually was in the hope of fetching a higher price.

Our life was a totally practical one, and from a very young age I accompanied my father as he worked. As children we always had to do our share of the tasks, our responsibilities growing as we grew. These included caring for milk cows and orphaned lambs, sawing and chopping wood, picking stones off the fields, brushing the yard, helping with housework and more. When my father had fences put up he had to make lots of wooden gates. I used to fetch and carry for him and was fascinated to see the gates gradually being built up and how everything fitted into its proper place. The processes and repetition left me feeling secure and inwardly satisfied. I can also remember having this same feeling around the age of four, watching my mother wrapping sandwiches for my brothers' lunch tins. It left me feeling satisfied and secure, seeing the wrapping so beautifully and perfectly done, the same every time, and how neatly it fitted into the tin; everything was as it should be.

A similar feeling is invoked in me as an adult when I have made something creative using my hands: a feeling of well-being, satisfaction… almost like being nourished. This feeling can last and sustain me for days and I can't wait to start the next project. It is as though something has been awakened in me – an interest and a hunger. I believe this is similar to what Frank R. Wilson in his book *The Hand* refers to when he says, '[there is a] pivotal role of hand movements … in developing deep feelings of confidence and interest in the world.[61]'

During my life I have at times felt some intellectual inadequacy, but on the other hand I am profoundly grateful to have 'grown out of nature' and for having had the possibility of having such hugely varied practical experiences and responsibilities as a child. Life on the farm and in the home was my real education, which has stood me in good stead throughout my life. I find it interesting that Richard Louv corroborates this for me by quoting from Finland's Ministry of Social Affairs and Health: 'The core of learning is not in the information … being pre-digested from the outside, but in the interaction between a child and the environment.'

I came across felting when I was about 30 years old, when I accompanied a friend on a day's felting workshop. I found the process fascinating and it was quite a few years later that I became fully conscious of the woolly connection to my childhood. I think this was because in the beginning I used chemically dyed, pre-combed merino tops. Although I enjoyed the process and was satisfied with the end result I felt something was missing. After some time I started using raw British fleece from a friend, and then some from my father. It was then that I felt the full satisfaction of transforming a dirty fleece into a beautiful finished product. This brought a whole new element into the process, which was infinitely satisfying. Using raw fleece seemed to bring it alive for me and I now know there is therapeutic value to the processes involved. I also started to experiment with plant dyes and gradually, as I built up knowledge and confidence, I found the dyeing and colours more and more exciting.

A brief history of felting

'The art of making felt by rolling, beating and pressing animal hair or flocks of wool into a compact mass of even consistency is assuredly older than the art of spinning and weaving' Berthold Laufer.[62]

Felting preparation

Felting is a process whereby wetted wool fibres are massaged together to achieve a flat or three-dimensional item or piece of material.

It is hard to know exactly when felting fleece to make a fabric began, as felt does not easily survive over long periods of time. There have been finds in Turkey of wall hangings that are estimated to be from around 6,500BC. It seems most likely that in the beginning, wool was gathered from the ground and bushes, or even harvested from dead animals, and was probably used for kneeling pads, for lying on, for lining footwear and later for placing under saddles. These uses could all eventually turn the fleece to felt, because there is the added moisture of sweat, along with movement and compression.

There are also finds from Siberian stone burial chambers where, due to a lack of air and the presence of ice, whole rugs were preserved along with felted garments, socks, stockings and cushions. Through the ages felt has also been used (amongst other things) for capes, mattresses, hats, armour and even lining for sarcophagi. In some parts of Asia carts and wagons were covered in felt tents and used as transport. Felt rugs were used in rituals long before woven rugs were used, and stuffed felt animals appear to have had some form of magical element to them. White felt seems to have been valued over other natural colours and used for special occasions.

In countries where spinning and weaving were not so prevalent, felting produced warm fabric with less work. As we know, Asian countries used felt to cover their Yurts or Gers and today it is still used in some places, as are felt boots, hats and cloaks. It works extremely well as an insulator in cold, dryer countries.

Sheep's fleece is made up of the protein *keratin* and the inner cortex expands when moisture is added; the fibres then give off warmth. This is a very clever way of nature providing sheep with extra warmth when the weather is damp. The natural oil that is excreted by the sheep, called lanolin, stops the rain from reaching the sheep's skin. It also protects the fibres and stops them from felting on the sheep. Fleece also has the property of holding moisture within it. It can hold up to 30% of its own weight without feeling wet.

Mongolian Yurt

The strength and thickness of felt is determined by the type and number of layers of fleece used and how well it is rubbed, rolled and shrunk. It can vary from fluffy and loose to a hard, dense piece, which will be more durable and repel water more efficiently. This felt can retain its shape and strength for decades. Felt made from wool is naturally resistant to burning and will only smoulder slowly. As felt does not fray it can be cut into pieces or trimmed and the edges re-felted or left rough.

Nowadays the art or craft of felting is enjoying a resurgence and we have more tools at our disposal than in earlier times. In a Russian museum of felt a demonstration was given of the use of a bow to help loosen and clean the fibres. The fleece was put in a pile over a fine grate and the end of a large bow was placed on the fleece and the string repeatedly twanged. The vibrations travelled down the string to the fleece and caused dirt particles to fall through the pile and through the grate below.

A bow could also be used to help separate and align the fibres, as fleece fibres travel in the direction of the root end, on account of the scales.

Alternatively fleece could also be beaten with sticks during the preparation process to help remove dirt and separate the fibres.

Felt was pounded with fists, rolled with hands, arms, feet and even pulled behind horses to harden it.

Protein fibres from sheep, goats, camel, yak, llama, guanaco and rabbit are all feltable. Each fibre has tiny little scales all along the shaft, which are there to help stop dirt from working its way up to the skin of the animal and also to help shed rain. These scales open up with moisture, aided by the alkalinity of soap; the rubbing pushes them together, the fibres entangle and the scales interlock with one another. A good crimp in the fibre aids the felting ability as the fibres become entangled with each other more easily. The finer the fibres the more abundant the scales are, though smaller. So, for felting, a fleece that has long fibres and has a pronounced crimp

Wensleydale fleece showing long, fine, lustrous fibres with crimp

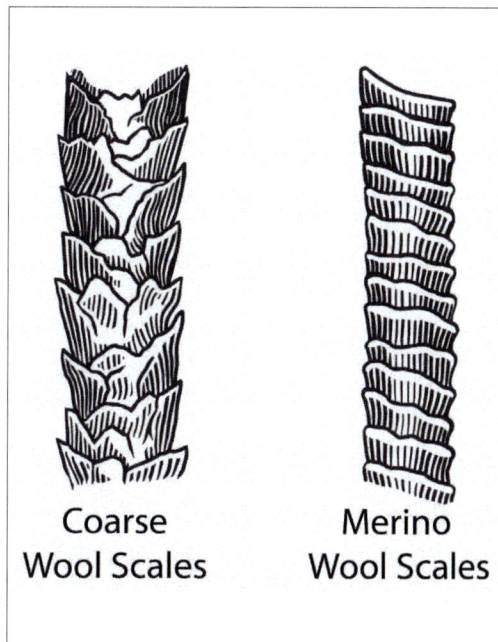

Close-up of wool fibre scales

should give good results. However, one has to take into account the final use of the piece of felt as the coarser fleeces are stronger and more hard-wearing, but are more difficult to felt.

Teaching felting

When I am teaching felting to a group of adults, I guide them through an awakening of their awareness to what is going on both externally, in the movements made by hand and body, and internally, in the way the felting process affects them emotionally, cognitively and physically, as we

Observational drawing of a sheep by Frances Graves

work through the different stages of the process. This degree of conscious, self-attention however, is not appropriate when working with children, even though they will have these experiences, some consciously and some unconsciously.

If, during a workshop, there are no sheep nearby, we look at a whole fleece laid out on the floor. People are often amazed at how big the fleece is once it is off the sheep. We touch, smell, look and perhaps accidentally taste the sourness, and describe our experiences of greasiness, warmth, softness or coarseness. We notice the difference in colour on the back and front, the length of the staple (fibre), where the fleece is denser or more open, the crimp or straightness, fineness or coarseness, and we look at the way the fibres are lying. We try to work out which end is the tail and which the neck. This all awakens our senses, helps us to familiarise ourselves with the fleece and its qualities and to think about the sheep which has given us this wonderful gift to work with.

To further make us aware of the gift of the fleece I like to share this poem with my group which has a sense of 'humble thanksgiving.' and respect for the animal.

The Washing of the Feet

I give you thanks, cold silent stones
And kneel in quiet awe before you.
From you, the plant in me has grown.
The washing of the feet, the washing of the feet, the washing of the feet.
I give thanks green grass and flower
And bend in reverence before you.
You let me win the beast's swift power.
The washing of the feet…
I thank you all, plant beast and stone
And bow in gratitude before you.
Through you my human crown is won.
The washing of the feet…
by Christian Morgenstern

Felting equipment

Felting of wool can be simply achieved with just a bit of soap and water and rubbed in the palms of the hands. This works well for balls and felting around objects such as stones. Equipment for felting larger items is relatively basic and most of it can be acquired from the household or bought from textile suppliers.

- Hand carders or drum carder
- A rush beach mat, old cane blind or even bubble wrap
- A towel is useful
- A piece of net curtain
- An old washing up liquid bottle
- Liquid soap or olive oil soap
- Source of hot water
- A table that can withstand water

Felting processes

Teasing

It would of course be easiest to begin with pre-carded tops for felting, but then the satisfaction of following the whole process from dirty fleece to a beautiful clean colourful piece of felt would be missed. In this day and age of instant gratification and the constant option of pre-prepared materials or premade objects there can be a lack of a sense of respect, gratitude and value for things. It can surely only be a good thing to foster the knowledge of where materials come from, how they are prepared and the time and energy involved.

The first stage in preparing the fleece for felting is to *tease* it. This consists of gently pulling apart the fibres with our fingertips, which allows the dirt to fall to the floor, and any little lumps and knots to be separated. The main gesture in teasing is that of one hand giving while the other takes, using the fingertips. The hands may meet in the middle in front of the chest area, or the taking hand may do most of the crossing and re-crossing of the midline. Many people have experienced a change in their breathing taking place while teasing as they feel their chest region opening up, and they relax into the rhythm of the movements. Teasing is repetitive and can be experienced as tedious or relaxing depending on one's nature.

We might ask ourselves if it is significant that when one is teasing wool with finger tips one's mind is busy; either in chatting with others or in thoughts that often remove us from the task at hand, perhaps even into a dreamy state. It is interesting to note that there is no other part of the felting process where the mind appears to be so active in this way, as in the teasing process.

Teasing wool

If we look at how we have changed the fleece through the process of teasing we see how it has become aerated, fluffy and looks like beautiful white clouds. This process could particularly appeal to those of a sanguine nature, as one can work quickly, building up an expansive, airy cloud of fleece while chatting with others.

As the wool expands in airiness so can our thoughts expand and wander. Our fingertips have a myriad of nerve endings, which link directly with the brain. One could say that the fingertips are the brain of the hand and Immanuel Kant,[63] who is still a central figure in modern philosophy, is said to have stated that the hands are likened to 'the brain transferred to the outside'.

This connection of the fingers to the brain is so important that as Professor Matti Bergstrom[64] says:

> *'If we don't use our fingers, if in childhood and youth we become "finger-blind", this rich network of nerves is impoverished — which represents a huge loss to the brain and thwarts the individual's all round development.'*

We have the well-known saying, something that our grandmothers may have said, that 'nimble fingers make for nimble minds', which resonates with elements of the previous observations.

Through Frank Wilson's[65] research it is now evident that the movement of the fingers, especially in children, stimulates the neurological pathways in the brain and contributes to the development of our cognitive faculties.

Carding

Teasing can be contrasted with the next stage in making felt, which is the *carding* of the fleece using hand carders. I notice every time carding is done that the chatting stops and the concentration deepens as people try to grasp the movements required to thoroughly card their pieces of fleece. It seems that this process is harder to grasp than teasing, and it often seems that the more people try to grasp the movements required intellectually, the more they struggle, and it is really through watching repeated demonstrations and often physical guidance that the movements become embedded in the bodily memory. Once this has taken place, rhythm is usually established and it becomes possible to enjoy a task that is much more physically demanding than teasing. There is often a sense of relief at this stage.

If we now look at the movements needed for carding, and where it takes place in relation to our body, we see that the work is carried out in the lower region of the body. We need to use our leg to rest one carder on, to give stability; this brings the sense of balance into play. The action of the arms is in a circular motion, as we make sure the fibres are all carded from end to end. We can hear the rasping sound of the carders, which lessens as people find the rhythm. Some

Carding Wool

people find this stage very frustrating, while others enjoy this more physical activity, once the movements have been mastered and rhythm takes over. There is a giving and taking from one carder to the other and the dominant hand is constantly crossing the midline creating movement from left to right and from below to above; we can see how the carder is taking control of the material and bringing it into a new order as the fibres are aligned. We might imagine our thoughts being ordered, as the dreaminess and chatter ceases. After carding, the fleece is lying flat in little bats with the fibres all lined up vertically. A certain amount of densification has been imposed on the wool.

Laying out

For this stage we divide the wool into four equal bundles. Using our mat of choice, the wool is laid out in little tufts, close up to each other. The tufts are laid out initially with the fibres lying in one direction, starting at the left side of the mat and working across to the right. The second row of tufts slightly overlaps the first row like roof tiles. When the first bundle is all used up the second layer of wool is then added in the same way but at a 90° angle to the first layer. The third is as the first and the fourth as the second. As we build up the layers in this way, working from left to right and top to bottom on the horizontal plane, we are imposing order on the material and working with a specific sequence. This activity and process could be looked on as a precursor to maths or reading. We are also working spatially in the vertical, with an awareness of what lies underneath and what lies on top.

Laying out crosshatched layers for a flat piece of felt

Laying out coloured wool

Any colour to be added can be put on top in any direction. Our thinking is called into play in the laying-out stage, particularly with a three-dimensional piece, as we concentrate on doing this correctly and make decisions about design and colour. Our feeling life is also involved as we choose colours and make up our design.

We now have a lofty, airy cushion of wool neatly stacked and ready for felting. It should look very pleasing and one can feel satisfied with all the work undertaken to get to this stage.

Rubbing – soft felt stage

A piece of nylon net curtain that is bigger than the piece to be felted is now laid on top to help stop the coloured or top layer of wool from moving around. It is important to remember that the wool will expand before it starts to shrink. A good squeeze of washing-up liquid from the bottle is needed and then topped up with hot water (the hotter you can work with the better, but obviously for children care needs to be taken with the temperature. Felting can work with hand-hot water, it just takes longer).

With the lofty cushion well wetted with soapy water we start to work it first by pressing down gently all over. Suddenly the loft has gone and the piece is flat. This is the next step in the densification of the bouncy, airy wool. Working gently with the palms of our hands we rub the covered, slippery, soft wool with the warm, soapy water. This can be a very sensual feeling. We have moved on from using the fingertips and the thinking part of the project to the palm of the hand. We use a rhythmical, circular motion as we move from the edges in towards the middle. It is easy at this stage to get lost in a warm, silky smoothness and watery dreaminess and enjoyment as our feeling takes over. This part of the process might appeal particularly to the phlegmatic part of our nature.

We need to gradually increase the pressure, however, and after some time a certain amount of frustration can be felt... will my piece ever be ready to turn over or to roll? We have to stick with it if we want a good quality outcome and gradually the will has to be more deeply engaged. We often hear expressions of surprise at how hard one has to work at felting, but at last – and usually with great relief – it is ready for the next stage.

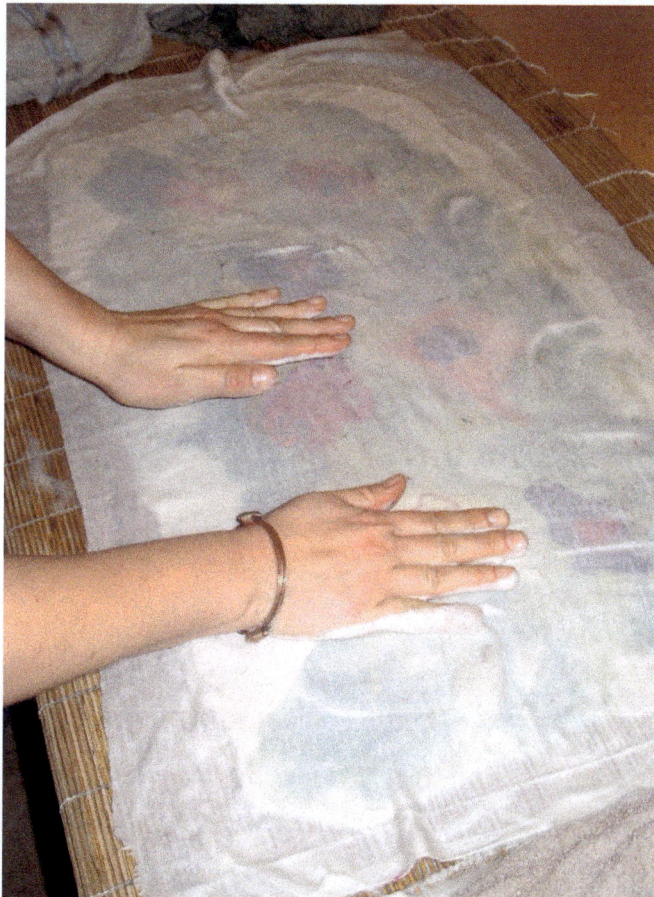

Rubbing – protecting work with a gauze curtain

Rolling

Each process in felting engages a greater degree of physical engagement as the material becomes ever denser. The whole body is engaged; we start with the fingertips and the head, move to the feeling and rhythmic system with the engagement of the palms, and then to the will while using the heel of the hand. We finish by using our limbs, perhaps even our feet. This progression can be seen to mirror the growth of the child as it takes hold of their body, their emotional life and their cognitive capacity. The airy, quick, expansive nature of the young child, with a somewhat chaotic will life, moves into the seven to fourteen-year period when feelings are predominant in understanding the world. Between 14 and 21 the young person is taking a hold of their thinking life and directing this into applied will activity as they move towards their path in life.

In the rolling of felt we are imposing our will through strength, determination, stamina and purposefulness. This activity asks us to move our whole body, which also helps to avoid sore muscles. Singing a good, rhythmic work song in time with our movements has an amazing effect; the more we let go in our singing the easier the task becomes. We get carried along by the rhythm. Group working and singing also makes it easier.

When the felt piece is well on its way it can even be worked on underfoot; rolled by foot or trampled and stamped on. Who better for this task than the choleric?!

We think of wool as being warm, soft, comforting and tactile. In the first stages of the craft it certainly is, but we can see the whole process as a kind of hardening/densification which we could say is mirrored by the child's gradual and natural development as they become ever more deeply involved in the material world, as they grow through the phases of childhood to young adulthood.

In the kindergarten, we might begin with the washing of fleece, which is a very sensual activity, done very gently in warm soapy water in a large basin or sink. This slippery warm softness can induce a kind of hypnotic dreaminess, conducive to early childhood. This is a good age to introduce playing with coloured wool, which can be dyed with plant stuffs, collected with the children from the garden. The dyeing process can just go on around the children as they play, best

Rolling – piece wrapped in a bamboo mat

done in a large pan hung over a fire in the garden. Felting a ball is also an excellent *first* project for this age group as it can fit neatly into the palms of the hands. With older children and adults it is entirely appropriate to approach the dyeing of wool more scientifically using plants gathered from the locality but also dyestuffs from further afield, e.g. cochineal.

Experience has shown that the dyeing process greatly enhances the activity and educational opportunities of the craft.

There are many projects, suitable for different age groups, which can be more or less complex depending on the age. For suggestions see Appendix 1.

Child's felted picture

Felted and embroidered bag by older pupil

Plant dyeing

When I first heard about using natural plant dyes I was very curious and felt this would be a much more interesting, healthy and ethical way to colour the fleece that I used for felting. It took me some time to feel confident enough to actually try it myself. Looking back on this time I cannot help wondering why I did not just start to experiment. I realise, however, that it has been very useful to have gone through this 'block' as I can readily understand why others may find it hard to get started; I have a good idea as to how much encouragement they might need.

Looking back now at my samples that I have kept since I began dyeing I can see how a lot of my colours started out quite pale, or I used dyes that were not very colourfast. My results gradually became more vibrant and with more shades of colour. From the plant materials I have used I have learnt which produce the best colours, how much to use and also those that are not colourfast. People quite often ask me if I use berries, but I have found that although they can give lovely colours they usually fade over time or when washed.

I have experimented with a few mordants, which are substances that make the dye hold 'fast' in the fleece. These are metallic salts such as copper, chrome (I have never used this) tin and alum. Alum is the least harmful of them all and this is the only one that I use now, as I can get all the colours that I need with it and the various natural dyes I use. Colours can be changed after dyeing by adding some acid in the form of lemon juice or vinegar, or adding alkaline wood ash water or adding some iron, which 'saddens' the colour by darkening it.

One interesting outcome I had in the beginning was a deer I made out of what I thought was dyed brown fleece. After drying it and when it was all felted, I discovered that the fleece had turned slightly purple. This must have happened because the PH was changed during felting by using alkaline soap.

Coreopsis flowers for dyeing wool

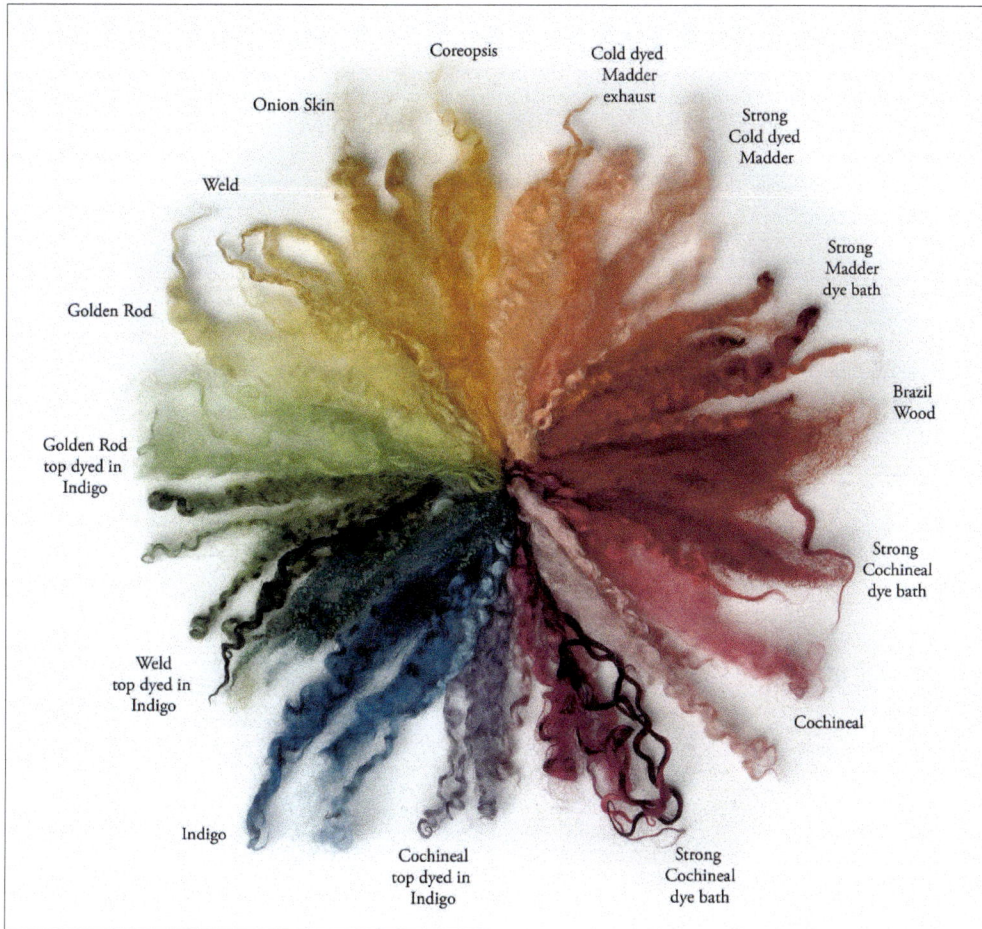

Samples of natural plant-dyed fleece

I am quite passionate about dyeing fleece and absolutely love it when I have done a big lot of dyeing using different colours and I then top dye some of them in another colour and hang it all up on the rack above the Aga to dry. The colours all run slowly from one to the next in a vibrant rainbow of silky curly fleece. This is particularly so when I use Wensleydale fleece which has a long, curly staple and a wonderful sheen to it. The fleece comes out of the dye pot, wet and flat. After it is spun, carefully outside in a pillowcase, it comes out all fluffy and three times the size; I am always amazed at how much there is. Looking at it all hanging to dry I feel incredibly rich and satisfied.

I have never tired from the excitement of indigo dyeing where the chemical magic takes place before your eyes. The fleece is extracted from the dye bath as white as it went in and then, as it is exposed to the oxygen in the air, it starts to slowly turn blue, or if the fleece was yellow it slowly turns green or from red to purple. Other magic in dyeing is when purple and pink cosmos flowers turn your fleece yellow. I love to surprise people with this. There are whole chemistry lessons available here in the dyeing process, as different colours are released from the dye materials depending on temperature or time soaked.

When I look at perfect chemically dyed merino tops (pre-carded in a long continuous tail) it looks a bit dead to me. In comparison, the plant-dyed fleece feels almost alive, looking vibrant

Coloured felted balls

and with many nuances of colour in every bundle. If you are dyeing yarn it is easier to get it all the same colour but for felting we do not need it to be uniform.

I grow some plants in my garden for dyeing such as coreopsis for an amazing orange, calendula for pale yellow. Weld, Goldenrod and onions skins give good yellows while carrot tops and nettles give a greeny yellow. Madder for delicate pinks to a lovely red to rich reddy brown. There are many, many more plant materials that can be used.

For me plant-dyeing fleece is endlessly exciting and rewarding and there are no guarantees as to quite what the end results will be. In fact there are no guarantees in felting either, but I have come to learn that so called 'mistakes' can become acceptable with a little mind shift, or that continuing to work on an item in some way can transform it into something equally useful and/or beautiful as the first intended item.

We also have the opportunity to learn the most when we make a mistake, rather than just getting everything right, as we then learn how to remedy what has gone wrong or how to transform the project. This, I feel, is a hugely important lesson for anyone but particularly children: to learn that mistakes are fine, perhaps even good, which can give the confidence to take risks and to let go of the fear of failure. Hopefully, further positive aspects could be to help overcome the propensity for a throwaway society through a growing understanding of how something can be transformed by our hands into a desirable and/or useful object.

Ideas for projects

Early years – felted juggling balls and felting around objects such as stones. From flat pieces: needle cases, little bags and recorder bags.

7–11 years – from flat pieces: sewing bag, pencil case and a large communal class project to make a piece for a tent.

Group Projects: A whole class communal piece to make up a farm scene. This could also be made from smaller individual pieces by soft felting and cutting out pieces to fit into the larger project.

Simple three-dimensional projects – Felt around objects such as cones, stones or simple templates to make animals to stuff and sew.

12–14 years – to wear: Crowns and waistcoats embellished with embroidery or appliqué. Hats, slippers, hot-water bottle cover and oven gloves using templates. Cut and sew from flat pieces.

12+ years (simple) *and 14+ years* (more complex): Three-dimensional randomly patterned bags, felted around templates, bags with flaps and intricate designs engaging the intellect, nuno felting and progressively more complex designs and patterns incorporating different mediums and techniques.

With each age come different possibilities and different relationships to the medium; always evolving. It is of course important to undertake these projects oneself before bringing it to the children, so have courage and start experimenting; it can become hugely satisfying for yourself as well as others.

'Eco-Literacy'

Bernard Graves

T he development of the 'eco-literacy'[66] movement is one of a number of attempts to draw our attention back to the 'book of nature'. It is by delving into this 'book' that we can realise that everything is joined up, every living organism is in some way related to another, and ultimately dependent upon it. Our school programmes and lessons would do well to reflect the same 'joined-upness'. A school offering a variety of integrated practical skills set in the outdoor classroom facilitates the development of eco-literacy.

To the sensitive hand, mind and soul, the mineral, plant and animal materials that are used in crafting each have something very particular to offer. They convey unique qualities, 'soul food' if you like, that both nourish and replenish us. In this manner, we have come to regard crafting as an intrinsically therapeutic and restorative activity for everyone.

It is the makers, with their ideas or plans in mind and tools in hand, sensitively responding to the varying resistances, that gives shape and presence to the materials used. The hand, our most sensitive limb, manipulates, with the eye and the ear confirming our every move. In return, our materials – be they wool, leather, wood, clay, metals or glass – inform us of their nature and something about ourselves. With attentiveness and openness to our actions, we can become receptive to new experiences and ways of doing things. In other words, we learn something new. Crafting offers us creativity, the means for both repetition and originality, and in so doing becomes a most valuable educational tool whereby we can contribute meaningfully in a world full of a plethora of factory made items.

Animal kingdom – skin to leather

When we come to tanning animal skins and to leatherwork, we find something entirely different from working with wool. This form of leatherwork is only appropriate for the teenager and adult. In my childhood, it was not uncommon to see a rabbit or hare hanging in the local butchers with its pelt still on... but this is now no longer the practice, and most people today would not dream of skinning one.

In leather work, one can, of course, start with prepared leather. An interesting practical chemistry process can be had, however, when involved with organic tanning. Ready-skinned deer or sheep pelts can still be acquired from a slaughterhouse or deer farm, processed and turned into leather using high tannin plant materials like oak or mimosa bark.

Working leather requires more tools and equipment compared with working wool. We now need a design and pattern, sharp implements, cutting tools and needles, and exactitude in our work to achieve a good finish. Working leather also requires a considerable degree of focus and three-dimensional thinking, particularly suited to older teenagers. In our experience, the process of skinning and tanning, sensitively handled, can speak very powerfully to the adolescent. Questions on the meaning of life and moral issues arise in the adolescent soul; questions of life and death, vegetarianism, etc. all come to the foreground while engaged in this activity.

CHAPTER 6

From Skin to Leather

Jeannie Ireland

Tanning and leatherwork – a personal journey

'It is easier to put on shoes, than to wrap the world in leather.' Chogyam Tungpa

'Leather: a material made from the skin of an animal by tanning or a similar process.' Oxford English Dictionary

The skins of vertebrate animals – including mammals, reptiles, birds and fish – can all be processed into a versatile, durable material through a variety of physical or chemical changes to the skins' protein structure. The uses to which this material has been put are almost endless and include clothing, footwear, bags, cases, rope, buckets, bottles, armour, tents, weapons, condoms, drive belts, furniture, sutures, saddles, gloves, hats, musical instruments, jewellery and sculpture. Not only could much be written on the subject of leather, but for many centuries it would have been written *on* animal-skin parchment, and wrapped in a leather binding!

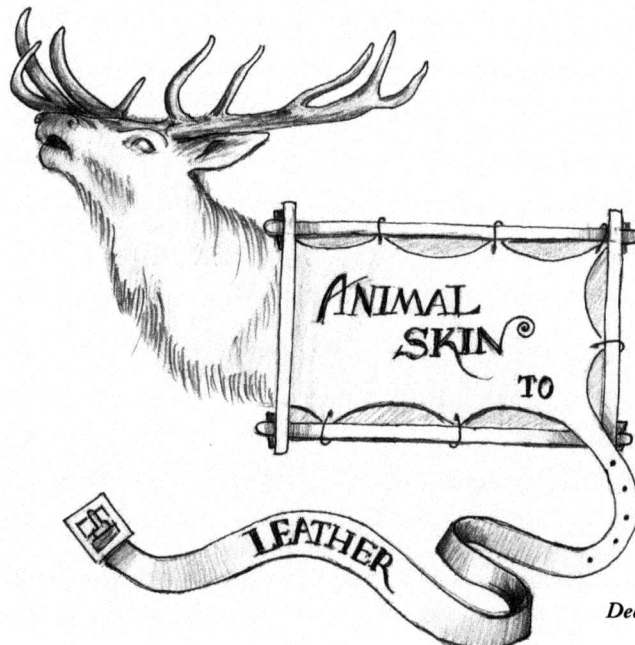

Deer and stretched skin

It was never my intention to become a leatherworker, let alone a tanner. I am told that my great-grandfather was a cobbler, so perhaps there was a genetic predisposition. Certainly craft ran in the family on my mother's side. Her father was one of the first generation of car mechanics, working on the treasured charabancs of the London élite in the 1920s. His father was, as already mentioned, a cobbler and *his* father a thatcher.

The craft genes that I inherited from my mother manifested themselves throughout my childhood. Looking back, I believe I am far more impressed now than I ever was in my youth by her imaginative use of all manner of materials to keep us entertained. She would make kites for us from garden canes and plastic bags. In amongst the bushes of the garden she would hide teddy-bear shapes made of chicken wire filled with moss so that their green fur grew as summer passed. I suppose that money was short, but I certainly had no sense of feeling deprived when trips out meant adventures in the woods. Mum would make camp in an old quarry, kindle a fire and cook sausages for us to eat beneath the trees.

When not busy raising three children, my mother was in the pottery studio. She taught and sold pottery well into her 70s. I grew up surrounded by hand-made ceramics and when something inevitably got broken, her response was always, 'Never mind, it's only mud.' Now that she has passed on, the pieces she made that are still in my possession are a powerful link to her, bringing her to mind every time I use a bowl or a jug made by her hand.

Despite this crafty background, I always intended to be a biologist. After graduation, however, I did not immediately find work and my career unfolded along a meandering path, wandering according to whim and opportunity. My first steps back into the world of craft occurred when I became involved in the reconstruction of an Iron Age roundhouse at the Chiltern Open Air Museum in Buckinghamshire. As well as building the house, we wanted to equip it with goods appropriate to the period and to dress ourselves suitably to inhabit it. The items we needed could not be bought, so we set about learning the skills to make them for ourselves. I found some courses in crafts and in this way I learned the basics of blacksmithing, spinning and weaving. Other skills were more elusive and it became apparent that if I wanted to learn them, I would have to teach myself. These were the very early days of the internet and information – though readily available now – was then desperately hard to find. Trial and error were to be my guides.

I began reading all that I could find on leatherwork and spent time at the British Museum staring at the blackened remains of Roman sandals from Hadrian's Wall and the few other available examples of early leatherwork. I assembled some basic tools – an awl made from a nail hammered into a piece of wood, a hole punch, craft knives and needles. For materials, I scoured charity shops, cannibalising anything I could find made of leather. As my historical interests migrated forwards into the Middle Ages, I discovered more examples for study and I began to make replicas of medieval belt pouches and shoes.

An opportunity then arose that was to take my life in a whole new direction. I met a Native American teacher who invited me to live with him and his family in New Mexico and to study a traditional Native American 'medicine path'. Such opportunities are rare and I did not need asking twice. A week later I had handed in my notice at work and by the end of the following month I was living in the mountains about a four-hour drive from Albuquerque, New Mexico. During this period I was to experience a whole new way of interpreting the world and our relationship with it. As a part of my apprenticeship I was to make my own shamanic tools – drums, rattles and medicine pouches. I had been vegetarian since my early teens and being confronted with the need to scrape skins and prepare rawhide was daunting. My hosts accommodated my refusal to eat meat with patience but scant comprehension – Spirit provided the gift of meat from Creation – why would I refuse it? During my time there I was to have many conversations on the differences between meat from animals reared in commercial units and those considered to be 'our relations' and hunted or reared with dignity and respect.

A deer pelt

When I returned to England I continued to work with rawhide and buckskin, preparing my materials from roadkill deer that I came across or that were picked up for me by friends. I was interested in trying European tanning methods, but information on how to do this was hard to find. A breakthrough came when I started working part time for The Hiram Trust, a charity established to promote practical skills education. I was employed as an administrator, but believe that I got the job more on the strength of my fascination with craft than on my administrative abilities! The Trust provided training for teachers to help them set up practical skills initiatives in their own schools. One of the elements of the course was *From Animal Skins to Leather*. In order to provide both our own materials and as a model for teaching, the Trust's director, Bernard Graves, set up a small tannery. I couldn't believe my luck! I had by this time led workshops at the Trust's annual Craft Camp and Bernard asked if I would be interested in delivering the *Animal Skins to Leather* element of the Practical Skills Teacher Development Course. A central precept of the course was to start each craft from sourcing raw materials. For leatherwork, this involved the participants in skinning a deer and going through the processes of making leather before they went on to work with the material itself.

When it came to teaching the first of these sessions, I found myself faced with a dilemma. Before I work with an animal in this way, my practice had been to hold a brief ceremony to thank it for its gifts and offer blessings. I was reluctant to forego this, but was also aware that others, not sharing my spiritual beliefs, might feel uncomfortable. In the end, I simply explained what I was going to do and why and then proceeded to 'smudge' the deer with Mugwort smoke, to thank it for its gifts and lessons to us and to wish it well in its ongoing journey.

At the end of the weekend, during our review session, many of the participants expressed their appreciation for the ceremony. The challenge of facing a dead animal was daunting and a show of respect and gratitude enabled them to feel they had 'permission' to continue.

I have now taught this process to a wide variety of groups, from teenagers with 'challenging' behaviour to those interested primarily in the science of the process. Each time, I am once again impressed with the depth of response provoked by this meeting with death and the dilemmas presented by it.

A cultural history of leather

Working with animal hides to produce leather was almost certainly amongst humankind's first craft endeavours. It is impossible to know under what circumstances people first began to take the skins from animals they had slain for food, in order to clothe themselves, but it was an achievement that was repeated across cultures and continents. Evidence exists, in the form of stone tools for preparing skins, which predates any surviving examples of actual leather. The shape and purpose of these tools has remained almost unchanged for thousands of years. Flint scrapers used for processing hides are amongst the most commonly found stone tools, in use from the Palaeolithic period onwards.

The remains of tanneries have been found in the ruins of Pompeii and in a pre-dynastic Egyptian site dating to 600BC. Traces of the plant material used in processing the leather were found in both of these locations.

A vivid impression of the reliance of our ancestors on animal skins is presented by Otzi the Iceman, preserved in ice in the Italian Alps for the past 5,300 years. His body was found to be wearing a coat of sheepskin, goatskin leggings, a calfskin belt, cowhide shoelaces and a bearskin hat. He carries a bow, with arrows held in a quiver of roe-deer leather. Clearly, by this period, the skills of making leather from both wild and domesticated animals was well-established.

During the Middle Ages, tanning was considered an 'odiferous trade', and was restricted to the outskirts of town. It is hardly surprising that tanneries smelled bad, considering that urine was used to degrease hides, and faeces (usually dog or chicken) softened the leather in a process known as 'puering'. The many different crafts associated with leather were overseen by guilds, which jealously guarded their own areas of operation. Shoes were made by 'Cordwainers' (from cordovan, high quality leather from Cordoba in Spain). Cobblers repaired shoes, or remade them from salvaged parts (the origin of the term re-vamp, the vamp being the upper part of a shoe). There were strict rules about how much new leather could be employed before the work became the preserve of the cordwainers rather than the cobblers.

In the modern era leather is still produced in significant quantities. Whilst new materials have been developed that fulfil many of the functions for which leather was historically employed, the quality and versatility of the material ensures its continued demand.

Leather-making processes

The skin of an animal, once removed from the body, is subject to decay in just the same way as any other part of the animal. In order to make the skin suitable for our use, this decay needs to be arrested and the skin stabilised. A number of methods have been found to achieve this. They include:

Drying – the bacteria responsible for decay require water; if a skin is dried, it will remain stable as long as it stays dry. The skin will become hard and inflexible and will need to be vigorously worked to render it supple again. Rawhide is the term for a skin that has been dried but not otherwise processed. If it becomes wet it reverts to its original form and will decay if not treated further or re-dried. Rawhide has a number of useful properties; it can be moulded when wet and will then hold its shape once dried – ideal for making drums and rattles. It is light but strong and has many uses for lacing and fastenings; the wooden walls of Mongolian yurts are traditionally held together with rawhide thongs. Parchment is also a form of rawhide, generally from sheep, kid or calf that has been smoothed with pumice and whitened with chalk to prepare it for writing or printing.

Salting – adding salt to a skin speeds up the process of dehydration and improves preservation, killing bacterial cells by drawing water out of them.

Freezing – freezing will arrest the decay of skins and can be used as a temporary measure until other preservation methods can be employed.

Brain Tanning/Fat Liquoring

Amongst the earliest methods used to preserve skins, it was discovered that rubbing the boiled brains of an animal into its own hide softened and preserved the skin. It is this method that was employed by some Native American tribes to produce the beautiful, soft buckskin clothing for which they are justly famed.

Brain tanning a deer skin

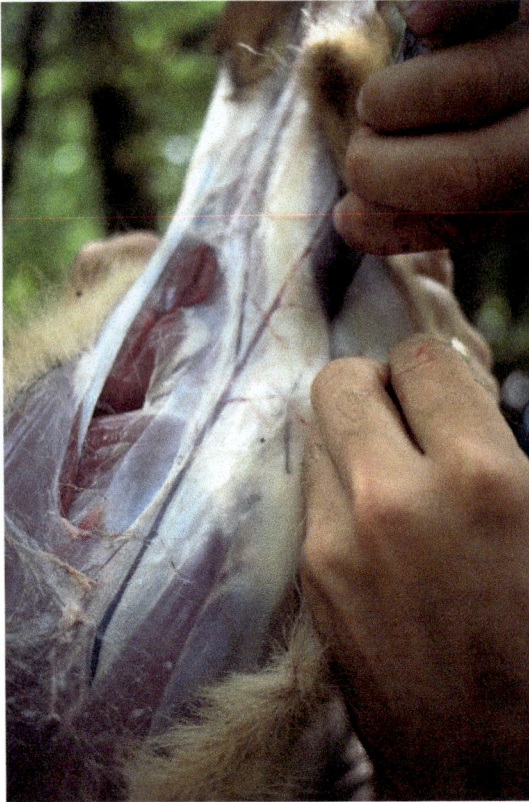

Skinning

The process works by introducing the oils present in the brain into the fibres of the skin, softening and lubricating them so that they will move over each other. Skins processed in this manner have a soft, almost fabric-like feel to them, but will become stiff if they are wetted and then re-dried. If the brain-tanned skin is exposed to wood smoke, additional chemical changes occur which make the product more stable and resistant to this stiffening. The smoking process also produces the yellow/gold hue associated with buckskin, which would otherwise remain a pale cream colour. It is generally held that the brain of an animal is conveniently sufficient to tan its own hide, although for thicker skins, additional oil is beneficial. Brain tanning is possibly better described as a form of 'fat liquoring', as no plant tannins are involved. In commercial leather production, fat liquoring with oil is sometimes incorporated into the tanning process in order to produce softer, more flexible leather. Chamois, or Shammy leather, now primarily associated with car-wash cloths, is also produced by a form of fat liquoring.

Tawing – another ancient method of preserving hides, tawing involves soaking them in a solution of aluminium potassium sulphate, or alum salts. This method was known in ancient Mesopotamia and had spread to Egypt by 1600BC. It was used extensively in the middle ages for producing soft furs and for 'points', the laces used to hold together medieval clothing. The leather produced is soft, supple and slightly stretchy. The process is not stable, as the salts can be washed out of the skin, leaving it to stiffen on drying. For this reason, fats and oils were often worked into the leather to complete the process. Today, tawed leather is still used in bookbinding, but is becoming difficult and expensive to obtain as its manufacture is now largely obsolete.

Tanning – the term 'tanning' is often used as a generic expression for making leather. It is, however, a specific technique involving the use of large, stable plant proteins – tannins – to infiltrate the fibres of the skin, forming ionic bonds with them. The result is a firm but flexible, hard wearing material that will resist decay. Tanned leather is used for a wide range of purposes including shoe-making and saddlery. A number of different plant materials have traditionally been employed, the best known being oak bark (the term tanning comes from the medieval Latin 'tannare', a derivative of 'tannum' = oak bark). The bark of birch, willow, sweet chestnut and mimosa (a form of acacia) have also been used.

Chrome tanning – developed in the mid 19th century, this method now accounts for around 95% of all leather produced. The process, originally used to stabilise catgut sutures used by the medical profession, was adopted by leather manufacturers in 1858. The technique involves soaking skins in a solution of Chromium III sulphate. It is a rapid process, taking less than a day and producing soft, pliable leather used extensively in clothing manufacture and upholstery.

Mimosa bark tanned deer skins

Unfortunately, the Chromium salts employed are highly toxic and its use has caused widespread environmental damage. Methods of removing the poisonous salts from tannery effluent have now been developed but tend to be restricted to America and Europe, whilst the problem remains considerable in the Developing World.

Tanning – The basic process

Of all the possible methods for preparing leather, tanning is amongst the most straightforward to use in the context of teaching practical skills. Tanning is possible on a small scale and produces a material that is ideal for making a wide range of leather goods. Whilst, commercially, Chrome tanning is much more prevalent, the toxic chemicals involved make it ill-suited to home or educational use.

The various processes involved can be broken down as follows:-

Fleshing – (sometimes referred to as 'de-fleshing'): The inner 'flesh' side of the hide is scraped to remove any adhering flesh, fat or membranes. This is generally done over a wooden 'fleshing beam' with a curved blade.

Unhairing – removing the fur from the hide: this can be done in a variety of ways including dry scraping or soaking in running water. More often, however, the fur-covered hide is soaked in a solution of slaked lime (calcium hydroxide). The strongly alkaline solution promotes the breakdown of the outer layer of the skin – the epidermis – to allow the hair to 'slip'. Once the hair has loosened it can be easily scraped from the hide.

Deliming – the hide is washed in water and then neutralised with an acidic agent such as vinegar. This is important as the following stage requires a mildly acidic environment.

Tanning – the hide is soaked in a solution rich in plant tannins. Whilst traditionally, ground oak bark was employed, this can be difficult to obtain. It is possible to buy powdered extract of mimosa root bark, which works very well. The bark of willow, chestnut or birch can also be used and are a little easier to obtain than that of oak as they grow more quickly and regenerate faster when cut. The solution used is fairly weak to begin with and is then strengthened as the tanning progresses.

Un-hairing a deer skin

It is allowed to continue until the tannins have penetrated right through the hide. This can be seen by cutting into the hide and seeing if a pale, untanned line remains at the centre. Chemical bonds form between the plant tannins and the proteins of the skin in a non-reversible reaction, at the end of which the skin has stabilised and become leather.

Scudding – this is a process by which the hide is worked over with the fleshing knife to squeeze out liquid from the swollen hide. It occurs during un-hairing and is repeated several times during the tanning process. It assists the tannin proteins to penetrate the skin evenly and also removes any membranes that were missed during the fleshing stage.

Fixing – the leather is rinsed to wash excess tannins from the surface, which might harden the leather and cause it to crack. A final rinse in an acidic vinegar solution helps 'fix' the tannins to the leather proteins.

Curriering – fats and oils are applied to the skin to replace those lost during the un-hairing and tanning processes. The method can vary depending on the desired finish but good results are obtained by immersing the still damp hide in an emulsion of oils and water and then stretching it on a frame to dry.

Working with leather

Leather is an incredibly versatile material from which a wide range of items can be made. Whatever the chosen project, however, there will be a series of stages that need to be undertaken.

Selecting materials – if there is a choice of hides, students will need to decide which one best suits the project they wish to complete. This will be determined by the thickness of the hide and its relative softness and flexibility. Even within a single hide there will be variations in thickness (thicker along the spine, thinner and more elastic towards the belly). If learners have only the one hide that they have tanned to work with, they will need to select a project that makes best use of its particular characteristics.

Pattern making – the three-dimensional finished work needs first to be visualised as the individual flat pieces from which it will be constructed. It is useful to have the student sketch how she imagines the finished piece will look and consider how that shape can be built up. A pattern can then be drawn on paper – this is probably the most important stage of the project and any impulse to rush ahead before the pattern has been thoroughly thought through should be resisted.

Setting out – positioning the pattern on the leather to make the most economical use of it whilst taking account of variations and blemishes.

Cutting out – carefully cutting out the leather pattern pieces.

Preparation – marking out the position of stitches and making holes for them, skiving, bevelling and any other adjustments required for the project.

Designing – transferring template

Detail – hole puncturing for strap

Construction – sewing together the component pieces using suitable stitches (saddle stitch is most commonly used, but others might be required depending on the project).

Finishing – working on the edges to produce a pleasing finished piece.

There are many additional stages that can be added, including moulding or wet-forming of leather, tooling or leather carving and dying or painting.

Given the wide range of options available, it is sometimes helpful to have students undertake a number of small projects such as key fobs, bracelets and coin purses to familiarise themselves with the material before progressing to something more demanding.

At its simplest, leatherwork requires very little in the way of tools – something to cut the leather with, something to make holes in it, some needles and a suitable thread. Armed with an awl, a rotary punch, a pair of scissors and a craft knife, good basic leatherwork projects can be undertaken. There is, however, a bewildering array of tools available today, each designed to make the work easier or to provide a better, more professional finish. How many tools you have and of what type will depend on your available budget and on the nature of the projects you wish to attempt.

Basic leather-working tools

The lessons of tanning and leatherwork

For anybody interested in working with leather, I believe that it is profoundly valuable to have gone through the process of obtaining your material from scratch – skinning an animal and working with the skin to turn it into leather. Even if you only do this once, it will inform you not only about the nature of the material, but also of its inherent value. This value derives both from the labour required to bring about its transformation and from its origins as part of a living animal.

In western society today it is very easy to become distanced from the implications of our relationships with the natural world. The realities of what happens in order to provide our meat and other animal products is hidden away, sanitised and presented to us in clean, barely identifiable packages on supermarket shelves. This makes it all too easy to ignore the implications of our consumption and to abdicate all responsibility for how that animal might have been treated both in life and in dying.

For many of the students I have taught this is their first close encounter with death and the experience provides rich opportunities for consideration of the ethics and morality of our relationships with animals and of our own mortality.

Leatherwork itself calls upon and develops a range of skills and proficiencies. *Planning and design* is essential before a project starts, together with an awareness of how the material will behave and what it is capable of. *Care* is required in the use of tools, both to prevent injuries and to produce an aesthetically pleasing, practical result. *Focus* is necessary as the various actions of cutting, preparation and sewing require precision and accuracy. Whilst it is often possible to change or develop a design as making progresses, the ability to envision the finished piece and understand how it can be constructed is very important.

As in all crafts, there are variations in the pace of the work. Periods of intense concentration alternate with more rhythmical tasks such as the back and forth action of saddle stitching or the finishing and polishing of edges.

Age appropriateness

The question as to what age it is appropriate to introduce a child to skinning an animal and tanning is open to debate. I believe that if a child grows up in an environment where she commonly encounters recognisable dead animals for food, she will not have problems with encountering an animal being skinned to make leather.

However, many young children today do not have this experience and have developed their ideas about animals from family pets and from television or films in which animals are anthropomorphised. This can result in them becoming distressed when confronted by a dead animal. For this reason, unless I am working with individuals or small groups where I know their background, I would not offer this activity to children under the age of 14.

For teenagers and young adults engaged in exploring their sense of self, their place in the world and their own mortality, the experience of skinning, preparing and working leather can be immensely powerful and rewarding.

Handcrafted leather bag

Frame, drums and beaters

Selection of handcrafted leather goods

Hand-made leather purse and wallet

Cross-curricular opportunities

The process also offers many opportunities of relevance to the wider curriculum, particularly the sciences. Biology is an obvious link, both in terms of anatomy and skin structure, whilst the chemistry of tanning is a wide subject to explore.

For younger students, there are numerous ways to introduce working with leather in relation to a wide range of subjects. It is possible to undertake projects related to history and myth, provided that some preparation of materials is done in advance. An example would be making rune amulets from vegetable-tanned leather as part of an introduction to the Vikings, or making small money bags when studying the Middle Ages. These activities will lay the foundations for more advanced projects in the future.

The two disciplines of tanning and leatherwork are very different in the nature of the learning experience but they are interdependent, and the value of exploring the origins of the material used in this ancient craft should not be underestimated.

Plant Kingdom – Willows to Baskets and Tree to Chair

Bernard Graves

In developing the school grounds as an educational resource, it has proved expedient first to ask the questions, what can our environment offer us? what materials and supplies are currently available? rather than – what can we make it do?!

We can then make our observations of the school environment, to see what it has to offer. Following these observations, we can plan on how to use these resources sustainably or indeed develop them further. If, for instance, a school wishes to have basketry on the curriculum, we could grow and sustain a small withy bed. Students can be involved in cultivating, harvesting and processing willows, thereby enhancing their experience and learning beyond that of only learning how to make a willow basket.

Speaking from my own experience, materials that I work with make a strong impression upon my senses as well as upon my emotions and sense of well-being. Mellowed willows, with their particular

Colourful willows by a stream

Basket-making hands

sweet-sour smell, fill the workshop with a pleasant aroma. The shades of willow barks – olive greens, browns, oranges and reds, along with the whites and buffs – all suggest different colour combinations and designs. The tactile nature of the withy rods is moist and supple, ready to be woven into almost any shape desirable. In the cultivation and preparation of withies, I am brought down to 'earthiness' and am connected to nature's seasons and the demands she makes of the grower. In this manner, in the sourcing of the materials and in transforming them into a basket, I connect with a living process: a dialogue between nature, materials and self.

In working with materials sourced from the plant kingdom, especially where we have cultivated them (such as dye plants for wool work or willows for basketry) the process can start immediately in nature. All craft activities working with natural, woody-type materials require long-term planning and seasonal work in cultivation and harvesting. Likewise, a lot more preparation time is needed in harvesting, sorting, storing, drying and, finally, processing the materials in readiness for working and using. In the cultivation and harvesting of willows and other hedgerow materials, we atune ourselves to the seasonal cycles of nature. This fact alone grounds us and puts the materials used into context. Understandably, a school cannot be expected to grow all the materials required; most will have to be purchased from elsewhere. Where schools have grown their willows, or can go out and cut their own, the joy and the satisfaction in the whole process is greatly enhanced.

Much of the craft of basketry relies on finding the right rhythm of working, archetypally weaving in and out, in front and behind the vertical side stakes in the basket. The bodily position of the basket maker, seated low to the ground, neither upright like the blacksmith nor lying down as if to sleep, but a semi-prone position, for me – this physical bodily position is indicative of potentially being in a semi-conscious state from which I can be seduced by the rhythmical nature of the weaving and enter into a kind of dream state. But the dream is always interrupted, as you always have to pick up the next withy rod to continue the siding or weaving. This experience of dreaming away was brought home to me when a student, in reviewing her work said, 'I just wanted to go on and on…'. In all craft activities, our moods can be profoundly affected by the alternating rhythm of dreaming and wakefulness – perhaps it is this oscillating rhythm that helps us find an inner calm and centeredness?

In basketry, as with all crafts, I relate not only to age-old traditions but, as a maker, I am open to receiving the many benefits and joys that come from working with this natural material. I become acutely aware of the disciplines required to work satisfactorily, the need to focus the mind, develop and apply skill along with appropriate strength, and a feeling for the emerging form. These are all eminently transferable skills to the weaving of life's tapestry.

CHAPTER 7

Traditional Basketry Crafts

Lucy Meikle

My journey with willow and baskets

I have been teaching and making baskets for 27 years and consider myself to be just as much a learner as are my students. We learn from each other, not just the craft techniques but about life, relationships, thinking, communication, motivation, reflection, boundaries, kindness, resistance, respect and reactions.

I consider my own childhood experiences to have been my main education, not my formal schooling, although that did give me a reference to what did and didn't work for me as a student.

> *'Many of the most important lessons in life can be learned but not taught. So even though we cannot teach these experiences, we can work to create an atmosphere to encourage learning'* W. Coperthwaite, A Handmade Life[67].

I grew up on a farm in Worcestershire, where I discovered a real 'sense of belonging'. I owned my own chickens from a young age, paying for their food and selling the eggs. The farm offered a wealth of natural, raw materials with which to build things and develop the imagination. I was always encouraged to draw and make things. We built complex dens tunnelled out of hay bales and planks. We modelled pots from clay gouged out of the river banks onto the front of our canoes. We lay in the stables with new born farm animals and only came in when we were hungry or had run out of daylight.

I was allowed to grow up in my own time and was surrounded by many positive role models. At the time of doing my exams, I remember thinking what a strange system it was; all I had to do was sit and memorise the facts (which I didn't understand), put them on paper for the exam and then promptly forget them (which I did!). I knew that none of it had sunk in and the only way to retain the learning was to do it myself and learn by my mistakes. Being able to go wrong and make mistakes is how I believe we learn.

I went on to study art for 5 years, which further developed my skills in how to really observe and advance my hand-to-eye coordination. I find that, having developed this capacity, I can turn my hand to many crafts, and enjoy making and mending the things we need for our home. Whilst at college I explored South American 'Braiding' methods which link to weaving techniques. I have always enjoyed observing how people do things and I try to relate to their experiences, which can help to develop empathy.

'Until recently, evolutionists thought that it is the uses of the hand, rather than changes in its structure, that have matched the increasing size of the brain. Thus a half-century ago Frederick Wood Jones wrote, "It is not the hand that is perfect, but the whole nervous mechanism by which movements of the hand are evoked, coordinated, and controlled" which enabled Homo Sapiens to develop.' Richard Sennett, The Craftsman[68].

After art college I went on to work at Kettles Yard gallery in Cambridge. It was an unusual gallery, as it ran a contemporary gallery alongside the home of Jim Ede. It represented art and beauty in the own home in daily use, and placed nature up with the top artists. A rounded beach pebble would sit side by side with a Gaudier[69] sculpture or a Brancusi[70], neither one being valued more than the other. Ben Nicholson[71] paintings, and the work of other St Ives artists, were loaned out to the public to hang in their homes. This helped me bridge the relationship between art and craft, as I could see a place for both. I looked to cultivate art as having both a practical and an aesthetic role. As a child, I cared deeply about how things looked, what materials they were made of, and always made presents, valuing the effort and love that goes into the homemade gift. I spent several years doing farm work with a travelling group of field workers who camped on farms around England, so furthering my love and connection with nature.

For a while I worked at Westonbirt Arboretum, home of one of the country's largest willow collections at the time, useful for getting willow cuttings. I also trained as a hedge layer and did some basket-making courses at weekends with many experienced basket makers.

I was then given the opportunity to train as a basket maker and offered a post tutoring in a Specialist Education College, Ruskin Mill College in Gloucestershire. This role facilitated a weaving together of my childhood experiences and influences, my love of nature and the environment, my interest in craft and using my hands, and my wish to serve people and contribute to a community.

'The real voyage of discovery lies not in seeking new places but in seeing with new eyes.' Marcel Proust[72]

I am passionate about making and its therapeutic value. To me, the benefits of a craft-/ land-based curriculum is common sense. From my own experiences, I have always found being creative nourishes and calms me, gives me a sense of well-being. This transformation is not only in the raw materials being fashioned into a finished product but within the maker themselves.

History of basketry

During the Palaeolithic Age (circa 7000BC) people made a variety of weavings. They would fasten their stone axes to wooden handles using animal tendons, strips of skin, tough grasses and bark fibres. Simple shelter and housing was made by using vertical posts as stakes and then weaving small branches and vines in and out of the stakes. These structures could then be smeared with clay or manure to keep out the weather. The Bronze Age provides the first evidence of container-like radial weaving.

Basket weaving is one of the crafts most widespread in the history of any human civilisation. It is hard to say just how old the craft is because natural materials such as willow, wood, grass and animal remains are perishable over time. The oldest known baskets have been carbon dated back to 10,000BC, and were discovered in Egypt. Occasionally, charred remains have been preserved because they can resist normal decay. The most common evidence of ancient basketry is an imprint of the weave on fragments of clay pots, formed by packing clay on the walls of the basket and then firing the pots.

The materials available in a given region would have influenced the styles and techniques that developed in that area. In Japan and China, bamboo and cane are the traditional materials.

In Britain, oak, hazel, willow and other wild materials were used for making the strong rigid containers and fish traps necessary in a hunter gatherer's everyday life. Fences and houses, too, were built from wickerwork or wattles.

Basket-making mostly remained a seasonal job, reserved for the dark days of winter. In lowland Britain in the 19th century, the weaving of willow, using different techniques, developed into a profession and ultimately a sizeable industry. In the 19th century the main growing and making areas of Britain were Somerset, Dorset, Gloucestershire, Nottinghamshire, Staffordshire, Berkshire, Suffolk and Norfolk, where everything, from cradles to coffins, was made.

'Borrow from cultures old and new and with our imaginations blend those borrowings to create new ways to live that are simpler, gentler, more generous and beautiful.' W. Coperthwaite, A Handmade Life.

Growing and gathering materials

Growing willow follows the turning of the seasons, with planting and harvesting done in the winter months. We can also go out to gather hedgerow plants such as wild dogwood, snowberry, clematis, spindle berry, hazel and lots more. This gives us a variety of materials, colours and textures to weave into our baskets and an appreciation of our local environment.

The willows, genus *Salix* (Salix means near water), has about 400 species with fossil remains dating from 100 million years ago. Willow has connections with healing, health, protection, the moon, water and love.

Willow can be easily planted in winter using 30cm cuttings (23cm pushed into the ground with buds

Free-form basket

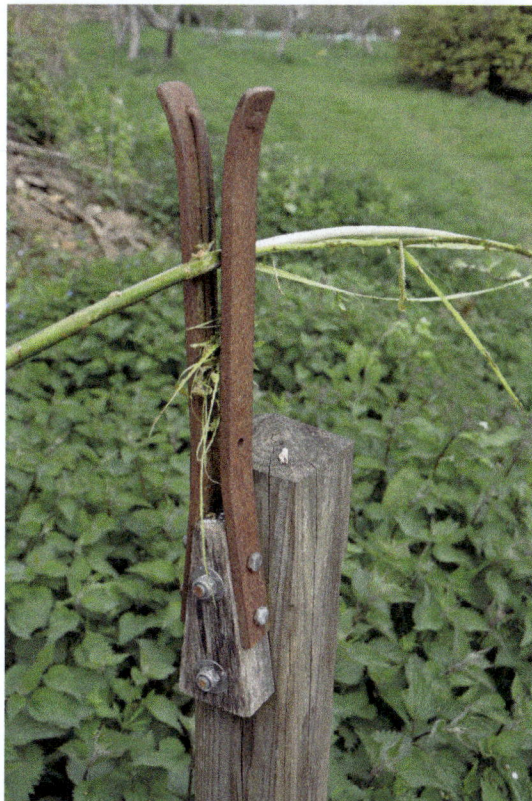
Willow Break – Stripping green willow that has been standing in water for four months, in May when the sap is rising, to make white willow

A selection of willow and hedgerow material

Four main tools used offer opportunities to be health and safety aware

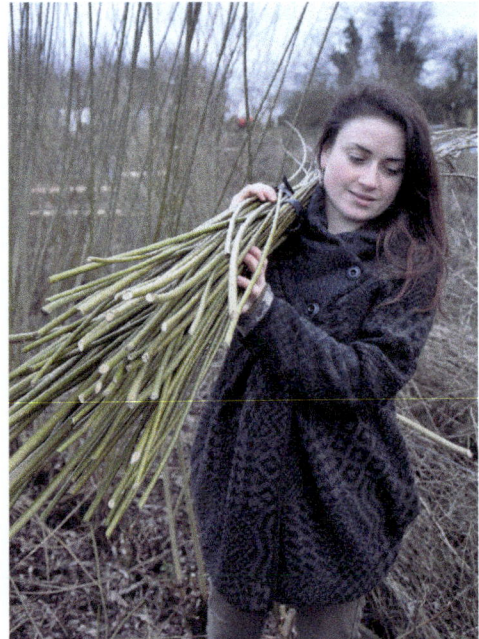

Harvesting willow

pointing upwards) and grown to provide a harvest each year of long, strong flexible rods. They can provide a variety of natural colours and there are some simple processes to vary colour and texture: green willow can be stripped of its bark to make a smooth white; brown willow can be boiled and stripped to make buff willow or can be boiled and left with its bark on to make steamed willow, a rich dark shade.

The willow is then sorted into sizes, to be sold in bolts of different lengths and colours. These can be used whilst still green and flexible or dried and stored, and then soaked in water when needed. Soaking and mellowing times depend on the size and type of willow. We use a tank to soak but an old bath works too. To mellow, we put the willows under a blanket after soaking which helps to make them more flexible.

Making the baskets and educational values

In the workshop, learners sit on the floor in a circle, facing each other. They work on large, wooden boards that rest on their laps, with the baskets in front of them and their willow and tools beside them.

Pairing weave – base

Joining on two new willow rods

Pairing the base

Inserting side stakes, applying your own will

Trimming base

Upsetting the Basket

A double French randing weave

Starting the border

Building up the strength and coordination of the hands, and hand to eye connection whilst manipulating the willow

This is the traditional way that baskets are made. It means that, not only are the learners engaged individually on their own creative project but, at the same time, they are part of a social circle, where the opportunities for conversation are able to flourish. The feel, sight and smell of the willow enriches the sensory qualities of the experience.

As learners weave their baskets, they are encouraged to incorporate their own interests, making their own individual, creative decisions about the design of their basket and thinking about the function of their basket and what they might choose to put in it. Over the years, learners have made an extensive range of baskets: dog/cat baskets, log baskets, fruit baskets, laundry baskets, coracles, rush hats, beehives, plant climbers, live willow shelters, duck-nesting baskets, etc. These have all started from the simplest weaves and then progressed to more complex challenges as the learner's skills grow.

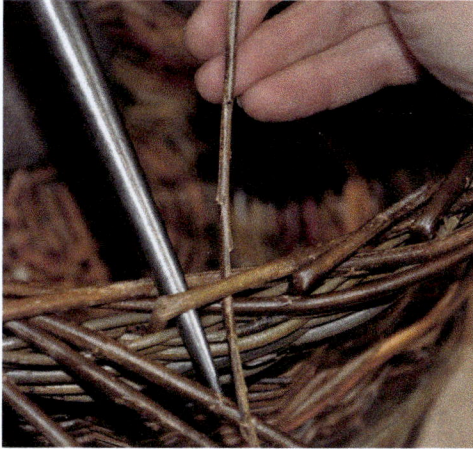
Using a bodkin to complete a border

Finishing off border

Using secateurs to trim the ends off

A finished border with roped handle

Where we can, we look to share our skills with other areas of the college giving students a sense of being able to contribute to the wider community and collaborate with each other. You may make a basket and add leather handles or use hazel wooden slates for the base of the basket. A willow coracle would need a wooden paddle and seat. Baskets can be made for the kitchens to serve food. Surplus willow can be used to make drawing charcoal.

> *'The need for imagination, a sense of truth and a feeling of responsibility, these are the very nerve of education.' Rudolf Steiner*[73]

It works well when the teacher has the flexibility to respond in the moment and take up unexpected learning opportunities as they arise. My first aim is always to connect and build up trust with each person.

Encouraging learners to take part in the whole process helps to develop their relationship with the world around them, socially and culturally. It is a reflective process, which engages their ideas, feelings and behaviour, and mirrors back to them the reality and consequences of their actions.

A 17-year-old student's reflection on the experience of basket-making

A lot of modern society and culture, I have found, is geared towards very superficial and transient goals. You go through life being told 'you must look like this' or 'you must look like that' or, in short that you must conform. For all that people speak of Equality and Fairness, people show a remarkable lack of upholding principles when confronted by someone unable to think or act like they do.

If you are incapable of following standard options, when what is obvious to others makes no sense to you, it is easy to fall into self-blame, bitterness and resentment, a lack of confidence in ever achieving anything at all.

However, learning crafts does offer some benefits to this. If you can't make sense of the world, you can make sense of the smaller things. I cannot sit in a classroom at a College and learn. I am probably not conventionally employable.

However, I can make baskets. I can solve the smaller problem of how to take a bundle of willow and create something functional out of it by the end. After failing at the conventional options of education, you can learn, by looking and listening and touching, how to make something, and that is an achievement; and in small ways the world starts making sense.

Once you have small achievements, once you know you can do something, it is easier to aspire to achieve something else. That is infinitely valuable. It gives you traction on the world.

Willow Weaving Student

Some learners choose to give their craft work away as a gift or use their baskets in the home, which can then be a daily reminder, consciously or unconsciously, of the challenges and achievements that have gone into their work. Learners may eventually benefit from selling their work and feel the sense of achievement that can bring.

Teaching students practical, transferable and recognisable skills illustrates their potential to create change in the world, encouraging them to take responsibility for themselves. It builds their confidence and self-esteem. The working environment is one of mutual learning and respect between teachers and learners, where we value diversity and look for equality of opportunities for all.

The full involvement in the whole process of each activity enables the learner to experience its intrinsic integrity. From sourcing (as in growing the material) to designing and making the finished article, the learners have an opportunity to grow, tend, plant, harvest, soak, sort and mellow the willow/hedgerow material before it is used to make baskets. Engaging the learner in all stages gives them an opportunity to develop a relationship with nature and a greater respect for the raw material that is worked into the finished product. If they can see the effort and care that has gone into it at all stages, this builds a greater personal connection and understanding of the value of the craft item they have made.

I encourage each student to progress at their own rate and incorporate other social, physical, numerical aspects and aspirations into their individual projects. If a learner would like to be able to improve their friendship skills I will plan to give them opportunities within the session to integrate and communicate with their peers, prompting and supporting them in their social development. The experience of basket-making in the workshop gives the learner an opportunity to embed their learning in context. Many of the skills are 'transferable skills' which can be used in everyday life or work situations:

- Planning and sequencing
- Time keeping
- Health and Safety
- Keeping one's work area tidy and organisational skills
- Improved concentration and focus
- Friendship and social skills
- Contributing to society / family (gifts or baskets needed at College)
- Improving hand-to-eye co-ordination and motor skills
- Overcoming challenges
- Recognising one's own achievements – building self-esteem and confidence
- Making Choices and becoming self-directing
- Managing expectations
- Building on communication skills
- Developing motivation
- Choosing realistic projects
- Integrated, practical literacy and numeracy experience
- Problem solving
- Empathy and understanding of others' challenges
- Compassion and helping others
- Ability to reflect and look for ways to progress
- Following instructions
- Sharing skills by teaching and showing others

The resistance and discipline of the raw material is its own unspoken authority. We can learn the qualities and capabilities of the willow rods; how far you can bend them before they kink or break depends on many things; how long they have been soaking, their thickness, age, careful handling and weather all play their part. With practice, we start to gain expertise at manipulating the pliable willow, giving us an experience of being in control that we can build on. If a rod breaks it can easily be mended, showing that healing and repair is possible not only in the basket but subconsciously in our own lives, something particularly poignant for learners who have experienced difficulties. In mending the basket and overcoming challenges we can start to heal ourselves.

> *Diminishing the fear of making mistakes is all-important in our art, since the musician on stage can't stop, paralyzed, if she or he makes a mistake. In performance, the confidence to recover from error is not a personality trait; it is a learned skill. Technique develops, then, by a dialectic between the correct way to do something and the willingness to experiment through error. The two sides cannot be separated. Richard Sennett, The Craftsman*[74].

I place a high value on experiential learning, learning by doing. The more senses involved in the learning process, the more knowledge is retained for longer. The more times new skills are reinforced and recalled, the more they are retained. I have observed its many benefits with our students as they transform and progress.

'Give the pupils something to do, not something to learn; and the doing is of such a nature as to demand thinking; learning naturally results.' John Dewey[75].

When we are basket-making, we are working with the three dimensions of space, using our whole body: balance, weight, limbs, fingers, smell, touch, movement, temperature, etc. With the movements, rhythms and gestures of basket-making we engage the learners. These rhythms, using different weaving patterns, can become reliable like the world turning and the seasons changing, in some cases becoming autonomous and driven by muscle memory. The effect can be very calming and can take one away from the complications of an over-active mind into more relaxed thought processes.

Learners can be the creators of order out of chaos, taking mixed-up willow rods and weaving them into a beautiful, upright functional basket. Confidence and self-esteem grow as the learner reflects on their achievements and looks to improve their skills.

My experience is that each basket is as individual as its maker, reflecting the basket maker's skills and struggles as they weave a container out of their imagination and into reality.

Baskets – a woven story

The Core of Nature is to be found within

Bernard Graves

We can recognise that there are tangible strands connecting us with nature and, inasmuch as we can regard the human being as both physical and spiritual, so too can Gaia be regarded as a differentiated being, comprising the inanimate mineral kingdom, the living plant kingdom and the sentient animal kingdom. We humans, as living, breathing and thinking beings, can grow in independence – not away from nature but with her, and she can help us find ourselves. We can also discover that through working with and transforming natural materials, we can discover vital aspects of ourselves. Our thinking, feeling and will for action can be informed by nature through the innate qualities of the materials themselves, together with the focus and sensitivity required.

J. W. von Goethe (1749–1832), in contemplating the relationship between man and nature, pointed to something profound which science has all but overlooked: 'Is not the core of nature in the heart of man?'[76] *By this, Goethe pointed to something profound. Rather than seeing the human being as separate from nature, he advocated that there was an intrinsic bond and that a study of nature would reveal the secrets of the human being, and that by an investigation of the nature of our human constitution, we would discover the secrets of nature's being.*

'The core of nature lies within the human heart' paraphrase from Goethe

Woodland and green woodwork

Woodwork has traditionally been part of many a school's technical or practical skills curriculum. Here, hard well-seasoned woods would be used to make finely jointed items such as a jewellery box, put together with a number of traditional jointing methods. There is, however, another woodworking tradition called Green Woodwork, which today is enjoying a revival. This approach works with freshly cut timber to make crafted items – from a simple rolling pin to a more complex steam-bent chair. The greenwood-worker shapes the wood using a variety of axes, a shaving horse and a pole lathe.

Like working with willows, sourcing suitable green wood materials takes us into the very heart of nature. Hedgerows and small woodland copses can provide us with material such as ash, birch and sycamore. These can be used immediately to good effect. The experience of the immediacy of harvesting the raw material and of the finished product is exciting and rewarding, the smell of the sap evoking memories of being in the woods, and the smooth lathe-finished item feels pleasant to the touch. It is also immensely appealing to the eye. The advantage of green woodwork is that it can be approached by all ages and all ranges of abilities, starting with simply stripping bark from freshly cut branches and then moving on to whittling and carving techniques.

As part of woodland management around the school grounds, wood can be collected and processed in readiness for various other activities, such as charcoal making, fuel for cooking fires and clay bread ovens, or it can be seasoned for use in all manner of wood construction projects, from primitive shelters to more formal timber constructions.

Working on a traditional pole lathe

A dedicated woodsman might change the three Rs ('Reading, Riting and Rithmetic') to the three 'Ss': 'Sawing, Splitting and Stacking'. One could think of these activities as prerequisite craft-literacy skills. I have witnessed first-hand in a school the great joy and delight of young children whose job it was to collect and process wood that was destined to be turned into charcoal, for use in the blacksmithing forges used by the older school students. The school had established a small charcoal-making industry, whereby children from the younger classes had the opportunity to engage in what is one of the oldest industries known to man and at the same time experience themselves as serving others. The same children also had responsibilities in growing and maintaining the modestly sized school tree nursery in full awareness of the need to replenish their woodland resources. I found this to be an exemplary model of education for sustainability.

Compared to animal and plant materials, working with wood requires not only more time and energy, along with the use of cutting tools, but special qualities of hand sensitivity and feeling are called for. This can often be seen as the woodworker runs his fingers and hands over a piece of freshly planned or scraped wood to judge the smoothness of finish. Woodcrafts, as described above, offer the opportunity for children and adults alike to work in, and enjoy, woodlands and hedgerows in their ever-changing seasons and cycles of work. Wood crafts also, in their increasing density of material, provide us with the pivotal transition from the softer, more easily worked animal materials to those like clay, metal and glass obtained from the mineral kingdom.

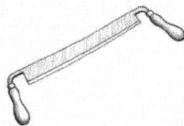

CHAPTER 8

Green Woodwork – From Tree to Chair

Richard Turley

"'The key was the wood,' Alexander recalls, 'I turned some wet wood and I was fascinated, it was so easy and so beautiful. Suddenly I knew it was the only way to make chairs, not with the hard dry stuff you buy in lumberyards.'" John D. Alexander[77]

Coppiced Sweet chestnut wood – Sussex

Personal journey to becoming a green woodworker

My first experience working with green wood was twenty years ago, in 1997, when I was fortunate to do a weekend course making gate hurdles with Syd Lukehurst, a third generation craftsman from Kent. Syd learned his craft from his father and grandfather, and he shared memories of working in the woods with them from the age of three. It had taken him twenty years to learn what we were attempting in a weekend.

I can still remember the care he took to arrange his tools and particularly in selecting the young ash trees we would be using. Syd took time to eye up the growing timber so that every part of the tree might be used with as little waste as possible; spiles, rails and braces came from the same tree and he was able to judge whether the rails would wind or cleave straight. This was a hard task in our overgrown, neglected woodland, and it made me realise what we had lost from not participating fully in our ancient woodland. There was a simple quality to the attention to functional details in these gate hurdles. Syd aimed to produce a hurdle that was light, strong and balanced and optimised the use of material. He was proud that his skills should be recognised in the community.

This weekend of hurdle-making started me wondering about the nature of intelligence. I had four A levels and two degrees and yet had little knowledge of how to interact with the natural landscape, which I knew my well-being depended upon.

Since then I have been teaching and making woodland craft at Ruskin Mill College with young people and adults, unconsciously mindful of this ancient wisdom of process and service in woodland landscape and community.

Traditional pole lathe set

Early years

I grew up an hour away from the Yorkshire Dales on the edge of Leeds. In the 1970s and 80s Mike Abbott was slowly rekindling traditional woodwork but I had no idea it was still practised. At school I made a footstool and book rack. We used plank wood, measured out the timber and learned to cut along lines with a chisel and hand saw. My dad was particularly pleased with the footstool. It felt good to have something tangible to bring into the house.

My parents had cycled to North Wales and Cornwall after the war and they told stories of their glimpses of rural life at the end of an era, before that of widespread tourism. My childhood was spent outdoors and my formative years were spent rock climbing, caving, mountain walking, hitch-hiking and wild camping with friends. An interest in landscape led to a degree in geology and teaching but I longed to work closer to the land. I first saw a pole lathe demonstration at a music festival. The Anglesey Bodgers in the 1980s brought green woodwork to alternative counter cultural events around Britain and later I would also set up lathes at local fayres and festivals. I found that most of the people I taught found a joy and satisfaction in the rhythm and movements that are involved when creating items on the pole-lathe.

I still explore the British landscape above and below ground, but have found teaching in the woods and workshop to be just as physical, challenging and creatively rewarding. I found work teaching at Ruskin Mill and continued to learn my craft alongside young people who were quite forgiving of my early failures. It has been exciting and innovative combining land work, craft and therapeutic education.

I doubt I would ever make a living solely from the repetitive making asked of the country craftsman of the past. My journey has been as part of a learning community, and although this has tensions and resistance just like the material I am working with, it teaches me and – as long as I take time to reflect and digest – I continue to be nourished.

Historical aspects of green woodwork

John Alexander first coined the term green woodwork in 1978. Alexander was particularly interested in how he could work efficiently with freshly felled wood. He investigated the character of wood as it dried and shrank, enabling him to gain intimate understanding of the mechanics of chair assembly. He demonstrated that, working with traditional tools and with knowledge of the qualities and dynamics of green wood, one could produce a chair that is strong, lasting, beautiful and relatively easy to make.

In North America, John Alexander and Drew Langsner[78] continued to study and develop green woodwork ideas. The craft had been kept alive and evolving in the east of the USA by country craftsmen. This revival of traditional techniques, which had seemingly lost out to technology, showed that green woodwork methods demanded attention and intelligent choices and provided work which inspired and was enjoyable. They wanted to revive the processes of the country woodwright for the benefit of city dwellers as much as those in the countryside. In the 1970s, Mike Abbott brought back to the UK (from the USA) this knowledge and, after working with the few remaining British craftsman, started the green woodwork movement we see today.

Fashioning furniture with hand tools may seem archaic and crude to those involved with today's technological design possibilities. However, Mike Abbott refers to a 'brutish elegance' afforded by a chair 'where every single element had been wrested from the tree with only hand tools'. He suggests that these chairs are faithful to tradition and linked to a cultural perspective, which may add value to those who use them. Working with the grain of the wood produces a chair which is inherently strong. The rebirth of traditional wood craft in the last fifty years is partly due to a growing need to live with more attention and care, with a deepening connection to this Earth.

Choosing a tree and deciding how its character and qualities will best serve its function makes us accountable to the world we live in, it offers meaning to existence and affords self-

Ruskin Mill greenwood workshop 2016

determination. As Peter Korn[79] suggests, quoting Victor Frankl: 'a craftsperson is able to decide what he becomes; in each moment he or she does not simply exist but can change their mental map and this can be highly motivating'. In green woodwork each artefact is unique and throughout the process you must be awake to choices. The path is risky and sometimes unforgiving but the maker can be autonomous and free from cultural habit. Craft is a living expression of culture, not just tradition and, to many, green woodwork could well be the beginning of a new wood culture, as both Ben Law and Barn the Spoon suggest in their recent books: *Woodland Craft*[80] and *Spôn*[81].

The axe is the principal tool of green woodwork and is as essential now as it was 10,000 years ago. Beautiful axes were made at Penmaenmawr in North Wales and in the Langdales of Cumbria and were used for 6,000 years of forest clearance. The stone axe has been shown to be highly effective and for two million years humanity evolved and adapted alongside the use of sophisticated tools such as stone axes and flint knives. By the Bronze Age, British wild wood was all but gone and woodcraft was already sophisticated. Northern European culture and intelligence developed hand to brain with the use of the axe.

The woodwright of Anglo Saxon times was central to the community. Simon Sharma[82] suggests that our collective memory identifies with a utopian 'greenwood' culture of these times. Until the Norman Conquest the greenwood 'was not an imaginary utopia; it was a vigorous working society'. It was far from wild, quite the opposite – pollarded, open pasture woodland. It was not a place of fear and darkness where one might lose oneself but a place where one might find oneself a place in the community. The greenwood was common land where social hierarchy was turned upside down. Greenwood provided for everyone Sharma writes: 'The mark of these western, woodland societies was not their separation from, but their connection with the rest of the world.'[83] Alongside furniture making, fuel was taken for glassworks and breweries, timber for town houses, coppice wood for tool handles and fences, wattle for building, oak bark for tanning, charcoal for iron work; swine were herded and fed on beech nuts and acorns in wood pasture, deer were hunted for venison, and hazel and chestnuts were foraged to be ground into flour. In Shakespeare's *As You Like It* the greenwood is a place 'where conventions of gender and rank are temporarily reversed in order to find truth, love, freedom and above all justice.' Alexander Langlands[84] quotes Sennett as saying that craftsmanship is a state of being engaged – how we interact materially with each other and our surroundings. Langlands tell us that 'Craeft' was a term celebrated for its wisdom, and Alfred the Great recognised this and set about promoting it.

The social order changed with the Norman Conquest and the value of the greenwood was taken by the ruling class. Forest laws took away the wood culture and community spirit of place from our ancestors. In 1217 the Magna Carta was signed under the Ankerwycke Yew, the oldest tree in Britain, and gave back some of the woodland rights to the people of England. Eight hundred years on, a new Tree Charter rooted in 60,000 tree stories collected from around Britain states that its intention is: 'to set out the principles for a society in which people and trees can stand stronger together.' The greenwood remains important for well-being in the collective consciousness of British society.

Medieval guilds preserved an ideal of fellowship and apprenticeship, and the woodwright was valued in the building and decoration of cathedrals. The individual wood craftsman's skills were nurtured and progressed from apprentice to master. Gothic style inspired by nature allowed freedom of expression for the woodworkers.

The age of industry

The Reformation, and then the Industrial Revolution, changed our culture but the country chair maker carried on, a relic of the greenwood spirit. He favoured simple design: round tenons rather than complicated heavy 'joyned' frames made the chairs light, strong and efficient to make. Jack Hill writes that the country chair maker used flexible ash rather than oak, probably from pollards or young 'maiden' trees, easy to cut and move. He worked with native skills and simple technology, part in the woods and part in village workshops.

Industrialisation brought division of labour so that by the 19th century the country craftsman was mostly part of a production line in factories. In his book *Country Chairmaking* (1994), Jack Hill[85] suggests that assembly-line standardisation meant a loss of honesty and of morality. Communities fell apart and melancholy started to be recorded as the population became landless and without place or spirit.

Even Chippendale had roots in humble country crafts, and his style revolutionised the culture at the time, as Norman Whymer notes in 1946. Whymer also laments the loss of the craftsman due to 'ill-controlled mass production' and the disintegration of the village unit which followed. For craft to survive it must be useful.

> '*The whole secret of a craftsman's work is that it combines usefulness with grace. He never adds meaningless bits and pieces to his work, simply to make it look pretty. He has no time for frills and fancies. The very beauty of his work lies in simplicity of design and grace of execution, and in such a strain must craftsmanship continue.' Whymer*[86]

Country craft chair making evolved in different regions, the designs and materials identifying people with their landscape. The craftsman needed to hold his head high in the village inn, so his work was honest. Work was toilsome – 144 chair legs in a day – but the simple, free and wholesome nature of the work must have made it possible. Today green woodwork changes our relationship to time and satisfies our physical senses, and the resistance that we experience when well-honed tools touch the wood exercises our emotional senses through experience of sympathy and antipathy.

The Arts and Crafts Movement did much to preserve knowledge of country chair making, and Phillip Clissett's[87] ladderback chair became an icon of William Morris's ideals. Ernest Gimson[88] set about making beautifully simply designed, functional and affordable ladderback

Chair with elm bark woven seat

chairs in his Cotswold workshop.

Today the green woodworker works alone; inspiration comes from tradition but he or she works to his or her own design.

Korn writes:

'Ruskin and Morris's craftsman was a skilled employee who produced the designs of others. For my generation craft was an opportunity to be self-employed, self-sufficient and self-actualized[89]*.'*

Peter Korn recognises the 'inward migration of truth' from Ancient Greek aspirations of heroic self-discovery through war to Aristotle's philosophical goal of life, to medieval service to the Cathedral and God and external truths. For today's generation, being human is about finding an internal truth. Green woodwork is a vehicle for this exploration of selfhood while the beauty of the greenwood process is that it is inherently in service to the community. For today's landless society, green woodwork reconnects us to cultural traditions, keeps ancient woodland alive, encourages new woods to be planted and creates functional, beautiful objects which last and afford a message of care and quality. From building dens, whittling pegs, carving spoons to pole-lathing a Windsor chair, green woodwork is there for everyone.

Materials – tools & process

The timber

Wood comes from trees – but trees are more than just trees. They live in relationship to a plethora of flora, fauna and fungi, and have their place in the physical landscape. Only the sun is transcendent to the woodland. Woodland is the pinnacle of ecological systems and its spirit is rich and diverse. To walk through a wood is to be immersed in impossibly vertical columns of water. One cannot help but be inspired, and throughout history woodland and trees have been sacred to cultures throughout the world.

Knowledge of the timber's qualities, ecology and uniqueness of character – such as grain, growth, moisture content, strength, suppleness, colour and taste – are all part of the experience of green woodwork. This intimacy is perhaps what attracts many to this craft.

There is also an element of risk involved. Although we are guided by an ideal form, working with the material means each piece will be different, just as the leaves of a tree are different while conforming to a recognisable species. Hand tools demand attention and focus at each movement. In the 1960s, David Pye in his book *The Nature of Art and Workmanship*[90] compared 'workmanship of risk' with 'workmanship of certainty' and noted that risk needs care and dexterity, and nurtures intuition, which will be absent in predesigned and perhaps mechanical workmanship. Workmanship of risk requires expression and emotional intelligence. When working freshly felled, green wood you are alert to changes; uncertainty exists and out of

Cutting freshly felled limbs

this can come new possibilities.

There is a grace and simplicity in following the natural lines of the wood and, as in Japanese carpentry, leaving a 'quiet' finish uncluttered by unnecessary ego. Conventional carpentry is often more about measuring on seasoned board and cutting out predesigned geometrical shapes. This is fine and needs skill and control but for me the green woodwork process can be less certain and engages the senses more deeply. As I work with the material its resistance brings feelings of sympathy and antipathy that I have to deal with; it makes me feel alive, and this is the genius of green woodwork in an educational and therapeutic context.

The tools we use are either for splitting along the fibres, or grain, of the wood (wedge, axe, drawknife and chisels) or for cutting across the fibres (cross-cut saw, bow saw, hand saw). These tools are extensions of our limbs; some are 20 years old or more and will last much longer. Their handles are polished by previous users. We also use tools for assisting us: saw horse, shaving horse, pole-lathe, jigs and measuring devices. These tools are easy to understand and use fundamental laws of physics such as ramps, pivots, fulcrums and levers.

To work effectively one must have tools which are sharp and an understanding of how to work with the minimum of effort. Using hand tools in this way teaches one to prepare well and to show care and respect. Posture is important and the rhythmic work coordinates us into our own body and breath. As the cross-cut, logging saw bites and the axe rings out, there is music in the work and shavings dance from a well-honed blade.

Tools of the trade: clockwise from top: turning, small splitting axe, side axe, turning chisels, drawknife, bowsaw/silky pruning saw, froe, wedge

The process: log to leg

Most green woodwork projects will begin by sourcing raw material from a woodland and sectioning it into a portable size. I try to fell in winter, as it is less disturbing to the ecology and also easier to clear up brash without leaves. In paying attention to the seasonality of the woods, learners orientate themselves to yearly rhythms and learn respect for these. Sometimes it is necessary to hold back, to wait and plan – all essential capacities for life that are not always experienced in modern society. Stems can be left long and returned to in spring and summer. Elm bark, for weaving seats, is the exception and must be gathered as the sap is rising in May and before the cambium sets and hardens in July.

> *After starting to cleave on the end grain of the log with a splitting axe continue using a wedge and maul or a froe*

A cross-cut saw is useful to cut timber into required lengths, and the timber can then be split or riven with wedges and an axe. One of the advantages of green woodwork is that cleft or riven wood is stronger than sawn, because the fibres remain intact and also the cell boundaries are not exposed to weathering and rot. Opening up the wood is like opening a book; you read a growth narrative. An old injury can sometimes be hinted at on the bark and show up as a knot inside the wood. To work green wood a straight grain is required, as is knot-free grain. These qualities in the wood require careful consideration of woodland management. Enough sunlight is required to produce strong, wide growth rings, but stems need to be close, so as not to branch out.

Riving releases internal tensions; if the timber was left round it would most likely split. From a triangular length of wood, we now hew it into a hexagon using a side axe and then shave into a cylinder with a draw knife. Each stage should be performed as accurately as possible or the next stage becomes compromised. Riving and shaving follow the grain and produce a strong piece. When the pole-lathe takes over we start to cut against the grain and weaken the wood; care is needed. Beauty without purpose is beauty without virtue.

Splitting a large log using wedges

Splitting using a froe

Side axing – hew off the corners of the triangular billet using a side axe

Side axed hexagonal billet

Side axed billet

Billet and turned chair leg

A shaving horse assists in holding the billet whilst the billet is shaved into a cylinder using a draw knife

Craftwork gesture of green woodwork

The physical movements become finer at each stage of the process, and more involved. Draw-knifing involves both pushing away with the legs to clamp the wood and pulling forwards and backwards whilst shaving. After each shaving is removed a reassessment is needed: perhaps a quick release and turn of the billet and another corner can be removed. The rhythm of the draw-knife can be entrancing and often the workshop falls silent at this stage. Korn recognises that the feeling of being in flow and working well for its own sake are particularly strong in doing craft. Green woodwork is particularly effective at allowing this state of being, which, once felt, can be recognised as a moment when transformation of self occurs – past and future concerns are lost and time stands still in the present, and in presence.

A fine finish can be achieved by shaving obliquely and allowing the shavings to curl around the knife. When using a knife to carve a spoon or a draw-knife to make a part for a chair, the process and choices are a conversation between the maker and the wood – but the design is always going to be determined by an empathy in the relationship. It is quite likely that the craftsman will find that, while he is free in his choices, the ideal has been determined and is perhaps inherent in the nature of the material and its intended function.

The pole-lathe also involves the whole body. The chisel hand moves in rhythm with the treadle and focus is needed on the cutting edge as the wood turns and the chisels form the leg. Design choices need to be made carefully as a leg needs to be repeated. Decoration should not compromise strength and should add interest without clutter. Here the green woodworker is giving spirit to the piece; however, this can be revealed simply, as the grain's flame flickers as the leg gently curves. Symmetry and grace are perhaps beautiful to us as recognised in the human form and in nature; however, we do not have to achieve perfection and each leg will be different, even if similar as in nature.

Experience of rhythm whilst working at the pole lathe

Once the parts are made, assembly depends on organised measurements, careful sizing, and observation of angles. Putting together a stool involves awareness of tensions and, when mastered, the piece squeezes together in perfect harmony. The tensions in the community of parts work together to provide a strong whole piece and glue should, in fact, not be necessary.

Throughout the processes there are many opportunities for measuring. One's own body is the best ruler; from elbow to fingertip is the length of a stool leg and a stool seat should be the width of your shoulders or roughly two hand spans. From this foundation more abstract concepts can be introduced, such as radius and diameter, and formal measurements used. Tenons need very careful measurement with callipers and need to be turned a couple of millimetres larger to allow for shrinkage. When looking down on a stool, the legs should just be visible, the angle can then be measured and an adjustable bevel used to ensure that all legs are similarly set. Because the process is uncertain there are opportunities for discussion and reflection.

As a tutor I have to gently facilitate the student's mental picture from fantasy to reality. Rather than using abstract plans we can observe chairs and stools for real and touch and sense how they function. Listening skills are developed both by following instruction and in hearing how the tools are acting on the material. Empathy is needed for others in the work space, and opportunities to help and teach new students can give responsibility, self-confidence and realisation of achievement. Therapeutically, the craft items may act as a 'transitional object' and, as Donald Winnicott[91] suggests, become a neutral and valuable focus for relationship. Certainly this happens as students show their item around college and, on taking it home and using it, link home life with college life.

Concluding thoughts

My workspace is open and on the edge of the woods, a small wood burner consumes offcuts to brew our tea. Green woodwork is ideally not a winter activity, when our focus is on managing the woodland. When the birds start to sing again it is time to start making, and students are immersed in sounds, colours and smells of the woodland environment. As they work, the rhythmic sound of the lathe and the ring of the side axe become part of the wood. At the start of each year, the shavings are raked out and used to mulch young trees, returning to nourish the soil and feed new growth.

The processes repeat the wheel of birth to death, the rites of passage in crossing a threshold to accepting the challenge, learning and mastering, and giving away the finished item only to start afresh. In this way I suggest the experience is transferable to other aspects of life.

Green woodwork projects

A useful project to start with is a mallet. This project introduces the basic skills of the craft, and can be owned and used by the learner. Mallets can be either made simply, out of a whole log with an axe, or a handle can be lathed and fitted to a head made from tough, grained wood such as elm. The mallet could be used to help in carving a seat for a three-legged stool. The challenge now is to make three similar legs. This will need restraint and courage to put some shape into their design. It requires acceptance of a good enough finish; small imperfections are honest and remain to remind you later of lessons learnt.

In the past, chairs were reserved as a status symbol and most people used stools. The back stool evolved into the side chair. A Windsor style chair with arms and back can take a week to make and so needs efficient and functional design as well as grace. If made well it will last, so it needs to appeal to all who will use it.

One can now start to explore different qualities of wood: flexible, fibrous grained ash for cleft, stick, furniture, diffuse, grained beech for lathing, fruit and thorn for spoons. You may find natural curves in the trees you have felled which can be used or else use steam to bend wood into

Long-handled mall and short-handled mallets

shape. Now you are beginning a long journey, travel slowly; have fun and create the world you want to live in.

The merits of craft and particularly green woodwork, perhaps because it is rich in process and sensual activity, is that it is intrinsically enjoyable. However, as Otto Solomon points out in his *Theory of Educational Sloyd* (1898) 'craft is not play but is green wood "work". Learners learn a work ethic and to love labour[92].'

Three-legged stool

Wood bowls and spoons

Mineral kingdom materials

Bernard Graves

Now with clay, metals and glass, we use materials obtained by various refining processes and procedures derived from the mineral kingdom. With these mineralised materials, we are faced with some of our biggest challenges. It is much harder to transform materials from the mineral kingdom (whether it be clay or metal) than it is to transform materials from the animal or plant kingdom (such as wool, leather or wood). As we 'descend' through nature's kingdom of materials from animal to plant to mineral, the order of hardness and density increases exponentially and so too, the demands made on the skill of the maker.

Youngster blacksmithing

When working with materials from the mineral kingdom, we need a greater use of technology and a good understanding and respect for the use of heat, whether fire in the kiln or forge. We need to engage in many more processes and tested techniques, all requiring specialised equipment and tools. We must also allow for much more time and greater efforts to be used in transforming clay into pots or to forge iron into useful items.

It is perhaps because we require the use of more technologies with these materials that the crafts of ceramics and blacksmithing are particularly appealing to adolescents. It is our experience that these hard crafts provide appropriate challenges for young people because, after all, they have 'descended' into their own 'matter', and in their outlook young people aspire to relate to the world of work. They also have the mental capacities to comprehend these more industrial processes.

These crafts specifically lend themselves to further cross-curricular activities: geology and chemistry from clay work, or metallurgy and ancient technologies when working with iron.

In many ways, by practising crafts, we undergo an experiential approach to the technological achievements of civilisations in their attempts, worldwide, to master the material world.

An interesting phenomenon to observe is the effect of heat, especially when blacksmithing: not only the temperature in the hearth, making the cold and inert iron malleable, but also the outer fire of the forge, evoking an awareness of the 'inner fire' that sometimes needs to be rekindled or quenched. The social metaphors, 'too many irons in the fire' or 'strike while the iron is hot' can be particularly apt for adolescents, who often need to sublimate exuberant behaviour.

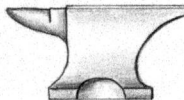

CHAPTER 9

From Clay To Pots

Sue Harker

My journey to potting

As humans, we are strongly defined by our childhood influences at home and in the environment that we were raised in. I grew up in Yorkshire in an artistic and practical family. I feel very fortunate to have grown up just before television came into the home, and before the relentless media onslaught of the internet age which is now upon us.

Life was simpler in my youth. It was the era of make-do-and-mend, where jobs were the order of the day – be it cleaning, polishing shoes or the wooden furniture, getting the coal in, or picking the vegetables in my father's allotment. We played outside, and in all kinds of weather. As children we were always encouraged to pull our weight in the house, to be responsible and practical. A particularly strong memory of mine is that of modelling the bright yellow clay in our small back garden in Leeds, and making up games with each other.

As a child, I led a double life. I attended a grammar school and later art college in the northern industrial city of Leeds. Leeds in the 1950s and 60s was a dirty, grimy place, and subject to sulphurous smog from all the coal fires and industry.

When I was nine years old, my parents rented a 400-year-old, nearly-derelict gamekeeper's cottage in the middle of a moor in the Yorkshire dales. This was a pivotal moment in my life. The cottage and the moors gave me a lifeline. We escaped to the cottage every Friday night for the weekend, as well as on every school holiday. Our various pets came too; rabbits, the dog… and the ferret. This wonderful place was where we really met each other as a family, and where I found great happiness. Here we played and reclaimed our childhood.

At the moorland cottage I was free from the shackles and regimented life of school and from the confines of railings and tarmac. I was free to roam. This freedom was not only a physical one but also an inner freedom, a freedom to be myself, to explore and play and discover, unhindered by the constraints of time and the expectations of others. I lived with nature as my reference point, my text book, my toy box and my playground, and with my imagination and intuition. Nature, with all her myriad life forms, was so exciting. I learned more there than I ever learned at school. That learning has stayed with me all my life. My eyes and heart were opened to the wonders of nature, and I did a lot of drawing. That deep connection to nature has never left me and it has been a compass throughout my life. On the moors I felt a sense of belonging to the land and the cycles of life.

Back in Leeds, on my way to college on Monday mornings, I experienced a stark contrast to our moorland life. I would walk past new tower blocks being built to replace back-to-back terraced housing. I can vividly remember wondering what it would be like to live in what, from the outside, looked like boxes, and I was deeply shocked to think that the children living there had nowhere to play. They were confined on top floors detached from the earth. I started imagining and designing playgrounds with caves, tunnels, trees and climbing frames. The effects of such short-sighted urban housing developments had created more social deprivation than the old 'back-to-backs'. It really brought home to me that, here in the city, our ancient bonds with nature had been broken. This disconnection came into all aspects of life, and particularly for those children growing up in the city. They would be growing up without knowing the trees, plants and birds, and without an opportunity to have a relationship with nature.

I went on to take a three-year diploma in Environmental Design at Bournemouth and Poole College of Art, where artists, craftspeople and architects worked together. The natural environment was still my overriding concern: how, as designers, we must strive to find that balance between the natural and the man-made in creating environments for living in, and to support children's healthy development. The digital age has only exacerbated this situation, leading to an increase in child mental and physical health problems.

I was fortunate in my final year to work with the potter David Ballantyne[93]. At the time, I was designing large scale murals and relief sculptures, but I found that the introduction to clay work brought about a profound shift in my way of working. It contrasted strongly with the heady intensity of the design studios. Through clay I became more grounded. In order to master the skills of working with this material I had to come out of my head and into my hands. The material became the teacher and my hands the focus of where learning unfolded. This was the beginning of a life-long adventure with clay and with fire. I had opened the 'book of clay' and it was beginning to reveal its secrets.

After college, I set up a workshop as a designer and maker of large-scale ceramics. After working on my own for some years, I became involved in community arts projects which then led me into teaching. I had never imagined myself going back to school!

After a formative period in the state system, I went on to teach in a Steiner school in the south-west of England, where I taught art, pottery and gardening for 20 years. When I arrived at the school, pottery was not on the curriculum and there was no workshop or equipment but the school was situated on clay, a fact discovered all too often in gardening lessons when the mud would stick to our boots on rainy days. I was not swayed by the view held at that time that to have such a facility would cost money that the school could not afford. This has been the thinking behind the closure of many pottery departments around the country in both schools and colleges over the past decades. Pottery as a school subject is still classified as 'non-academic', which could not be further from the truth. This view totally overlooks the enormous scope for cross-curricular or integrated learning when working with clay throughout a school's curriculum.

I soon found that the lack of a pottery workshop at the school was not, in fact, an impediment but was an opportunity. To have a finished pottery workshop with electric kilns and power wheels in place, with clay pigments and glazes bought ready-made, is to start at the end. Children learn far more by experiencing the evolution of the potter's craft from its beginnings. They learn first-hand about their local environment, its distinct geology and the materials around them. By building their own kiln and firing with wood, they develop a resourcefulness as well as a deeper connection and relationship to their surroundings. This is, after all, what potters used to do before the industrialisation of the process.

What is more remarkable is that it needn't cost a penny! Everything we required could be sourced within the school grounds.

At the Steiner school, craft was greatly valued as part of the core curriculum; every child had the opportunity to engage in crafting. Making and thinking go hand in hand.

Hands working clay – "The hand is the window to the mind." Immanuel Kant[96]

Over the years, I developed the 'outdoor classroom' and integrated crafts into the school curriculum, making full use of the local environment and the abundant resources around the school grounds. By the time I left the school, clay and the outdoor classroom had become a part of numerous projects within the school curriculum. The freshly dug clay was used over time to make cob for bread ovens for use in cookery lessons. It was used for wattle and daub structures in the grounds, for bricks for pottery kilns and for lime kilns for chemistry. The processed clay was used in numerous ways in class projects, such as in Roman mosaics, for tiles, for modelling pyramids in history lessons or animals, musical instruments, making 3D maps, clay tablets and, of course, pots; the possibilities are endless.

School is essentially an artificial environment and it is where children spend most of their waking hours. It is therefore incumbent upon teachers to bring into the child's experience as many opportunities as possible to learn directly, at first hand, from the natural world. This is a child's birth-right as a human being.

History of pottery

The study of pottery's development has contributed greatly to our knowledge of different cultures and periods of history. This is testified to by the enormous ceramic collections in museums around the world. Pottery is the oldest synthetic material made by humans and is related to the

Examples of early pottery

control of fire, which is thought to date from 600,000 years ago. Because of its permanence, archaeologists have learned much about human culture and beliefs from the shards of pots found in caves and burial sites. In some cultures, a lovingly formed vessel would accompany a person into the afterlife. Some of the earliest recorded human artefacts ever found are the Venus figurines from the upper Palaeolithic period. These statuettes are dated to around 27,000 years old and are mostly found in central and Western Europe.

The earliest pottery fragments discovered so far were found in caves in China and were dated from approximately 20,000 years ago. The making of pots was a great technological step forward for ancient peoples, transforming life, allowing foods and liquids to be stored and pots for cooking, eating and drinking, and eventually for trade. Clay could, of course, be used in many ways, and our prehistoric ancestors employed clay and earth colour in the decoration of their caves and bodies, and in the modelling of cultic figurines and animals.

Clay fired or unfired was used in building. Clay tablets were used by the ancient Sumerians in the development of early cuneiform writing. Each period of history and continent has its distinctive, iconic pottery with its unique decorative symbols and designs. The technological advances in glazes, kiln design and firing enabled more enduring and sophisticated forms to be created. The exquisite achievements of the Chinese and Korean master potters are still unrivalled to this day. Chinese ceramics were more highly prized than gold because of the enormous human investment of effort, time, skill, dedication and knowledge of the master potters – some of whom were elevated to 'national living treasures'. Whole villages and communities grew up around pottery production. In England, Stoke-on-Trent became a centre for the pottery industry.

Even today clay is indispensable in the manufacture of an infinite number of goods for the home, industry, pharmaceuticals, building and, of course, pottery and art. One does not have to look far to find something made from clay or with clay in it.

To study the history of ceramics is to study the fascinating history of mankind's diverse cultural inheritance, and the appreciation of the aesthetics of form and decoration. We can also learn to value the skill, dedication, wisdom and courage of our ancestors.

As we read on, we can see that pottery is inextricably linked with science. The earth sciences are clearly in evidence: geology, mineralogy and chemistry. To design and fire a kiln, and work out its proportions and scale in order to harness the transformative forces of fire is a lesson in physics.

Clay, clay glorious clay… What is clay?

Clay is all around us. It can be found in natural exposures such as cliffs, escarpments, river banks or in artificial ones, such as quarries, railway and road cuttings, or road works. A study of local geology and industry will identify its whereabouts.

Clay is an ancient material, millions of years in the making, and each clay has a different story to tell about its geological origin. The raw materials for pottery are found abundantly all over the world because the granitic, igneous rocks from which they derive account for much of the earth's crust. These hard igneous rocks are decomposed by millions of years of weathering by sun, rain and ice. The decomposition of feldspar accounts for the formation of clays.

There are two main groups of clay, primary and secondary. The primary clays are always found where they are formed. The almost pure white china clays of Cornwall are a good example. When these primary or 'mother' clays are transported by the natural forces of wind, glaciers, rivers or seas they pick up impurities, iron and other minerals, as well as organic matter. Their journey further pounds and crushes them so that by the time they are laid down, often thousands of miles from their place of origin, they are changed in colour, texture and particle size and have become highly plastic. These are the secondary clays, the earthenware and ball clays.

A natural inland clay seam – Sussex

A large clay seam on the beach near Weymouth, England

Finding and using local clay for pottery connects us directly to the massive forces and time scales of the geological processes that formed, and are still forming, the earth. I love to tell the pupils that the clay they are handling could be several hundred million years old and it was possibly being formed when dinosaurs roamed the earth. Ichthyosaurus bones were found in a field near our school which, along with the oolitic limestone and sea fossils in our clay seams, supported this theory.

Clay is a joy to handle; it is a wonderfully malleable, impressionable, versatile material. It is the remarkable plasticity that makes it unique. Clay can be smooth, silky and tactile or it can be more gritty and earthy, inviting a vigorous, robust response. It has many colours that come from the minerals in it, iron being the most common. It can be white, yellow, green, grey, blue or red. It is one of the most important materials used by mankind because of its unique ability to take on any shape and the fact that it can become permanent once fired.

Waters in clay and their role

Clay is a fine-grained material composed of flat particles of silica, alumina and water, $AL_2O_3+2SiO_2+2H_2O$. The particles are extremely fine and plate-like. The finer the particle, the greater the plasticity of the clay.

Water is an essential constituent and can account for as much as 40% of the weight of workable clay. There are three types of water in clay. The water of plasticity, which allows the clay particles to slide across one another, is 20% of the clay mass and dries out in the air. The pore water is 10% of the clay mass and is trapped between the particles. Pore water is only driven out with heat at 120ºC. The chemically bound water, which is 10% of the mass, is only removed by heat at around 600ºC. Above this temperature, the chemistry has changed and the clay becomes irreversibly ceramic, though it is still very porous in texture. The usual temperature for the first or bisque firing is around 950ºC.

Crystalline Hexagonal structure of clay

Illustration of clay platelets

Three types of water weights involved in plastic clay

clay particle

pore water 10%

bound water Layer- 10%

water of plasticity 20%

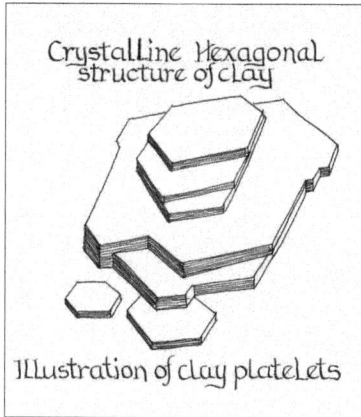

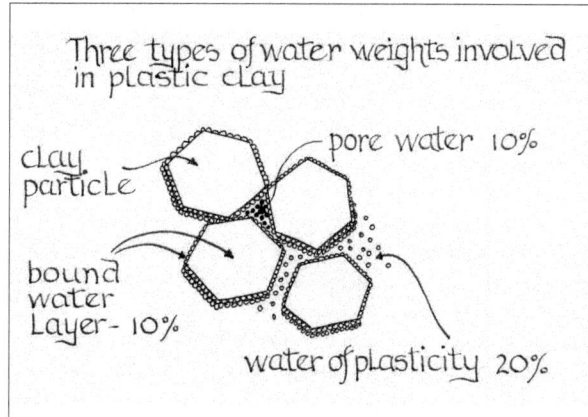

Magnified clay platelets – Alumina Silicates AL2O3+2SiO2+2H2O

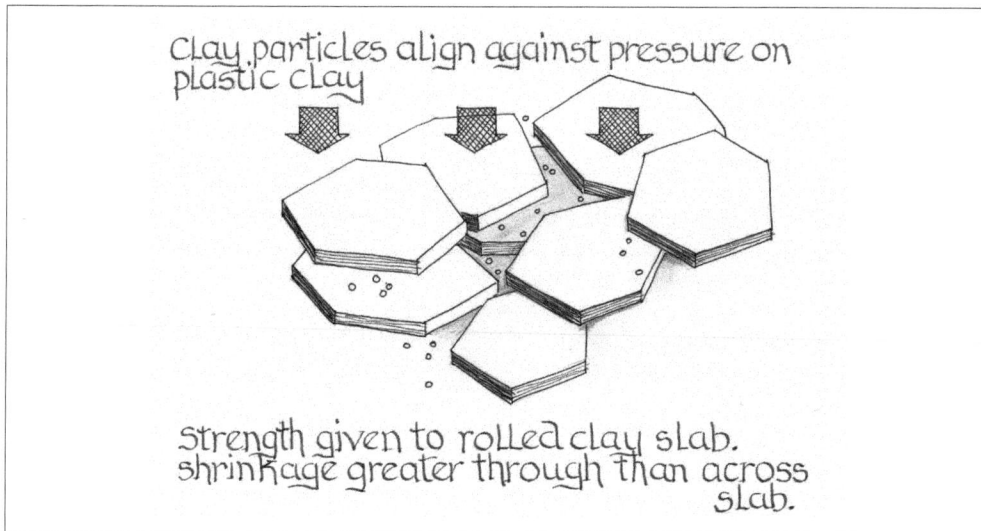

Clay particles align against pressure on plastic clay

Strength given to rolled clay slab. shrinkage greater through than across slab.

Clay particles align against pressure

From clay to pot – 'Entering the Earth'

What follows is a description of how teaching pottery can be taught as a whole-process – from the sourcing of clay to finishing and firing the pots.

The first thing I do with pottery students is to prospect for clay in the local landscape. We get well acquainted with our local geology. Several sites are tested and 'potholes' dug.

A clay pit can be made in the midst of a wildlife haven, amongst trees and plants and the pit itself becomes a joy to go to, as was the case where we dug clay at school. Supplied with buckets and wellies, the children tread a singular path through the lush, waist high plants to the clay pit. They learn not to make too much of an impact and they develop respect for the fact that what was previously an undisturbed and wildlife-rich corner of the school is the home of many plants and animals. They learn that we clay-diggers are visitors with a specific purpose and goal to undertake, but it is vital to make the pupils aware of our potential adverse effect on the surrounding ecology. Clay makes a mess!! The craft of pottery can have a heavy footprint or impact.

Winning clay – digging naturally occurring ground clay, Sweden

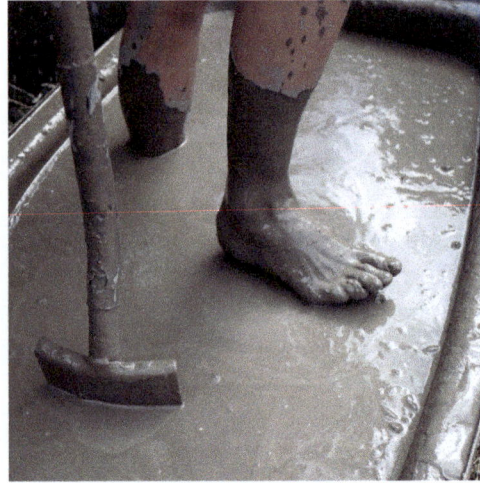

Puddling Slip

Puddling clay and mixing in straw or sawdust for kiln building

From the colourful, light-filled surface above the clay pit, the pupils descend down into the cool, dark and damp, earthy depths. What an assault on the senses! The pit is invariably full of water and frogs, and the nostrils awake to a pleasant infusion of musty, earthy, decomposing organic compounds. The strata of the earth can clearly be seen: on top the organic topsoil, interspersed with plant roots and worms supporting the life above. Beneath the topsoil the slightly yellower subsoil is embedded with limestone and fossilised shells. Below this can be found the greenish-yellow clay which is good for cob, bricks and kiln-building when used as it is unprocessed. As we dig progressively deeper, the clay becomes more compacted and 'blue'. This clay is the best for pots. Here at the clay pit is a nature lesson, a geology lesson and an environmental science lesson. Clays can also be experimented with that have been sourced from further afield.

Digging the clay is physical work, but for the younger children it is an immersion into nature and is lots of fun. The older pupils relish the huge physical challenge of extracting large quantities of clay and hauling the heavy buckets and barrow loads back to the pottery workshop. It requires teamwork and lots of strength and energy.

Refining clays using water and sieves

Refining clays

Freshly dug, local clay can rarely be used for pottery straight from the ground. The clay is full of small stones and organic debris and needs to be processed or washed. This activity invites delight and revulsion in equal measure – and it is messy!

The clay is mixed with water, is stirred or *blunged* with wooden paddles or bare feet into a slurry and is then strained through sieves into a luscious, silky, creamy *slip*. Clay at this stage evokes an irresistible urge to sink ones hands into it up to the elbows and to revel in its beautiful cool, creaminess. In our local school clay, all the tiny limestone grit needed removing. Once processed in this way, the clay slip is dried for a few days on cloths laid out over plaster until it is firm enough to handle.

Kneading

Once firm enough, the clay must be kneaded and at this stage it can be tested for its degree of plasticity. I ask the pupils to bring in other clay samples they have found for testing too. To test it, a sausage of clay is made and curved round to see if many cracks appear. If it cracks too

Hand kneading clay

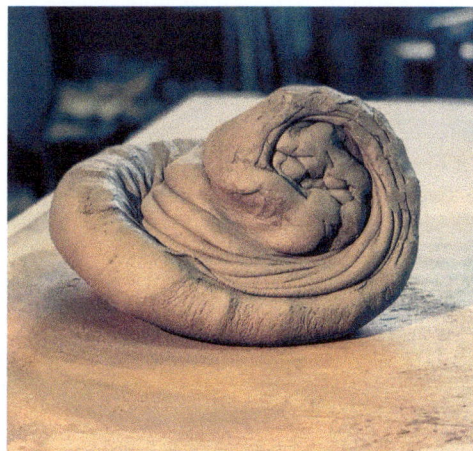

Spiral kneaded clay

much, it is too 'short' and will need a more plastic clay blended into it. The clay may need to be 'opened' a little by the addition of fine sand, particularly if most of the fine grit has been removed by sieving. This adds 'body' to the clay and aids in the escape of water and gasses from the clay during drying and firing.

Each student kneads his or her own clay. The kneading is critical for preparing the clay for pot-making, and it is a difficult skill to master. At the beginning of each pottery lesson the pupils knead their clay before getting to work. This serves several functions; it equalises moisture content and eliminates lumps and air. Most importantly, it aligns and moves all the clay particles in a spiral arrangement, which improves its workability and breathes life into the stiff cold clay, waking it up. The difference in the clay is tangible. It also helps the pupils to come into their bodies and limbs, and particularly into their hands. The spiral-kneading technique is hard to master. It requires a rhythmic motion and co-ordination of the application of pressure – by leaning into the clay – with the lifting and turning of the clay. The potter must have sensitivity in the hands, working together to contain the clay while in effect turning the whole mass inside out without trapping air in. It takes practice but, once acquired, is a fluid and powerful action. To be able to judge when the clay is ready also takes experience. Our clay is now ready for shaping.

Making a pot – pinch pot method

There are many ways to make a pot.

Pots can be made by pinching, coiling, slab building or throwing on the wheel. Whatever one's age, it is beautiful to start with the immediacy of the *pinch pot*. This can be made with as much of a conscious eye for form, surface and function as with any other pot, and yet it is a uniquely intimate and personal process; the pot's shape is determined solely by the individual maker's hand and direct response to the material. In the preparation of the clay the activity has been very physical, exerting large motor movements in the limbs. For the pinch put, the hands are now the only tools required.

'In our hands, we have the subtlest of all machines.' John Ruskin[94]

Every part of the hand is used for pinching pots, starting with the palms. Sitting comfortably, either on a chair or the floor, a handful of clay is taken up and formed into a ball that fits comfortably within the space of both hands clasped around it. The ball needs to be shaped into as perfect a sphere as possible by patting with the cupped hand and smoothing the 'skin' of the clay sphere to an even, uninterrupted whole. This is a great exercise in hand-to-eye co-ordination and it is the first step to bringing a conscious and strong form to the formlessness of the clay.

Each hand now works independently in a synchronised rhythm; the non-dominant hand holds and turns the ball, rather like a potter's wheel, while the dominant hand shapes the clay. First the thumb must find and push down into the central axis of the sphere as it rotates, while the fingers on the outside of the sphere contain the curve of the outer wall. The ball of clay is then very gradually opened up from the bottom to the top with a subtle pinching action as the ball rotates. Maintaining a rhythm, the speed of turning, the pressure exerted and the space between each pinch is tantamount to achieving a form with even walls and a relatively level top. Without the rhythm, the form is in danger of becoming contorted and weak. Through quietening the mind to the discipline of the rhythm, we can create a space and become conscious of the emerging form through collaboration between hand, eye and clay, without forcing or imposing ourselves on the clay. We need to be totally present in ourselves.

As the sphere is hollowed and the walls grow thinner, so the form grows in size and great care in handling is needed to maintain the integrity of the form, both visually and structurally. At this point a basic language of form can be introduced. The forms can become more 'open' as

Pinch pot method

in a bowl or 'closed' as in a cup or vase form. Attention is drawn to the inner concave space in relation to outer convex surface. We are so used to handling mass-produced pots that are identical; pinching a pot by hand can lead us to a more natural, organic, pleasing form that feels 'right' in the hand.

While working on the pot, the pot is held in the hand throughout. When the form is complete it may be too soft to support its weight and must be laid upside down on the table to firm up a little. When firm enough, it can be gently upturned on the table and allowed to 'find' its own foot, not too wide and not too narrow. Sometimes a foot can be made by adding a coil to lift the form. A lovely way of decorating these pots is simply impressing found materials like leaves or shells into the surface.

As the form dries, it becomes 'leather hard' and the surface can be burnished to a smooth shine with a pebble.

Relationship of the Pot to Human Being

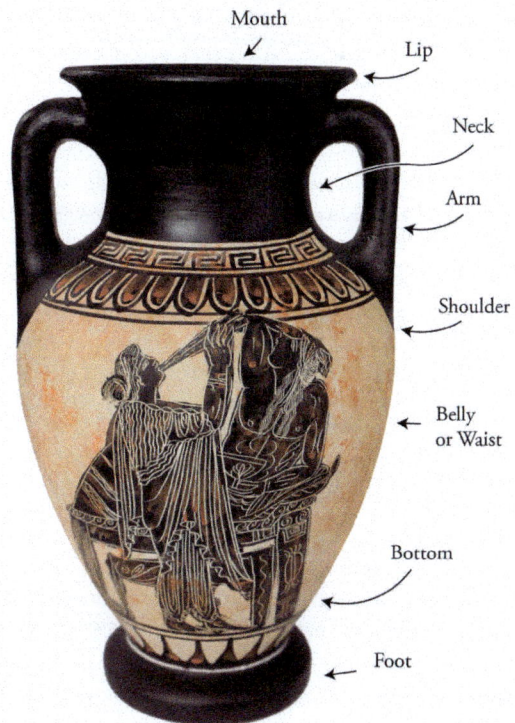

Mouth

Lip

Neck

Arm

Shoulder

Belly or Waist

Bottom

Foot

Coiling a large pot

Coil pots

As the pupils gain confidence in handling clay, they can undertake a more challenging project such as making a coil pot. This is a more physical encounter with the material. It is an up-building and formative process, and I feel that it helps to work on the pupils' own formative forces. The discipline of the process working through them has a strongly incarnating effect because they are working the soft clay up into three-dimensional space against the forces of gravity. They need to have awareness of all the parts of the pot to bring them all to a harmonious whole. Along the way, we look at classical pot forms and discuss the relationship of the pot to the human being. A pot has a *body*, a *foot*, *belly* or *waist*, *shoulders*, a *neck*, *lips* and a *mouth*. It also has *arms* or *lugs*. The *head* is the individual potter imbuing the pot with their own personality or character.

When coiling a pot the clay must be well joined, the walls must be even, the form strong. As with the pinch pot, very few tools are required when coiling pots apart from the hands and a few simple tools such as a simple scraper of wood or metal, a wooden beater and a pebble to burnish. There is lots of scope to look at traditional designs and decorative techniques such as carving, applying coloured clay slips or impressing and modelling the surface.

Wheel work – ancient & new

The potter's wheel stands amongst the most original inventions and holds a fascination and appeal. The origin of the potter's wheel is inconclusive, but could be about 5,000 years ago in the Middle East. Its advent meant not only a far greater output of pottery generally but also, with its immediacy and dynamic force, a different sense of form and range of shapes.

Teenagers are eager to test their skills on a potter's wheel and it is hard to hold back their enthusiasm. It is preferable if they can learn on a *kick wheel,* where the whole body is engaged and they are in total control. Throwing a pot on the wheel is significantly more difficult to learn then either pinching or coiling pots. It demands practice, total body awareness and concentration.

Thorough kneading is essential and the spiral that the pupils have kneaded into the clay is opened up again by the centrifugal force of the spinning wheel.

Pupils must be firmly centred in themselves to harness and control the forces of the wheel. Every nerve and muscle is focused on the moving clay as it is formed by the hands and fingers. The whole body is involved in the process; feet and legs set the wheel speed, the arms and hands control pressure and centring. A momentary lapse of focus can spell disaster. Practice is essential for success. Wheel work can have a very therapeutic and centring effect as the pupils gain mastery and their skills develop. It is very absorbing and the pottery workshop falls silent, save for the rhythmic whirr of the wheels.

'The acquisition of skill is not a moment of rapture but a deeper more harmonious quality in the person.' Anon

The firing... Baptism by fire!

Making pots is only half the story, now the pots must be handed over to the transformative alchemy of the fire. The pupils must build and fire a kiln to convert the clay to ceramic. There are many ways to fire the pots depending on type of clay and the effect required.

Pupils love the drama of smoke and fire. The younger pupils can build a simple, low temperature, self-firing kiln with a few old house bricks and some sawdust – a fuel source that is plentiful and free. This will reach temperatures of 600ºC degrees and above, a dull to cherry-red heat. This is an excellent first kiln and the carbonised results work beautifully with pinched and burnished pots.

Pots can be fired in a bonfire, which does require a degree of expertise and achieves temperatures of over 700ºC, orange-red heat.

Relatively small pots can be fired in a 'paper and clay slip' kiln that can be built entirely with found or waste materials. It can be built and fired in one long day or built one day and

Artisan potter throwing a pot on a traditional potter's wheel, India

Throwing a bowl on an electric potter's wheel

fired the next. It is another self-firing kiln and can easily reach bisque temperatures of around 900-1000ºC, yellow-orange heat.

This kiln is dramatic in both sound and sight when it is firing at peak. The pupils can witness their pots bathed in the swirling vortex of yellow-orange flames and can really experience the transformative power of the fire invoking a genuine respect and awe. The pots are given over to the fire for it to work its magic. The opening of the kiln the next day and finding their pots still warm in the ashes of the kiln and observing the effects of the flame on their burnished pots is always a surprise and delight. The burnished surfaces licked by the flames reveal a subtle palette of sensuous, warm colours of the earth. While still warm, beeswax can be rubbed into the surface and polished to enhance the colours and shine.

The older pupils, who have made larger pots, need a bigger kiln which can be built to last several years. They can study kiln design and different fuel sources, their combustion properties and environmental impact.

Wood is the most environmentally sustainable and is carbon neutral. Waste wood from saw mills and wood yards is plentiful.

Bonfire firing

The older pupils can also be responsible for firing younger pupils' pots. Their wills and developing strong bodies and thirst for adventure will be engaged in the building of a large tunnel or dragon kiln with hazel, willow and cob, all sourced from the grounds or nearby. They will already have collected and seasoned and stacked wood for a whole day's firing.

Firing a kiln is an art and a science. The pupils will experience a prolonged high-temperature firing, reaching temperatures of 1000°C and over, yellow-orange to straw-yellow heat colour. They will learn to control and judge the rate at which the temperature increases. The kiln is a living being. Each moment the pupils must be awake to the kiln, the sounds of the flame, the amount of

Construction of paper slip kiln

Paper slip-kiln firing 950°+C

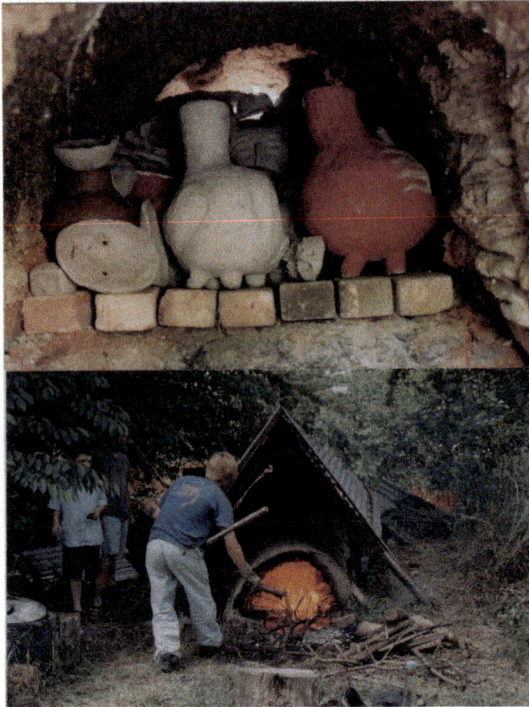

Inside a dragon kiln and firing

smoke from the chimney and the colour of the flame, to judge when and how much wood to use in stoking the kiln at just the right moment. Too sudden an increase in temperature and the pots are in danger of exploding, too little and the temperature drops.

This firing is an event and can be experienced by the whole school on festival days or during breaks. To learn how to master fire on this scale makes an unforgettable and deep impression and it is the grand finale of the clay work process.

Glazes – to glaze or not to glaze?

The wide variety of surface treatments possible with unglazed ware, such as in the projects above, is sometimes all that is needed. Glazes become necessary for functional tableware to create a hygienic covering and in the case of porous earthenware, to render it waterproof. They also open up a whole realm of decorative possibilities, especially at stoneware temperatures. Glazes can be bought readymade without a thought about what is in them or they can become the start of a whole new world of exploration and understanding of glaze chemistry by making one's own. That said, earthenware glazes are an exception and the ingredients have to be purchased because the main constituents of the glaze, about 75%, are lead or boron which cannot be used in their raw state and which need to be combined industrially with silica into a frit.

It is at stoneware temperatures of between 1200 and 1300ºC that many beautiful glazed surfaces can be created using raw materials that can be found locally. A very simple, beautiful glaze can be made with just wood ash and local clay. The fun is to discover what materials there are in your locality and to test them in different proportions.

Most stoneware glaze materials start as rocks, e.g. feldspar, limestone or granite, flint and quartz, clay, which are ground to a fine powder. Monumental masons and quarries may be a good source. Some glaze materials may live in the kitchen cupboard, such as salt and soda. The metals in the form of found oxides such as iron oxide (rust) or some made in the chemistry laboratory from copper or chrome can be added to bring colour to the glaze.

Working with these different materials is a great opportunity to understand more deeply the geology and the chemistry of the various rocks and their effects in glaze composition and it is fascinating area of work involving practical application of chemistry.

Raku glazing – Japan 'Joy in the crack'

An exciting introduction to glazes and the colours and surfaces achieved by the different metallic oxides is the raw immediacy of Raku firing. The term Raku means 'enjoyment or happiness' and originated in Japan 400 years ago in the making of tea ceremony bowls. Nowadays raku has become a much-explored medium and can lead to experimentation with different effects.

Ash-glazed jug

The kiln is simple and the temperatures for melting the glaze is low, between 850 and 1000ºC. The firing is extremely short – 30 minutes or so – during which the glowing red-hot pots are drawn from the kiln with tongs and the still molten, glazed surface is either cooled in the air or oxidised, to bring out the colour of the metal: greens and turquoises for copper, blue for cobalt, white for tin, or smothered in a variety of combustible materials to starve the glaze of oxygen or reduce the glaze to reveal metallic lustres of copper, silver and bronzy golds. The effects are unpredictable and dramatic and create an openness to the unexpected and accidental. The metals are the stars of the show.

The journey from clay to pot

The journey from digging clay to retrieving a finished pot from a kiln is not so much about the end product and the creation of beautiful pots, although that is of course an important part of it! To work clay with respect, the pot will have integrity, truth, honesty. The humble clay can be elevated to something beautiful. We can give voice to the clay.

But for the pupil it is more than a pot. It has meaning. The pot represents the pupil's journey and how the pot came into being. The gift from the earth of the ancient decomposed rocks and aeons of geological time in the clay, the sacrifice of the wood, the water for processing and shaping, the air and the power of fire to transform it. The hard work and obstacles overcome by the pupil herself. Through developing their wills and working with the discipline of the craft and all the elements, they have created something of worth. This can provide a huge sense of achievement; the process lives in them, they have grown. They are transformed.

Craft comes from the German word KRAFT which means power or strength. Working with materials and the hands provides insight, knowledge and skill. There is a striving for harmony,

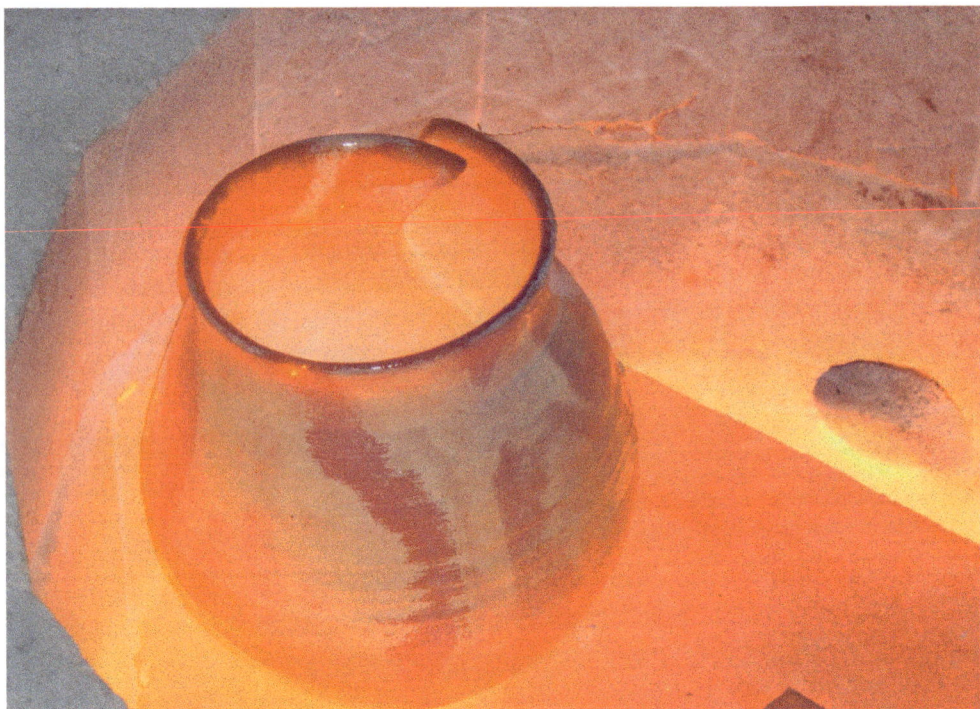

Raku glazing – ready to take out of kiln

Horsehair Raku-fired pot with lid

function and beauty. As Ghandi declared from his spinning wheel, 'the work of the hands is indeed an apprenticeship to honesty[95].'

As with other crafts there is a sense of responsibility here, a reflective process. The material becomes the teacher. The learning is on a deep level. It can raise questions about our dependence on, and relationship to, the natural world around us and how what we do needs to be done sustainably and ecologically and with respect for all life.

'The highest reward for a person's toil is not what they get out of it but what they become by it.'
John Ruskin[96]

CHAPTER 10

Pit Forge and Blacksmithing

Arian Leljak

Iron and my journey

'We can do so simply by asking, though answers are anything but simple, what the process of making concrete things reveals to us about ourselves.' R. Sennett, The Craftsman[100]

Blacksmithing heath

My father had a small engineering workshop in the spare bedroom of our flat where I grew up in Zagreb, Croatia (then Yugoslavia) in the 1970s. Though out of bounds for the children, I would often sneak in there when he was at work and 'make things'. Oily, and often unintelligible, bits of machines, tools and equipment lay there in a mysterious yet purposeful sequence. Try as hard as I might, this sequence could never be deciphered by a curious 10-year-old. Working around this very grown-up world of mechanical objects, I received my first lessons in metallurgy… if forced, drill bits and files will shatter whilst nails will bend and screwdrivers flex with magical toughness. As these were my father's 'means of production' rather than cheap objects of leisure (he was proud of his West German-made tools) asking him about a broken drill bit would have been an unwise admission of my experimenting, so these lessons remained a tacit knowledge until much later in life. Nowadays, this body-based, visceral knowing of how things work on an elementary level is rapidly disappearing; dozens of participants in my blacksmithing workshops over the years come with less and less 'feel' for the materials, and correspondingly more *hunger* to *do something with their hands*.

The need to engage with simple, tangible work – which produces useful items via an accessible process – appears to conflict with our object-saturated western lifestyles. Evidently, a life where access to ready-made material objects facilitated by cheap overseas production and (relative) wealth has given rise to a profound paradox: we have never had more material possessions while also experiencing a decreasing understanding of and relationship to them. Notions of 'I got too much stuff' and 'need to de-clutter' somehow also give rise to the need for renewed engagement and understanding of the nature and the production of the man-made world around us. 'We want to feel that our world is intelligible, so we can be responsible for it.'[101]

My teenage years led me (as they tend to do) to leave behind my early mechanical interests and pursue, instead, studies in biology, pharmacy and veterinary medicine. But I found academic studies overly abstract, and overly impersonal. I chucked it all in and arrived in the UK in late 1989 to pursue an organic farming apprenticeship in East Sussex. The farm was adjacent to a college which ran a sculpture school, where I enrolled 18 months later.

As I understand it now, the meaning of my stint on the farm (less than half a mile up the track from the college) was to engage in and learn about the land, the great and complex context from which all our resources are obtained. The wealth of minerals, animals and plants on the farm was a rich source of materials which we art students carved, cast, cut, burned and forged.

It was an old-fashioned art course, which meant we made objects out of natural materials: paper, wood, clay, plaster, copper and iron. There was much labour and debris, and less emphasis on conceptual work. Peter Pechman – an old, wiry, East German blacksmith – would turn up to teach us three-week blocks in blacksmithing. With few words of English, he demonstrated the work of an artist blacksmith, rather than that of the welder/fabricator/engineer. He got us all to forge a nail and then, with a glint in his eye, pointed to the archetypal forming processes behind it: *contraction* (the head), and *expansion* (the point). I saw, as if for the first time, the commonest of objects in terms of the underlying forces which shaped it. What was revealed to me was the difference between the finality of a completed item and the endless potential of the creative processes which could be applied in future processes of making.

My teaching career started a few years later at a Special Needs college in the south-west of England. Having found my own learning a slow and arduous process I was fortunate to engage in setting up a forge in an 'outdoor classroom' workshop, employing the most simple (yet most revealing) tools, techniques and materials. This relative technological simplicity was an excellent means of making the learning process accessible, tangible and meaningful for those to whom learning was exceptionally difficult.

Everything that I have learned over the past 20 or so years since setting up that outdoor classroom has convinced me that such learning processes are the most relevant for everyone to do – young and old alike.

History of blacksmithing

Early workers of iron were able to use the metal from a unique and peculiar source: in meteoric form. Coming to the Earth in the form of meteorites, and containing a mixture of iron and nickel, this 'cosmic' iron was fairly pure and was immediately usable – it required no processing first. This was a very rare form of iron, and in those early days of iron-work it was more precious than gold.

The first smelting of iron ores dates from around 1500BC and it was practised in several areas of the Middle East: Turkey, Iran, Iraq. This marked the beginning of the Iron Age; it is the first use of technology in both smelting the iron out of its ores and then forging it into artefacts.

Ironworking spread across Europe and Asia relatively quickly through the use of easily available ores. In Britain the Iron Age dates from around 500BC, in the Far East from even earlier.

Most tribes in the Americas did not have Iron Age technology before the arrival of Europeans, and they were essentially still living in a Neolithic culture up to that point.

An important aspect of the early ironworking process is its environmental and social integration. The requisite fuel for ironworking was charcoal and, in the Iron Age and Medieval contexts, the smith and the charcoal burner shared the same community. Their interchange of skills and goods had a direct and mutually beneficial relationship. Other crafts intimately connected to the forge are leatherwork (the bellows being made of animal skins) and woodwork (for the making of tool handles, workshop shelters, work benches, etc.). In return, the smith would serve those crafts with the multitude of metal tools they required.

Since the Industrial Revolution, which by some accounts starts in England in the 1750s, charcoal was replaced by coal as the preferred fuel of iron production. This change of fuel went hand-in-hand with a degradation of the social and environmental connections so integral to

Engraving of Egyptian blacksmiths pit forging using clay pot and leather bellows

Iron smelting

Forging a bloom of iron

early iron work. Deforestation in the UK, for example, had much to do with iron making. Shipbuilding was another major wood-demanding industry.

The Industrial Revolution, ignited by coal-fired blast furnaces, also saw the gradual replacement of hammer-forged, wrought iron by mild steel – which gets rolled into lengths by machines.

The need for human labour was significantly decreased. The single remaining blast furnace in the UK, at Port Talbot in South Wales, produces 10,000 tons of iron per day and is managed by a handful of workers. Technological progress always increases production but it decreases – sacrifices even – human involvement and concrete experience of the process.

Smelted lump of wrought iron

In contrast to industrial production, many Swedish farms in the 13th century had their own smelting pit, where local iron ore would be smelted and forged into wrought iron items. Skills which enabled this to happen were part of the local, situated, communal knowledge. Today, the increasing complexity of all technology means that there is no such thing as 'local' production, based on environmental and social skills and resources. Production is 'globalised'- the Port Talbot blast furnace in Wales uses an American-designed technology to process thousands of tons of Canadian, Brazilian and Australian ores into iron for export to global markets.

Perhaps of greatest significance for the individuals involved in industrial iron production is the high level of separation of the skills needed to facilitate such production. A *division of*

Wood heap seasoning

Clay-covered charcoal clamp

labour has produced individuals who are 'knowledge' workers; designers, engineers, metallurgists. Typically, they are not involved practically with production, which they influence instead via their 'thinking' work. The 'shop-floor' workers, on the other hand, are not required to know the whole process, and they, typically, have a practical skill relating to some defined aspect of it.

My experience of facilitating blacksmithing workshops over the past 20 years has taught me about the extent to which individuals benefit from integrated, situated and experiential learning opportunities. This appears to be based on a widespread need to take part in the ***whole*** process of *making* – of crafting. This is the need to heal the rift between the head and the hand, between the designer and the maker – even if only temporarily.

Pedagogical applications

'All I know is a door into the dark…' Seamus Heaney, The Forge[102]

There has been a gradual resurgence in the craft of blacksmithing in the UK since a low point in the 1970s, when this craft almost disappeared completely.

The process of working with iron has, at its very core, an immediacy of transformation; the cold, hard and rigid material is brought to *life* by heat. At a bright yellow temperature (1200ºC) it acquires a soft, malleable, plastic form, which yields under the hammer before hardening again (as it cools) into a solid shape. This process of heating and cooling is done repeatedly until the final form is achieved. In no other craft is this transformation quite as immediate and quite as central to the process of making.

Alan Evans[103], the eminent British art blacksmith, once said to me: 'Think of it (iron) as plasticine; if you can model it, you can forge it.' For lots of people this process of heating/softening and cooling/hardening brings to the senses exactly the kind of visceral understanding which modern technology has hidden away from us. It contains a huge educational and developmental potential. It requires, however, that we step back in time and engage the methods and processes which have been known to us for 3,500 years and which almost anyone can replicate – almost anywhere, at almost no cost.

The essential elements needed to set up an educational forge workshop are as follows:

- a container for a fire of some sort and some way to blow the air so that we nearly double the temperature of naturally burning fire (from 750ºC to 1300ºC).
- some iron for forging and a reasonably solid lump of iron to use as an anvil.
- some charcoal for the fire
- a hammer
- It is that simple.

There are countless ways to achieve the above and over the years I have come to appreciate how technologies from different eras provide the appropriate learning context for groups of various ages and abilities. There appears to be a link between a personal/developmental stage of the participant, and the historical/technological stage used as working process.

Iron Age technology – first forges

Nothing is simpler, more accessible or more appropriate for young learners than a clay-lined pit with two pipes and a pair of hand-bellows. Many forms of this forge, using the same principles, are still in widespread use today in Africa and Asia, where roving or village smiths repair and make iron items for everyday use. I have built countless 'pit-forges' over the years, never taking more than an hour or so to construct one from clay and stones. I have, and still do, use it in a variety of contexts: mainstream school projects, forest school settings, home education programmes, Special Education needs providers, Craft camps, Family workshops, and even as part of therapeutic intervention for young people with challenging behaviour.

A pit forge hearth

Erica working leather bag bellows at pit forge

Rhythmically striking iron on an anvil

Iron Age technology offers highly harmonious physical engagement based on simple gesture of fanning the charcoal fire, and making small, discrete items in a relaxed and cooperative social environment. This reflects the times before time mattered, and where production was related to an immediate and limited need.

Medieval technology

The main change when a developmental step is needed from the simple immediacy of Iron Age technology is to increase the size of the fire, materials and tools. This is reflected in the development of the bellows, for instance, where significant changes occur quantitatively and qualitatively if we employ the double action concertina type. As with all technology, these bellows are much harder to design and make in the first place, but their use is much more straightforward. There is much less practical skill needed in using these bellows although they require more strength and stamina to operate.

With reduced physical coordination needed to fan the fire, the challenge becomes that of managing the much hotter fire correctly. As we are now easily able to reach temperatures beyond the melting point of iron (1535°C) and thereby increase the risk of destroying our work, a different human capacity is tested: that of attention and focus. Any lapses in concentration are immediately and brutally exposed; a hissing, sparking piece of work disintegrating in the fire.

Medieval forge is, in one sense, the archetypal picture of the blacksmithing craft: darkened workshop space, bright yellow blaze in a brick hearth, large anvils and hammers, sweaty foreheads.

This development in the potential for smithing provides excellent challenges for teenagers and adults who wish to experience the archetypal forge process. Not many will describe this activity as 'therapeutic', certainly not whilst in the midst of it. Despite the significant increase in physical commitment, this aspect of smithing pales in comparison to the amount of complete focus and attention needed.

Medieval picture of blacksmith's forge

To get some sense of this process, imagine a length of inch square steel, heated to a very bright yellow heat in the forge by a strong and steady levering action which operates the bellows. With one end of it held by hand in a pair of tongs, the other (the hot end!) is then rested upon the anvil. You then hammer the piece with complete focus and determination as it becomes orange in colour, then changes to dark orange, then bright red. At around cherry red you will need to place it back into the coals.

The Village Blacksmith

Under a spreading chestnut-tree
The village smithy stands;
The smith, a mighty man is he,
With large and sinewy hands;
And the muscles of his brawny arms
Are strong as iron bands.

His hair is crisp, and black, and long,
His face is like the tan;
His brow is wet with honest sweat,
He earns whate'er he can,
And looks the whole world in the face,
For he owes not any man.

Week in, week out, from morn till night,
You can hear his bellows blow;
You can hear him swing his heavy sledge,
With measured beat and slow,
Like a sexton ringing the village bell,
When the evening sun is low.

And children coming home from school
Look in at the open door;
They love to see the flaming forge,
And hear the bellows roar,
And catch the burning sparks that fly
Like chaff from a threshing-floor.

He goes on Sunday to the church,
And sits among his boys;
He hears the parson pray and preach,
He hears his daughter's voice,
Singing in the village choir,
And it makes his heart rejoice.

It sounds to him like her mother's voice,
Singing in Paradise!
He needs must think of her once more,
How in the grave she lies;
And with his hard, rough hand he wipes
A tear out of his eyes.

Blacksmith at forge

Toiling, – rejoicing, – sorrowing,
Onward through life he goes;
Each morning sees some task begin,
Each evening sees it close
Something attempted, something done,
Has earned a night's repose.

Thanks, thanks to thee, my worthy friend,
For the lesson thou hast taught!
Thus at the flaming forge of life
Our fortunes must be wrought;
Thus on its sounding anvil shaped
Each burning deed and thought.

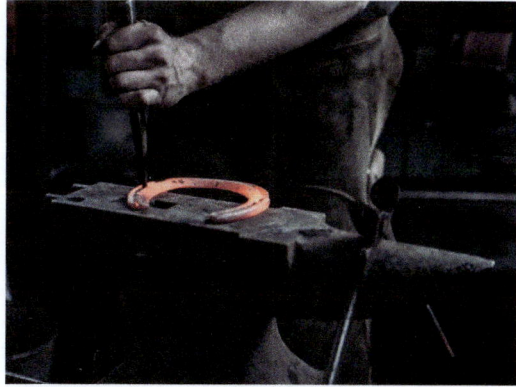

Blacksmith forging a horseshoe

Henry Wadsworth Longfellow [1807–1882][104]

At this stage you continue with the bellows, with your mind reflecting on the action performed, and the next sequence of hammering. All this takes place whilst remaining alert and aware of the steel in the fire, never letting it slip from your consciousness for a split second. When just below the melting point, again you draw the piece out and: 'Strike while the iron is hot!' This age-old saying captures perfectly the craft gesture of blacksmithing; right action is applied at the right time, with complete clarity, determination and accumulated skill. These qualities are not inherent, they are learnt through many hours of practice, and many burnt pieces of work.

'Strike whilst the iron is hot'

Landscape as context for craft education

Iron Age and medieval technology workshops can, if at all possible, be significantly enriched educationally if placed in an environmental context. Woodland is the perfect place, as it can tie in with charcoal production, and charcoal production involves woodland management, which in turn encompasses a number of other crafts, e.g. green woodwork. The local landscape may contain iron ore so you may try an iron-smelting process. Or you may find clay and build your pit-forges for free. This may lead you to use the forge to make some of the tools for woodland work, e.g. Make an axe; use the axe to cut down a tree; use the wood to make charcoal; use the charcoal to make an axe. This cycle gives education through craft an enhanced meaning and engenders for the learners a sense of service, cooperation and interdependence which – in this case – is *experienced* rather than simply *understood*. The meaning which is experienced concretely, through practice, is of different value to any kinaesthetic learner. They are the ones that chronically underachieve at school, despite endless efforts by the educational authorities and researchers to close achievement gaps.

Children at pit forge in the woods

Medieval and modern blacksmith's forge

Medieval bellows, and other tools and equipment from this period, facilitate bigger and more efficient working, but the technology remains well within direct human experience. You can look at the moving leather and wooden parts of the medieval bellows and appreciate its double action operation, and with a small amount of mental effort realise how a very simple system of two valves enables a constant blast of air into the fire.

18th-/19th-century blacksmith's workshop & tools

Inside a Victorian blacksmith's workshop

As this technology develops further, the air is typically blown into the fire by a fan, either manually operated or using an electric motor. Either way, the important thing is that the relationship to the intensity of the fire is separated from the smith who is now 'free' from this effort, and is able to concentrate on production of forged items. This both enables focus on end results and also disengages the maker from a direct relationship to the size and intensity of the fire they are using.

The learning opportunity here is in the ability to increase production while being able to concentrate even more strongly on the multiple elements of the process – but, again, without direct involvement in them.

The challenge is more that of supervision of what the machines are doing, and less of monitoring one's own physical state and effort. As such, the reflecting nature of craft, which informs the maker as to how well they are aligned with the process, can diminish, and the kind of modern 'multi-tasking' can appear in place of focused work. 'He's got too many irons in the fire' perhaps captures this well.

At the stage where a person is ready to pursue a more serious vocational training, the use of a plethora of powerful electric, and even computer-aided technology, becomes appropriate and useful, though this can never replace the gradual building of skills via an embodied, physical training over a long period of time.

Inside a blacksmith's workshop today – forge powered by an electric fan

Power hammer at work

Plasma cutter at work

Educational rationale – the blacksmithing craft gesture

I always make a point of observing the reaction of visitors to my workshop. Long before a stream of questions and comments begins, there is a particular moment when some people simply pause and watch with a mesmerised expression. I experience this as a kind of visceral resonance between the person and the craft process before them. It is as if their body is saying, 'I want to try this!'

Other people remain untouched; perhaps they find their 'resonance' when observing woodwork, or pottery, or bread-baking. Such is the nature of the 'Craft Gesture', as described in the previous section, on the observer.

What, then, is unique to forge work as an educational experience? Physically speaking, forge work demands a strong sense for coordination between the left and right hands. The hands often perform different tasks within the same process, e.g. one hand holding the piece on the anvil and rotating it between the hammer blows, whilst the other strikes in an up-and-down sequence.

Next is the strong rhythmical sense in the hammering action. Unrefined strength, and uncoordinated movements, are a major obstacle to fine work; a consistent rhythmical hammering sequence allows for the all-important adjustments which are observed and accommodated *between* each blow. This observation and fine change in the angle at which the hammer falls upon the piece takes place within much less than a second! This is why *control*, rather than *strength*, is the primary skill.

Psychologically speaking, the most important capacity is that of *balance*. This is the ability to remain calm, collected and in control, despite the huge variety of strong sense impressions inherent in forge work: brightness and intensity of fire, heat, loud high-pitched anvil ring, clapping of the bellows or whine of the fan. It is as if one part of you needs to be completely committed and physically involved with the processes around you, whilst the other part needs to remain *outside* of these sense impressions and quietly 'direct' the proceedings. It is about remaining cool-headed in a very hot place.

A modern blacksmith working

All this requires discipline and determination, and above all else, *focus*. Lapses of concentration are exposed in a dramatic fashion; molten metal, burns, injuries etc. The type of focus required is, nevertheless, reflective and persistent, rather than reactive and impulsive – this only leads to further loss of control.

This kind of focusing brings about the hugely important quality of *consistency* to forge work; the heat needs to be just right *every time*, the technique applied needs to be as *precise* as possible, the aim needs to be crystal *clear,* and all this needs to take place at exactly the right moment: 'Strike while the iron is hot!'

The small loss to any of these qualities causes the work efficiency to drop, and not by a small margin. Such loss is experienced as frustration – educationally – and bankruptcy in a commercial sense. To illustrate this, a small project like a coat hook will take a smith 10 minutes to make, an inexperienced student may need two to four hours. Such are the contrasts.

Finally, and perhaps most importantly, more than in any other craft, the sense for concept, the idea, the design, needs to be clarified completely *before* the project begins. In no other craft have I experienced the attempt to 'try something and see how it goes' to be less productive. Instead, the *thought* of what is being made, or what is the next step in the process, determines how good the final result will be. When the piece of steel is at near-white heat as it comes out of the fire, you simply have to know exactly what action needs to be performed, and then perform it, immediately.

Overall, the gesture inherent in forge work, and the 'lesson' iron can offer is that of 'awakening'. It is about being quietly focused, clear-minded and practically committed.

Take a look at a piece of hand-forged ironwork, perhaps a well-made gate somewhere. You will see a strong structure, which has served its purpose for decades, if not centuries. But you will also notice variety of gracefully curved shapes: leaves, ribbons, scrolls. Far from looking cold and rigid, these forms bear witness to the very nature of iron, that of malleability, flexibility and its process of being made pliable by fire.

Cutting hot Iron

Iron presents qualities of strength and firmness, but be it an axe, a leaf, an animal motif or any other, its form always speaks of a fire and heat process which inherently celebrates the iron's ability to mould flexibly and gracefully. These are the very qualities that are engendered in a person who commits to working with it.

Old wrought iron railings

Crafting: A Descent into Matter – transformation of materials

Bernard Graves

To help formulate the integrated approach to education we are describing, and to provide a relevant context for a craft curriculum, a colleague of mine, Aonghus Gordon[102], formulated the proposal described below. In this proposal, we see how an integrated craft curriculum can be the catalyst between landscape and materials, nature and the maker. Crafting is the means whereby the maker facilitates the transformation of nature's materials, giving them a new context in life and new purpose.

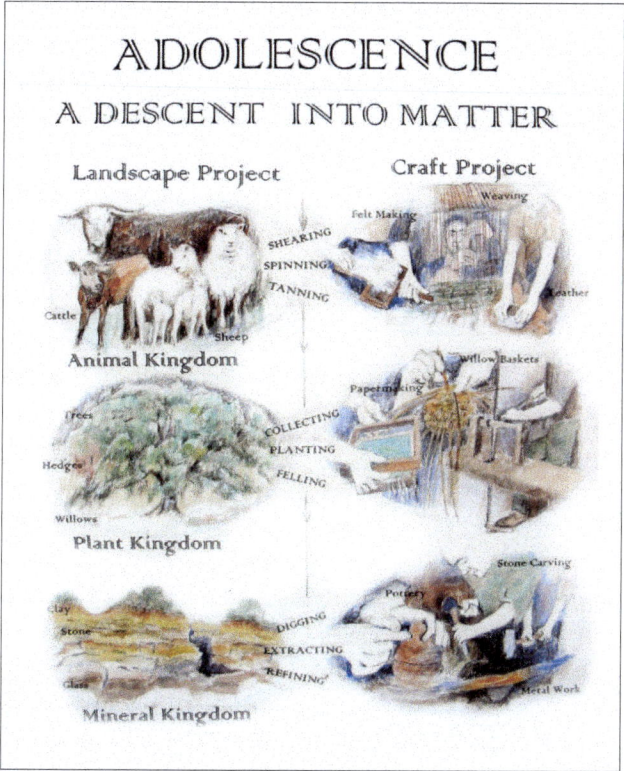

ADOLESCENCE
A DESCENT INTO MATTER

Landscape Project — Craft Project

Felt Making — Weaving

SHEARING
SPINNING
TANNING

Cattle — Sheep
Animal Kingdom
Leather

Trees — Willow Baskets
Papermaking
COLLECTING
PLANTING
FELLING
Hedges
Willows
Plant Kingdom

Clay — Stone Carving
Stone — Pottery
DIGGING
EXTRACTING
REFINING
Glass
Mineral Kingdom
Metal Work

A Descent into Matter
(Original by Kay Wedgebury RM (commissioned by Aonghus Gordon, Ruskin Mill College, 1994)

In the illustration above, the kingdoms of nature are ordered, showing their respective raw materials and processes necessary to prepare the material in readiness for the craft activity – often a craft in its own right. Where the preparatory processes (such as the growing and harvesting of willows in the school grounds) can be undertaken, pupils can benefit from the fuller experience and knowledge of the materials used to make a basket.

A further explanation at this point on the phrase 'A descent into matter' may be helpful.

*'**Matter**' – the materials used in various crafts, which range from soft materials easily worked by hand, such as wool, to those sourced from the mineral kingdom, like the metals that offer much more resistance and require the use of fire and more complex technologies not only to process them but also to work them.*

*'**Descent**' – the journey undertaken to process and transform materials into an artefact, increasing in length of time and arduousness; there is also a noticeable progression in the unaided use of the hands to using tools, as one proceeds through using materials from the animal to the mineral kingdom.*

From this follows the insight that the innate qualities of materials and craft processes are best suited to different age groups of children, according to their strength and skill.

However, though wool is eminently suited to the ability of a younger child to work with successfully (as in felting), more senior pupils can be challenged to work with the same material but using more complex techniques and designs. They can also start to encounter the more resistant substances such as metal, and the fiery processes required to transform these.

Finally, we come to describe glass and traditional, leaded, stained-glass work. Our transformative journey has led us from working with soft, gentle and warm materials like wool to the more resistant cold materials like iron. Beyond the metals, the manufactured stained glass used in traditional, leaded glass-work offers a unique opportunity to give aesthetic and pleasing design to an otherwise inert

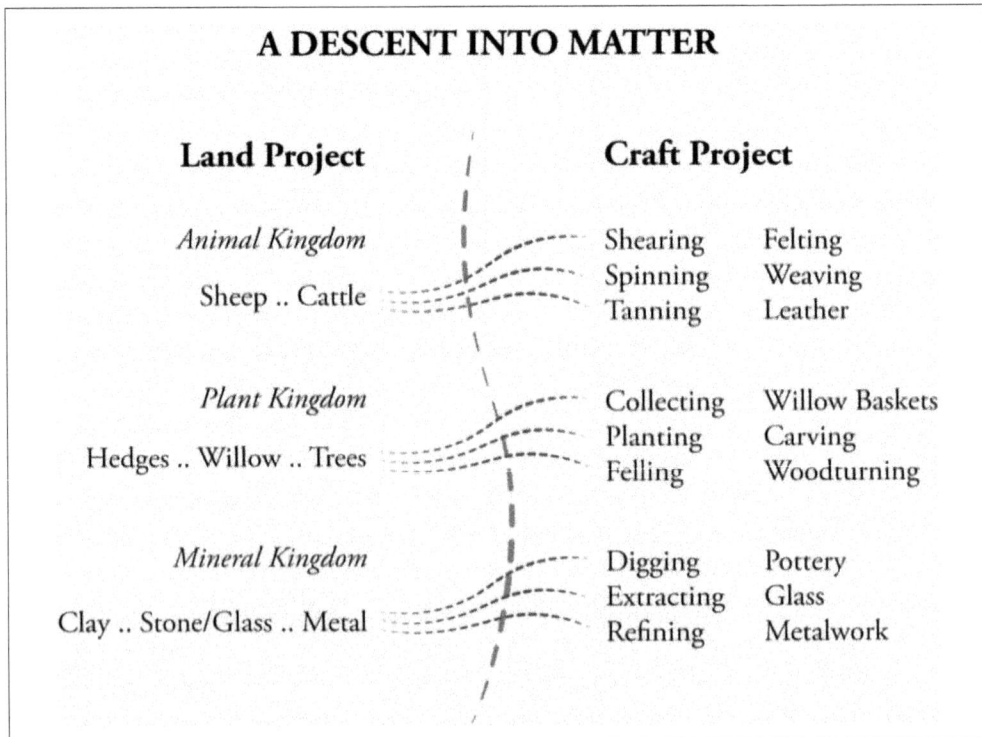

A DESCENT INTO MATTER

Land Project	**Craft Project**	
Animal Kingdom	Shearing	Felting
	Spinning	Weaving
Sheep .. Cattle	Tanning	Leather
Plant Kingdom	Collecting	Willow Baskets
	Planting	Carving
Hedges .. Willow .. Trees	Felling	Woodturning
Mineral Kingdom	Digging	Pottery
	Extracting	Glass
Clay .. Stone/Glass .. Metal	Refining	Metalwork

A Descent into Matter (after Aonghus Gordon, Ruskin Mill College, 2000)

mineral-based material. *Refined from silica, quartz and pigments made from metal oxides, glass can be made more or less translucent or opaque with its colourful secrets best revealed when natural light is allowed to pass through it.*

Unlike all other materials that can be harvested or refined from natural resources, producing glass from the natural ingredients of silica, quartz, seaweed and metal oxides is realistically beyond even the most resourceful of craftsmen, as complex industrial processes are required to produce sheets or panes of glass. Thus, we are challenged to use a material already manufactured and cut it to suit our design. Compared to other crafts, there are relatively few hand tools required, but this is balanced with the increase in designing and drawing skills necessary, as well as accuracy, for cutting both the glass and the lead for holding and hanging the glass pieces.

When the basic techniques for glass-work are mastered, great creative potential is available for crafting – for truly artistic work expressed in colour and form in flat window hangings and three-dimensional pieces which may be lit up from the inside by candle or electric light. At first glance the techniques used to put a piece together may strike us as a rather clinical and cold process which, compared to a blacksmith in a hot forge, it most certainly is. However, upon completion and through illumination, the piece warms and inspires through the interplay of light and colour, and this is a truly transformative experience.

Agate, quartz crystal and glass piece – Johannes Steuck.

CHAPTER 11

Stained Glass

Johannes Steuck

My journey to stained glass

I left Fine Art college in 1978, having completed a sculpture course and with the vague sense that I somehow needed to add skill and knowledge of materials to 'ideas'. The emphasis at college had been very much on 'thinking' and the actualising of thought. I wanted more – a kind of creative journey through materials and a conscious development of skills and tool use.

I spent more-or-less the whole of 1983 doing ceramic mosaics, working as an un-official community artist in Camphill Thornbury. Having immersed myself in Sufism in India, I needed time to re-evaluate my relationship with Christianity. Mosaic-making provided me with the means to do this, as this is an artform that really came into its own in the early Christian era. I was inspired by early Christian imagery, icons and painting – particularly anything from the Byzantine period. This phase of my work was a going-backwards in time, as it were and was countered by developing a contemporary technique, i.e. using randomly chipped shapes of tile of different thicknesses.

My approach allowed for more expression and a more painterly style. Mosaic making prepared the way for subsequent explorations with stained glass. Both are sharp, brittle and unforgiving materials whose surface or intrinsic colours cannot be mixed but need to work together, side by side, to create subtlety and tone.

Interestingly, making mosaics was a personal, and largely unconscious (in-so-far as I did not have stained glass in mind) re-living of a process that had unfolded on the greater stage of history. One can imagine a sort of 'metamorphic process' in which the natural rounded pebbles used in Macedonian floor mosaics become the square stone tesserae of Roman villas and courtyards. These underfoot mosaics are transferred in time to the interior walls of early churches as glass paste, and are finally transfigured into stained glass by the Romanesque and Gothic Renaissance. Thus, there is a process of a 'shift' through location and material which moves from dense, light-reflecting stone flooring, through semi-opaque glass paste wall decoration, to light transmitting coloured glass. Substance is refined!

I moved back to the Cotswolds In March 1984 and by about June of that year was well on the way to acquiring basic stained glass skills. I had finally moved from Thornbury (the place where I grew up) to be near the then 'emerging' Ruskin Mill College. The College has today become a well-established institution, giving practical training, guidance and a therapeutic environment to young adults with complex needs. I took a gardening job at Cotswold Chine Home School, a Steiner School for those deemed to have challenging behaviour. The principal (an enlightened man) wished to commission me for a stained-glass window. I had never done any glass, but as 'luck' would have it, living right next to the school was the stained-glass artist called Edward Payne. His father, Mr A. Payne had also been a local stained-glass artist.

Detail of face mosaic, 2013

Edward Payne[103] was 79 when I began my once-weekly, two-hour training sessions with him. Born in 1907, his life had spanned the greater part of the 20th century. He was a living bridge to a bygone era; a time when Britain still had an Empire, when decency and respect were still the general currency of human social interaction (at least at home). This was a time before the great machinery of commercialism had spun away all other values in its wake. He was probably one of the last living representatives of the Arts and Crafts movement, a movement started in the 19th century and manifesting strongly in William Morris[104], John Ruskin[105] and Christopher Whall[106]. The advocates of Arts and Crafts proclaimed the ideal of 'the total work' – that the artist should be both designer and executer. For Morris, Ruskin and their contemporaries, the artist/craftsman was the ideal person; inspired, contemplative, skilled and practicable. He should be responsible for both 'concept' and 'object'; the artificial barrier, the great divide between artist and craftsman erected in the Renaissance, should be pulled down.

My semi-conscious longing, which came to the surface after leaving art college, i.e. to add skill and knowledge of materials to my artistic endeavours, seemed to be realised at this time. Mr Payne embodied everything I could have wished for in a teacher. He was tall and bespectacled and, it would be no exaggeration to say, embodied 'shining goodness'. Both his age and his

Mr Edward Payne, Stained Glass Artist, 1906–1991

temperament made him slow. It would probably be more accurate to say he moved at a speed that was not rushed, that was not modern, not governed by the urgent shortcuts of economy. Entering his house and studio was always special; the hustle and bustle of everyday life simply fell away and one could get on with the far more interesting business of 'being'.

Mr Payne took me through the basics of traditional stained-glass window making; design, colour sketches, cartoon, glass-cutting, painting, firing and leading-up. Much of his teaching was by way of example and focused on demonstrating through a 'this is how you do it' approach, rather than through a detailed breakdown of a process into its logical components. This meant I had to fill in lots of gaps, do a lot of self-learning. It also meant I was left very free. I was free to develop my own methods and free to make my own mistakes.

Madonna and Child – Edward Payne, 1987

Stained glass did not come easily to me. It was in many ways inimical to my nature – precise, exacting, disciplined, indirect, demanding both skill and patience. I am not naturally a very skilful person; in fact I am probably quite dyspraxic. I had always envied people whose movements were smooth and well synchronised, people who could, for instance, turn the key in a lock while skilfully transferring something held in the right hand to the left (possibly using their teeth) and then give the door a gentle nudge with a knee and slide in. I would always have to drop whatever I was holding; the key was always the wrong way around and I would usually have to unlock and lock the door several times before gaining entry.

I assisted Mr Payne in his last big commission; the four windows for the Cirencester hospital chapel. He was 83 and in need of physical assistance but was as creative, conscientious and exacting as ever. With painstaking care, he had constructed a cardboard model of the chapel's interior with little strips of 'stained glass' to give an impression of the outcome. One peered into this tiny model and saw with what infinite care and patience he had constructed his doll's-house panels; window glass, mosaicked over with colour and painted with black line. I was responsible for painting some of the lesser features, mainly patterns, and was permitted to paint one picture panel; Jacob wrestling with the Angel. This panel was inspired by an El Greco[107] painting. The two lancet windows flanking the altar depicted religious scenes; the two at the sides, badges and emblems.

A natural history of glass

'Glass is a natural substance, a super-cooled siliceous liquid, that is, a liquid that becomes solid without having the usual freezing point'[108].

Glass is a substance, usually transparent, lustrous, hard and brittle, made by fusing soda or potash or both with other ingredients. It usually consists of mutually dissolved silica and silicates that also contain soda and lime. Glass occurs naturally as volcanic glass or obsidian, and as dung-shaped nodules after lightning strikes in deserts. These are called fulgurites, the lightning being attracted to the desert by buried iron and fusing the sand on its way through. Glass sometimes comes to earth from outer space in the form of Tektites. The Moon is covered in glass marbles.

A cultural history of glass

The making of glass objects probably began around 8000BC. The discovery of glass is attributed to a Phoenician barbecue, to quote from Pliny the Elder:

'A ship belonging to traders in soda once called here, so the story goes, and they spread out along the shore to make a meal. There were no stones to support their cooking-pots, so they placed lumps of soda from their ship under them. When these became hot and fused with the sand on the beach, streams of an unknown liquid flowed, and this was the origin of glass'. (Pliny, 362)[109]

Although Pliny was a Roman this is a very modern interpretation of 'history', i.e. attributing an important discovery to chance. Thus, at the very beginning of glass making, and indeed at the very beginning of everything there is a conundrum: was it chance or inspired discovery? Random event or intention? Did our ancestors simply stumble into their inventions or was there something else involved? We don't really know, but there is something very random about chance and if we apply it to our own lives, we might feel vaguely disappointed.

Teaching stained glass

Back in the Horsley valley, Ruskin Mill soon transformed itself from being the gathering place for a handful of craftsmen and artists practising their craft to a training college for young people.

Detail of stained glass panel (Johannes Steuck)

Molten glass

I taught mosaics and stained glass. As so often in my life, I was put into the strange position of having to 'jump ahead', to teach stained glass when I was very much a beginner. If I had aspired to be a craftsman this would have been anathema; the very idea of passing on unperfected skills and instilling 'bad practice' in the next generation would have made the true practitioner wring his hands and cry out in agony. But then, I never thought of myself as a craftsman – I was an artist using stained glass as a creative medium and, as such, I had no scruples about teaching. My strange torturous journey was the strange and torturous journey of my students. It forced me to rationalise all the various processes and to develop an appropriate curriculum.

Stages of making

Here I will give a brief overview of the processes and stages in stained glass making.

Semi-precious stone panels.

Right from very early childhood I was interested in crystals; indeed, at one point I wanted to be a jeweller. This devotion to minerals, to precious and semi-precious stones, resurfaced shortly after my training in stained glass. This was in part triggered by a tiny piece of stained glass that my wife Jeanie owned (made by her aunt Olga in America) into which was incorporated a tiny slice of agate. How true it is that we choose our influences! A thousand others may have seen this object and not responded to it at all; for me it was a Damascus moment. From then on, semi-precious stones, particularly agates, became an important source of inspiration, the idea being that the stone itself could set up a kind of chain reaction or ripple, a little like casting a pebble into a pool. Setting the agate meant creating an environment around it that, from then on, would be its home.

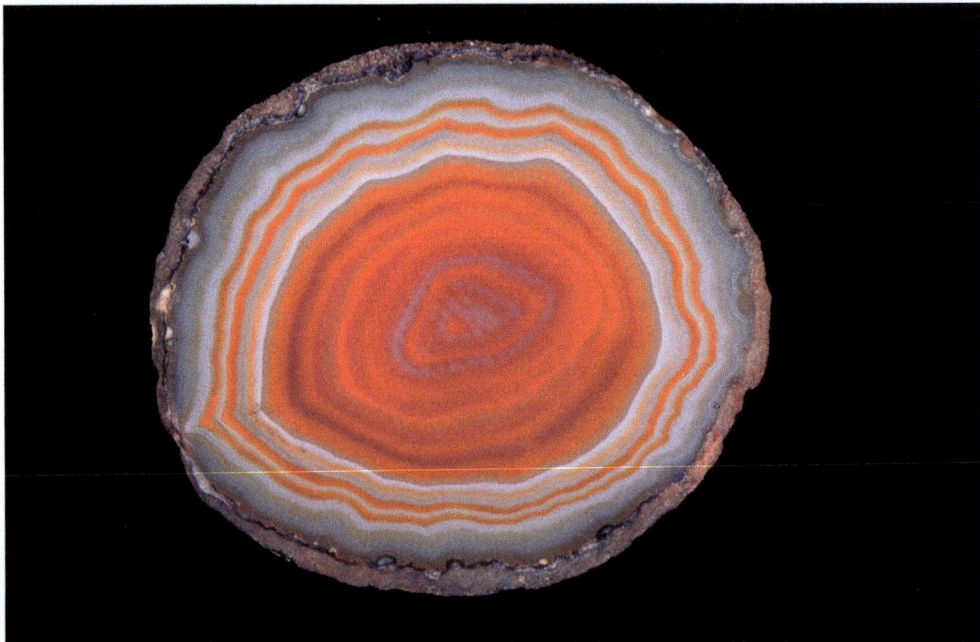

Semi-precious Agate
Most semi-precious stones useful for setting into stained-glass panels come from the quartz family. They include rock crystals, citrines, amethysts, carnelians and agates. These stones all have something in common: their essential component is silica.

I used this process as a first step in my approach to stained glass teaching. Instead of the student being faced by the terrifying prospect of a pencil and a blank sheet of paper, she had a beautiful stone to play with. The stained-glass object also had a certain 'organic flexibility'; in other words, it did not need to conform to a rigid right angle but could expand and shrink a little as it absorbed inaccuracies.

Incorporating semi-precious stones into a stained-glass panel is like returning to the roots of the craft, using silica in its natural form. The first step is to contemplate the stones, familiarise oneself with their features and characteristics. Next, they need to be placed appropriately; a design is then created around them.

When the initial design has reached a certain level of completeness, the student can do some glass cutting. The resistance and difficulty encountered in cutting glass are a good lesson in simplification. The student learns very directly what is possible and what is impossible; she not only comes up against her own limitations, but also pushes up against the limitations and potential of the material. This experience then feeds back very quickly and directly into the design. The design is then traced, and transferred into a cut line and templates.

The birth of stained glass

Now the student is ready to start cutting the stained glass. This is the time to look at it, appreciate it, marvel at it, learn a little about its history, manufacture, composition and cost.

Interestingly, stained glass is the only art form to arise out of Christianity. All other art forms (painting, sculpture, etc.) have a long pre-Christian history. The earliest stained glass is from the 10th century, although only small fragments survive. Stained glass really came into its own in the Romanesque and Gothic era. Suddenly and magically (with a little help from the Rosicrucian Alchemists) this new art form appeared. Chance or intention, who can say? If we wander about in a cathedral we can perhaps pick up a few hints. The overall effect is one of darkness illuminated by light. We gaze up at the stone patterns and traceries, the blotches of coloured light on the floor, and we may think trees, sacred groves. Perhaps the beautiful gothic church with its rhythmic and fluid architecture, its relationship to light and space, is nothing but a kind of crystalized sacred grove. The humanisation and Christianisation of a long Pagan past.

Traditional production of glass

Originally all stained-glass would have been mouth-blown or spun. If mouth-blown, a glob of molten glass is inflated by blowing, is stuck into the furnace again and shaped into a 'cylinder'. This cylinder is cut, and the two curved pieces are reheated and folded out, creating flat surfaces. Spun glass is produced by centrifugal action. The heated glob of glass is spun rapidly at the end of a rod, resulting in a disk. This disk is then cut up into plates.

The colour in stained glass is due to the inclusion of metallic oxides or metallic elements in the glass. Copper produces blue, as does cobalt; green is made from iron, yellow from selenium and red from gold. This is colloidal gold, as gold does not oxidize and therefore has to be incorporated as an element. The price of gold is currently so high that certain forms of pink or rose glass are no longer produced. This brings us to the matter of cost. Stained glass is expensive; great economy should be exercised. Make sure the cuts are not wasteful!

When first confronted by brightly coloured bits of glass, it is easy for the student to go into a kind of feeding frenzy, to stick every available colour into her panel. Restraint is the key here. She should be guided by the subtle colours of her stone; it should not be blasted into dullness by a zapping with over-bright or lurid colour!

Once all the glass cutting has been completed leading-up can commence. The leads or cames are stretched, opened and laid flat on the work bench nearby. They are placed between the coloured glass, framing each piece. Leads, or cames, come in various shapes and sizes. Broadly

Lead
Lead has been mined since ancient times, as its ore, galena, is easy to smelt. Galena is a combination of
lead and sulphur with traces of silver. In fact, it contains enough silver to make extraction worth-while.
It appears in the periodic table of elements as Pb, which are the Latin initials for Plumbum. It is used for
roofing and was extensively used for pipes. Lead, being a 'radio-active' material, has a half-life. This half-
life lasts for 120 years. All the leading in churches and cathedrals has to be renewed after this period. The
melting point of lead is 327°C.

speaking there are two types: round and flat. The round is slightly more expensive but works
better, does not kink when bent. Modern leads have been cast in iron moulds and milled, they
also contain other metals. They are stronger, more durable, and solder together better than the
old leads. In the olden days, leads were cast into special stone moulds using willow withies or
reeds to create the grooves.

The next step is soldering. Modern electric soldering irons are probably the best thing to use.
In the olden days, before the use of gas and electricity, soldering irons were heated up in braziers.
They had wooden handles, an iron shaft, and broad, pointed copper heads. They would be heated
in succession, more than one on the go at a time, and passed to the Master by a useful small
boy or girl. Pre-literate, or should one say, selectively literate societies possessed an abundance of
useful small girls and boys. Training started early, and it is quite clear that the kind of excellence
attained by craftsmen in the past is no longer generally achievable. We start too late and have
become confused by intelligence. I guess everything has its price, and to save children from the
abuses of the Industrial Revolution, it was essential to instigate universal education. What is
possible now, is to become a craftsman consciously.

I found that the semi-precious stones came into their own when a small gap is created around
them, when the lead and glass do not 'thrust' themselves into their proximity. This is where
another metal can come into play. This other metal is copper.

When hammered, copper assumes the hardness of steel; if it is annealed (heated to a low heat
and quenched in cold water) it becomes soft and pliant again. Copper can be used to bridge the
gaps between the flat semi-precious stones, such as agates, and the stained glass.

The final process is puttying. It has three purposes: weather proofing, strength and aesthetics.
If you are working on a large window, it is worth using stained-glass cement. I remember
Mr Payne concocting an elaborate cocktail of ingredients; whiting, plaster of Paris, a little red
lead, lampblack, white spirit and boiled linseed oil. Nowadays it comes in a tin and has the
consistency of very thick treacle. It is brushed into the gaps between the glass and the lead with
a stiff brush. Sawdust is applied to soak up some of the excess liquid and then cleaned off. The

Tin

Tin has been used since very early times, 4000– 5000BC. After copper, it is the other main component of bronze and was extensively mined in Cornwall. It occurs as the ore cassiterite, which, when pure, forms clear, brilliant tetragonal crystals. Like lead, tin has a low melting point, 232.8ºC. It has a few interesting qualities. When a stick of pure tin is bent, a strange crackling sound arises, this is called the 'cry of tin' and is due to its crystalline structure. When exposed to very low temperatures for a long time, it will crumble into dust. This was a very sharp lesson for Napoleon on his retreat from Moscow, as the tin buttons on his soldiers' uniforms disintegrated leaving them virtually, 'hanging onto their trousers'. Float glass is manufactured by floating a layer of molten glass on a layer of molten tin. This makes it possible to create a comparatively large expanse of absolutely even, flat glass. Tin has the quality of always 'seeking the level'.

Native Copper

Mined since very ancient times, copper pre-dates the bronze age. It is sometimes found in its native state, when it has a branching, plant-like form:
'Pure copper can be rose-red, sunrise-red, reddish-yellow or brown-red. In transparency of extremely thin sheets it is a shadowy blue-green, complementary to the orange-red of the polished metal'. Pelikan, the *Secrets of Metals*'[111].

sawdust dries out the cement and makes it possible to more-or-less 'confine' it to its appropriate place. A small panel is better puttied with ordinary bog-standard linseed oil putty.

Transforming materials, transforming self

My work with semi-precious stones began to have a very profound effect on me. Not only was this way of working a useful teaching aid, it gradually led to a place of silence. The painter, when he is confronted by 'rose', if he is honest, has to admit that anything he may do, however clever, can never in any way come near to 'rose'. Yes, he can create something that guides the eye and mind into a greater appreciation of 'rose', capture some particular angle never yet explored before, but 'rose' itself is unattainable. We can express it, but the thing itself we cannot make. And thus it is with agates, quartz crystals, fluorites, amethysts, carnelians, calcites and tourmalines. These stones need to be celebrated, placed in among colours and shapes that do not smother them or vie for attention. My contribution had to be thoughtful, sensitive, humble almost. I became the stones' servant. These ancient jewels were perhaps millions of years old, formed under extreme conditions of heat and pressure, buried for aeons beneath the Earth's crust and then wrenched out, cut, polished and carried into the light. I felt there was something very fitting in this combination of glass and jewels. In a sense, glass is our 'jewel' – this extraordinary substance, not quite rigid, yet hard and brittle, a threshold through which light becomes coloured light. As Goethe so poignantly says: 'Colours are the deeds and sufferings of light'[110]. The Phoenicians had invented it and the Egyptians were the masters of its use in combination with gold and semi-precious stones.

Aspects of making

To generalise, one could say there are three basic, traditional art/craft making processes: *Modelling*, *Carving* and *Construction*. *Modelling* involves all those making activities where the material is of one kind and whilst moist or pliant, is bent, pulled or in any other way manipulated. Pottery is a classic example and by a long stretch, modelling could include forge work. *Carving* also implies the 'oneness' of the material, and involves the reduction of its mass, the removal of material and refinement. *Construction* is a synthetic process, where different elements and materials are brought into relationship with each other. Stained glass is definitely in that category.

The basic elements brought into relationship with each other in stained glass are glass and metals. Lead and glass are polar opposites, lead is dense, soft, malleable and definitely not see-through. Glass is brittle, hard, sharp and transparent. They are 'wedded' together by tin, which becomes temporarily liquid to achieve this. The putty reinforces this unity.

If we run through the stained glass making process again mentally, we can observe how it really does involve all our faculties. The first step is the design, which could be a very contrived thing or a semi-conscious splurge. This initial design is then defined and traced, involving choice, selection and boundaries, a much more intellectual process. Our feelings are strongly activated when we choose our colours. The will is engaged when we start cutting the glass and leading-up, meeting resistance.

Running through the entire stained glass making process is a kind of switch between positive and negative, between something that is lively and creative and something that is dull, possibly boring and repetitive. We pour our energy into the design; this should be as colourful and interesting as possible. The next bit, all the tracing, is perhaps not so exciting. Yet something interesting has occurred; all the positives, the colour patches, have been reduced to negatives, to lines. When the templates are cut out, the negatives become positives again, temporary planes that define the boundaries of the glass. The laid-out pieces of glass have negatives between them, the gaps that will be filled with lead. This moving between positive and negative is good for the mind; it keeps it fluid, flexible and creative.

Painted glass face portrait

ART IDEAS

INSPIRATION

SKILL KNOWLEDGE

CRAFT MATERIALS

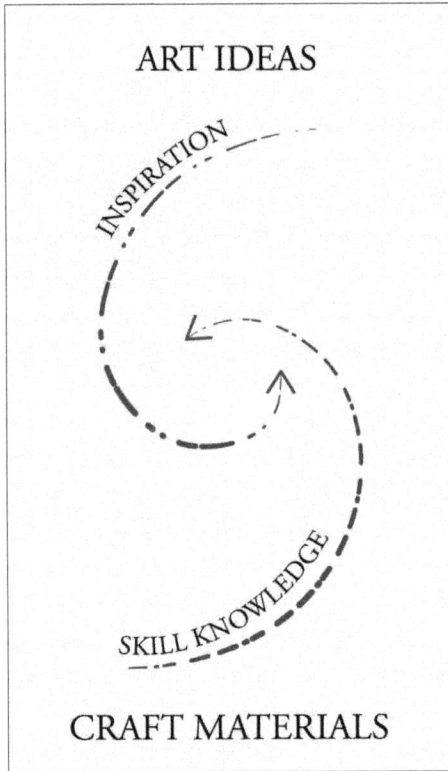

Art/craft interaction

Resistance, mastery and improvising

Having practised stained glass for many years now, I would say that there are three distinct phases: Resistance, Mastery and Improvising.

Resistance

Resistance is certainly something I encountered! As I said, there was always something slightly cack-handed about me; cutting glass and accuracy did not come easily. Resistance is about suffering, cutting yourself, leaning on glass splinters, having to endlessly re-cut misfitting bits of glass. Resistance is about filling in holes, pushing yourself against the material. Resistance is about not knowing – is it my lack of ability, the bluntness of the cutting wheel, or just bad luck that blocks me from doing the job properly? Above all, resistance is about learning and a commitment to learning. You have a goal, something worth achieving, and resistance tempers your ardour, holds you in check, develops your skill and knowledge, confronts you with your limitations and expands your potentials.

Mastery

Mastery is something that happens in time, through a process of repetition and a striving for excellence. For me it happened very gradually over the years and could never be taken for granted. You can have good days and bad days, good moments and bad moments. When I was working very intensely with mosaics, I had a much clearer experience of mastery. Sometimes a kind of 'Zen' state would pervade me in which I worked automatically. This state was accompanied by a mood of emptiness: not negative emptiness, vacuity, but the emptiness of *not thinking*, filled with joy. It always took a long hard slog to reach this state and then, almost imperceptibly, and never as a matter of course, an easy effortlessness would set in. The memory of the movement had somehow embedded itself in my organism, and could be summoned by the unconscious. At this point, the work would flow unimpeded; every fragment fitted perfectly, was just 'right'.

Mastery means mastering the materials and processes, but it also imposes limits, restrictions. One of the side effects of mastering a craft is the possible sapping away of spontaneity. The kind of 'devil may care' attitude, where the whole emphasis is on process and in which there is very little focus on 'outcome', vanishes. There's a drying up; one's energy is directed towards the practicable rather than the experimental. This is something Mr Payne warned me about, saying, 'You must carry on drawing and painting; the craft of glass can kill your creativity.'

Improvising

On one level there is a fundamental difference between art and craft. In craft, there is a striving towards excellence: the perfect teapot, for example. The masterpiece stands as a kind of archetype that needs to be constantly reattained. In this sense, the craftsman is a conservative. The artist is forever trying to shift the boundaries, trying something new. There is no external measure of excellence, there is only the 'creative resonance test'. This basically means, do I like this? Do I find this stimulating? Does it have potential? The challenge is to unite these two tendencies, which could be called knowledge of materials and skill, with creativity and inspiration.

I came to the craft of stained glass from the perspective of an artist and had to struggle very hard to master craft skills. It was in my nature to experiment and innovate, so I suppose the three stages of Resistance, Mastery and Improvisation happened for me simultaneously. The important thing when making anything is somehow to retain an openness. Never 'seal' the piece completely at the design stage. Keep it fresh, allow for changes, play with the colours. As mentioned before in Aspects *of making*, stained glass making goes through stages of negativity and positivity, the boring and the exiting. By exercising a certain degree of self-control, and metering out the creative input, you can end up with something lively and energetic rather than with something whose dynamic has already been exhausted in the design stage.

Crystal glass lampstand

Concluding thoughts

Bernard Graves

T here is no doubt in my mind that, in as much as schools can develop their unique practical skills and craft curricula, with sourcing materials from the immediate environment, we help to open up awareness for, and provide ways in which children can become actively engaged in developing and maintaining the school grounds. This approach of a shared vision for the school environment as an educational resource will have the added benefit of bringing different departments of the school together and can rightly be regarded as a model for sustainable education.

Traditional English slewed basket

'Descending and Ascending' path of crafting

The intrinsic educational and remedial value of the picture of a 'descent into matter', transforming materials as an educational and socially healing process, becomes apparent when we become aware of how different materials require different sensibilities and ways of working. Each material and craft process demands something specific in the way of skills, knowledge and understanding.

All that we bring to bear in the moment of creativity allows for something new and unique to arise. The artefact, the pot that emerges from the clay, the basket that comes together from a pile of sticks, the hook or knife that is shaped in the forge: these are the conjoint results of our skills, efforts and nature's intention.

It could be said that nature harbours all the potential artefacts that we could make. In return for our crafting, we not only 'ennoble' the raw material with shape, design and purpose but the maker, in return, is blessed with knowledge and enrichment of experience.

In crafting, our hands, heart and head serve as the instruments for the realisation of the idea, for instance, of a felted or leather bag, a hedgerow basket, a steam-bent ash chair, an earthen pot, a hand-forged knife. Through these activities, we have the opportunity to revisit and discover for ourselves the creative exploits of our ancestors in their endeavours to transform materials and provide for their everyday needs.

Traditional Crafts may be considered to belong to the cradle of civilisation and although they were responsible for our early technologies, their practical relevance today may well be questioned. Yet we believe their justification lies in the fact that craft, a work wrought by the hands, affords us creativity, joy in the making and a more profound sense of value and respect for both nature's materials and the material things with which we surround ourselves.

CHAPTER 12

Lighting Fires

Jonathan Code

Lighting fires

A chapter on fire-lighting would be well-placed – it could be assumed – at the *beginning* of this book on *crafting,* which details specific craft materials and practices, and is perhaps mis-placed at the end of such a section. After all, so many crafts rely on fire, heat, warmth of some kind in order to prepare materials for crafting (as when obtaining iron from ore), to work materials (heating the iron in the forge) or finish crafted items (fire clay pots in the kiln). Fire is – from this perspective – both the 'alpha' and the 'omega' of crafting processes and we must master fire's making before we can master other craft processes.

Lighting fires

Essential as this role of fire is to the making of crafted items, it is apt to *follow* the previous chapters on specific craft processes with a modest chapter on fire, due to the particular emphasis we are wanting to give in this book to the transformation of materials *and of the maker*.

The moment human beings mastered fire – a date which has been mentioned in previous sections and which is still something of a moving feast – a transformation of materials and of the immediate environment was afforded *along with* a radical transformation of the human being themselves. What do I mean by this statement?

Transformation is a mutual process – or its potency is that it has the *potential* to be so. If, as so many of the chapters above have articulated, we *participate* in the process of transformation with our whole being, and do not hand it all over to machinery and industrial processes which remove us from the immediacy of the event, *we change with the clay*, with the steel and with the wool. But we do so in accordance with the nature of the material and its means of transformation.

Let me come at this from another angle.

A noteworthy feature of this book on *crafting* is that it arises out of a collaboration of quite special and unique authors. The authors of this book are not only skilled in the transformation of materials and substances – they are not only craftsmen and women of remarkable ability and insight – they are also experienced and skilled *educators*. These capacities do not always go hand-in-hand, and are not to be taken for granted. It is one thing to fashion a beautiful pot out of clay, to transform the hide of a dead animal into a beautiful pair of shoes, to bring out of a tangled mass of wool a beautifully felted picture – it is quite another thing to be a 'midwife' or mentor to a developing human being *while also* mastering the transformation of materials.

Education is, from this perspective, an art and craft in its own right, and one that takes some mastery. Such an idea has been alluded to in a phrase that regularly resurfaces in discussions about the aims and objectives of education – and it takes as its core metaphor the act of making fire.

> *'The mind does not require filling like a bottle, but rather, like wood, it only requires kindling to create in it an impulse to think independently and an ardent desire for the truth*[112].*'*

The idea that education should be focused on *kindling flames* rather than *filling vessels* is a very old one. Although it has often been attributed to the poet W.B. Yeats[113], it can already be found – if we dig a bit deeper into historical sources – in Plutarch's *Moralia*, in the last lines of his *On Listening to Lectures*[114]. The fact that this phrase still crops up in discussions about education today[115] testifies to the fact that educators continue to ponder about the aims and means of their trade a good 2,000 years after Plutarch voiced his own views on these questions. It seems that we are still oscillating between 'filling' and 'firing'. It is no doubt clear by now, if you have been reading through the book to this point, that we are strong advocates for education to focus on the latter – on 'firing' and not 'filling'.

In this chapter I am going to explore this idea of *education as kindling*. I will consider it, to begin with, by describing the practical task of fire-lighting using traditional tools (essentially, four bits of wood and a piece of string!). This is a process that I have worked with for many years with a great variety of learners in an equally diverse range of settings. Learning how to 'make' fire – in a practical sense – is that aspect of fire-lighting which could precede chapters on other crafts. It does so, as previously mentioned, in a pragmatic sense. Fire is needed to light the forge, the kiln, and in most (if not all) workshops, to heat the kettle! When discussing this aspect of fire-making, we can think of it in terms of the gateway to many of the other crafting processes.

I will follow a discussion about the practical demands of fire-lighting by reflecting on some of the inner experiences that lighting fires evokes in those who undertake it. These experiences are both my own – what I go through with each and every fire-lighting session – and those that have been fed back to me by fire-lighters over the years. This section rightly *follows* from experiences in kindling flames but also (though through inference mainly) experiences in *crafting*. I propose that all crafting is fire-lighting or 'kindling' – in the fullest sense of the term; all *making* is about finding, nurturing and following an *inner* flame, while we simultaneously work to transform materials outwardly. This is where education and making meet: in the realisation that we are creators and makers, and by kindling our flame through *crafting* we alight on something that is deeply human, and strive to master the ways and means of keeping it alive.

Kindling flames

I grew up in Ontario, Canada and spent my holidays at a small, quite rustic cabin on the edge of Frontenac Provincial Park. The cabin is, quite literally, within a stone's throw of a deep and very clear lake (from whence it gets its name – Big Clear lake). Summers at the cabin often involved canoe trips and camp fires; in fact they still do. Evenings out camping in the Park are spent under the stars while watching the flicker and glow of flames, the warmth of the embers growing brighter as the darkness closes in around us. These fires are inevitably linked with food; the neat gas flame of the cottage cooker is given over to the much smokier affairs of camp fires.

In winter, the same lake that takes our canoes during the summer is transformed into a vast icy expanse, supporting skates or skis. Fires become essential for warmth, for drying out wet winter gear, and for buffering the temperatures outside the cabin walls which can well drop to -20°C.

Fire accompanied me, in this way, through my childhood and youth. I feel I really came to 'learn' about fires' ways through all those years – and vastly contrasting seasons – at the lake. Fire was deeply connected to the preparing of meals, its nurturing a crucial role for keeping warm, its flickering flames connected to times of deep contentment. Fire could, of course, have quite dramatic and destructive faces as well – as during the summer when an island on the lake burnt to a crisp, its trees and shrubs only a charred reminder of what the forest there had once been.

Through all those years of getting to know fire, however, it was always brought to life for me through a match or a cigarette lighter. It was inconceivable to set out in the canoes without carefully stored matches, conscientiously protected from moisture in any manner of containers. When I first stumbled across the process (and challenge!) of kindling a flame by friction I was already in my 30s.

At the time, I was working as a teacher in a land-based college nestled in the Horsley Valley in the south-west of England. Watching a colleague of mine deftly work a fire-bow and spindle, and in some few minutes call forth a glowing ember, and out of this ember a flicker of flame, and from this flame a fire… I was completely captivated. I felt I had just witnessed a much-belated rite of passage, one that I had somehow missed (along with most of my peers) while being initiated by desks and tests instead. Even with all the fires I had ever kindled by the side of a lake I had never done so through friction.

I was instantly determined to master this seemingly magical act for myself and soon set about learning the kindling craft. I say craft because lighting fires in this way is not done with the flippant flick of a lighter's wheel, or the strike of flammable minerals that tip a matchstick. Lighting a fire with a bow and spindle involves a range of knowledge and skill that can only be acquired over time, and through a good deal of determination. It also involves the fire lighter being engaged wholly in the preparation and performance of her craft.

I learned fire-lighting myself, and soon found myself teaching it to others in a variety of different contexts. Every time a fire is lit through these age-old techniques of kindling, I am struck by how this activity invites us to learn about ourselves – about our heart, mind and hand – as well as about fire's ways.

Preparing

We talk about *making fire,* but I am convinced, after years of facilitating the kindling of flames, that we do not make it at all. Instead we can at best attempt to create the necessary conditions for it to arise. We can hone our technique, get better at choosing tinder, improve our tools and timing, but fire's flaming is a grace and gift beyond our wilful grasp.

Our best chances for enabling fire are with taking the time for careful and considered *preparation.* Adequate preparation is of the utmost importance, and although it does not guarantee that a fire will be realised, poor preparation almost certainly means that it won't.

We begin by sourcing the 'tools' of the trade: hearth board, bow, spindle and bearer. Tinder must also be gathered, dried and stored so that it is at hand when the kindling act is attempted. The time, attention and careful consideration given to both tools and tinder imbue them with a kind of quality rarely given to purchased goods.

Preparation, depending on the context in which the fire-lighting is to take place, often unfolds days or even weeks before the fire-kindling moment. Our first awakening, in fire-lighting terms, is thus to the significance of *time.* In an age of the instant download and the lightning quick response, an act of gathering that won't bear fruit or flames for some months to come cultivates the capacity to act without the addiction to immediate outcomes. We learn to be present in the potential of what is being prepared.

Preparation brings us strongly into our senses as we walk into woodland with the questions: where will I find good hearth wood? what is the best wood for spindles? for bow and bearer? We wake up to ash, to hazel and willow; we have a new sense for thistledown and leaf litter. The woods and dry matter that best suit each of these key components of our fire-lighting kit will vary depending on our environment but wherever we are, as we prepare we are brought to a heightened awareness of the context in which we aim to undertake the act of kindling.

Stepping into the world of our senses, we also slip into the myriad cycles of becoming and passing away, participated in by all living beings. This is a very different kind of time from the

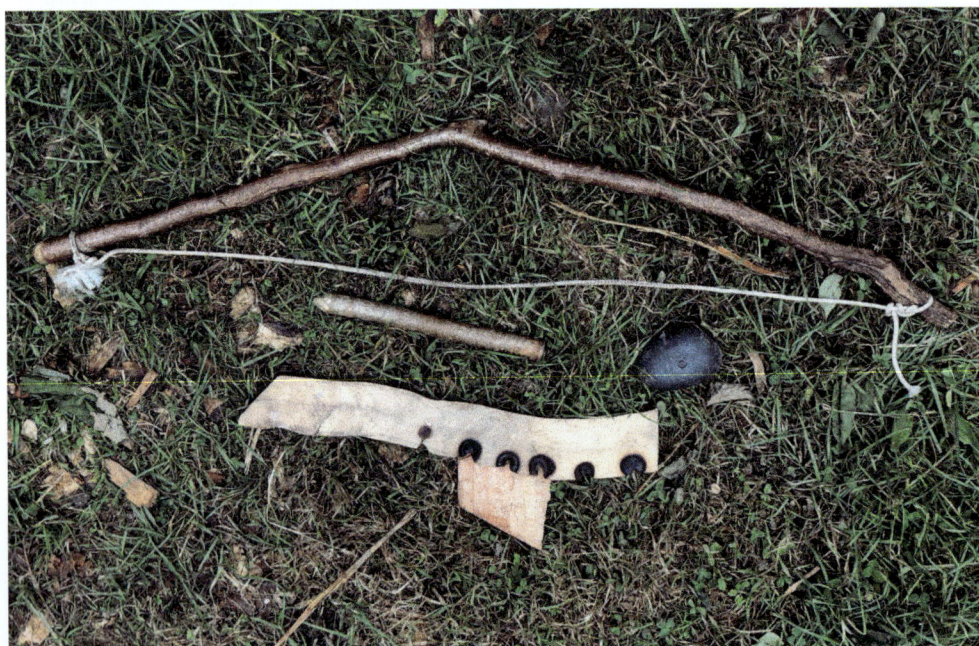

Fire-lighting kit: Bow, hearth and drill – made from local woods

one measured in tick-tock hours, encountered in the classroom's hermetic enclosure. It is a time marked by the setting and swelling of bud, the sap's run into leaf, the flush and wither of flower and the fruit's fall. As would-be kindlers we need to relearn these rhythms, as they speak to us of the right moment for gathering rods for spindles, for sourcing tinder, for seeking out the fire-fungus[116] and old-man's beard[117].

Preparation is for outer intentions, though it is simultaneously an inner practice; it bridges the two. It prepares the preparer, and readies her for what may come. As the hearth board and spindle are selected, the bow strung, the tinder gathered and set to dry, the working of hands feeds the imagination and builds anticipation for the practical task that lies ahead.

First findings

Fire-lighting with fire bows has experienced something of a renaissance of late. It has been brought back into the public eye by proponents of bush craft and skills for wilderness survival[118]. It is sometimes featured as the quintessential skill needed if you are stuck in a tight spot with only a knife, or if you are really wanting to go 'back to basics' in your search for the do-it-yourself life. In terms of detailed information about suitable woods for fire-lighting and pointers for good technique, much can be gained from these sources, which are readily available in this time of open access information. These will also vary (available woods, for instance) depending on your context, so it is good to take the advice from bush craft sources and adjust according to your own situation.

As an educator, my interest in bringing fire-lighting into the lives of learners, and into this final chapter in a section on crafting, differs from those of the bush craft context or as a tool for wilderness survival.

For starters, I invite participants in the process to get into groups of three or four. Fire-lighting enables (or provokes!) a social process along with the practical task. After an initial demonstration from myself of the technique for using bow, bearer and spindle, and how to 'bed'

Collaboration – group fire lighting

or 'seat' the spindle well into the hearth board, I suggest that one member of each group takes responsibility for holding the spindle upright while two other members take either end of the bow. These are suggestions, of course, and I do not think an overly directive approach is at all helpful at this point.

The whole purpose of working in this way is to leave the group to navigate the process themselves, with carefully timed and managed input from a skilled facilitator. The fire-kindlers will meet with difficulty, with 'problems', with any number of vagaries in the process, and they will have to solve them together. I have seen fire-lighting taught in such a way that all the equipment is so prepared and the process so prescribed from the outset that the group may as well have been given a box of matches. But fire is not given, and we need to learn its ways before it will appear for us in our fire-kindling efforts. Over time, the group will find the right choreography, the right roles, and the moment they do so the three individuals merge into one and smoke will appear!

Later on, and in their own time, participants in these facilitated fire-kindling sessions can work to master the craft themselves. In order to do so, a deceptively simple set of parameters needs to be grasped. The process unfolds archetypally in the three planes of space – the hearth board on level ground sits in the horizontal plane of the earth's surface. The spindle stands in the vertical, held at the top by the bearer, the bottom in a dish in the hearth board. As the spindle is brought into rotation by the action of the bow, a strong focus and ability for holding this vertical

Ember forming

is essential. The bow moves rhythmically in the frontal plane and though a change of rotation occurs on each alternating pull of the bow, the spindle must never pause or stop. Fire-lighting is thus a perfect activity not only to establish these dimensions of space (in the younger kindler, for instance) but also to gain a creative relationship to them *in ourselves*. We can only find the right relationship between the planes of space in the kindling process if we find them within our own body and being – and fire-lighting invites us to master these if we are to become kindlers of flames.

When facilitated with a sensitive degree of input from one who knows the process well, and who can lead the group through to the realisation of fire, the outer process can be a potent experience of our almost magical abilities to transform materials into the means of transformation – for the emergence of fire!

Radical pedagogy

Lighting fires is radical pedagogy. It is radical because it challenges a number of trends that have come to define education and, indeed, cultural life today. It is radical because it 'roots' participants once again in *two* realms to which we could be more deeply connected, at a time when there is an increasing alienation from both.

The first realm that we encounter, which has been briefly sketched out above, is the 'outer' world from which the materials for the fire-lighting craft are sourced. This realm is also where our kindling efforts will take place.

The other realm that fire-lighting touches upon is an inner one. In the course of attempting to kindle a flame, a wide range of emotions are encountered. These are, in fact, evident in every kindling session I have ever accompanied, and they follow a similar (but not the same) sequence.

It begins with *anticipation*, an eagerness to try out a task as ancient as culture itself, and one that somehow goes to the heart of what it means to be human. The tools for the craft are taken up with excitement but often with a bit too much eagerness or exuberance. Early attempts soon give way to *frustration*, anger even, and perhaps a not-so-well-hidden struggle with despair. The journey is not all downhill, however; it is rather a set of peaks and troughs. The first waft of smoke lifts the spirits and gives confidence that good technique is starting to be grasped. This stage needs to be sustained, however, if the first smoke trails are actually going to carry through to an ember. The saying 'where there is smoke there is sure to be fire' is perhaps a bit misleading here, or it needs to be couched with 'if the fire-lighter persists in his or her craft'. Perseverance is key to success at this point in the process.

A number of signs speak to the progress of, or problems encountered by, a fire-lighting group. In cooler climes, the 'coats-off' stage is a clear sign that a good deal of effort is being expended. Coats are cast aside with abandon, hindrances to the necessary subtlety and freedom of movement for limbs. Sometimes a group will spontaneously break into song, a rallying cry to renew commitment or an expression of the common intention and will that is being discovered. Changes in the sounds of the group while they work, and of the spindle as it is spun on the hearth board, are indicators of the potential for flames. A noisy spindle is a sign of trouble. The sound of harmonious working is, in contrast, almost silent but to the experienced ear it is still audible. Even when the technique is grasped and the three work as one, fire may yet remain elusive. The colleague who introduced me to the craft has said that, at times, and after many years of kindling flames in this way, there are still days when he struggles to get the process right. Fire is fickle, and it cannot be forced.

If all goes well, an ember will arise: a pile of black powder turned out of the union of spindle and hearth board. If this pile of powder produces a persistent trail of rising smoke it is likely to contain a cherry-red heart, fire's embryo. At this point the group must be very wary of panic or haste. All too often it is assumed that speed is now of the essence, when it is quite the contrary.

Anticipation

Where there's smoke there is fire

Too much haste and the ember will be lost, knocked off into the dust or placed in a tinder nest that is too loose and ill-prepared. Time, in fact, can almost be felt to stand still with the arising of the ember. A slowing down is advised. If it is a good ember it can be slowly fed with more black powder. Once it has clearly established its fiery core it can then be taken on the point of a knife and lifted into the tinder nest. It will have integrity – if those handling have this too.

A tinder nest is a tight bundle of dry plant fibres. It is called a nest because it has every appearance of a bird's creation. Made of dry grass or hay, lined with thistledown or other findings, it should be made so that the ember can be placed in it without getting lost. There is a distinctly maternal or parental mood that arises in the group as the ember goes into the nest. A tenderness arises, along with an oblivion to the muscle ache, the bruised knuckles and sore knees that may have been part and parcel of getting this far.

With a steady breath, the ember can be encouraged to spread. It takes hold of the tinder, grows, gets hotter and hotter until the moment approaches when a flame springs forth from dry matter and – magically – fire dances in front of the kindler's eyes. All previous efforts are replaced by elation, a jubilant celebration amongst the kindling group and a bone-and-soul satisfying feeling of warmth and accomplishment.

Fire-lighting thus takes us deeply into our own burnings, each stage of the outer journey mirrored in kind by the building of an inner ember and fire that it is then our own responsibility to tend and sustain.

An ardent desire

Fire-lighting encapsulates the possibilities and pitfalls of learning in a simple, yet also profound, task. Handled with care, it can quite literally spark a host of experiences and insights that bridge the all too often sundered realms of mind and matter, of the sacred and the profane. It braids together hand, heart and head – theory and practice – and puts all involved in contact with a timeless act that lies at the very roots of culture and consciousness.

Giving birth to fire

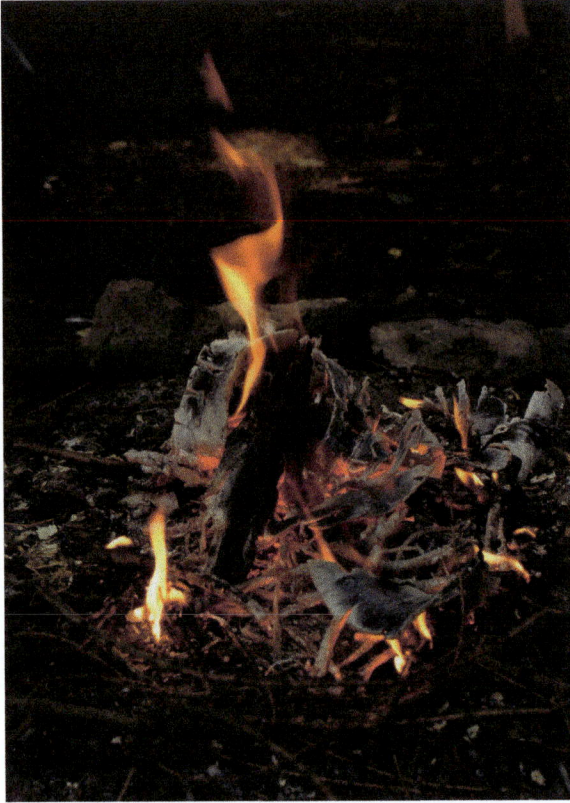

Fire is raised

Fire-lighting has become for me 'an instance worth a thousand bearing all within itself' (to borrow a phrase from the poet J.W. Goethe[119]). As an educator, I am something of a generalist, facilitating learning in a wide range of subjects, but I find myself returning again and again to the fire-lighting task. I have, to date, facilitated kindling sessions for a growing list of learners, including children and adolescents in schools, agricultural apprentices, teachers-in-training, managers in organizations, and academics in their campuses of higher education.

Fire-lighting, mind you, is not what I teach – I am not a fire professor, nor do I run kindling classes for children as part of their prescribed curriculum. I have, however, found it to be an ideal process to work with in a wide range of educational encounters for the many fruits it offers.

Very often the people who I meet in educational settings have never started a fire with a bow and tinder. It was not taught to us at school, we had no initiation rites involving fire, and nor is it one of the many practical tasks or chores required to manage a modern household. Everyone is thus a fire-starting novice; we set out on the same footing.

For those of us who are called to the teaching profession, fire-lighting holds in it a wealth of possibilities for the threads it draws to other matters. Fire is woven throughout history – both natural and cultural. It features in philosophy, flares forth in all the world religions and can be found in literature both factual and fictional. The practical task of lighting fires readily sparks contemplations in chemistry, studies in physics, and forays into botany. And when it comes to the practical arts, kindling a flame leads directly to the forge and the furnace, the kiln and the kitchen.

Needfires

There is crucial consideration and contemplation to include at the end of this chapter on fire before you, dear reader, have a go yourself at kindling a flame.

Ernst Lehrs describes, in his supremely insightful book *Man or Matter,* the ancient practice of lighting a 'needfire':

> '...if sickness broke out among the cattle, a widespread practice was to extinguish all the hearth-fires in the district and then to kindle with certain rites a new fire, from which all the local people lit their fires once more. Heavy penalties were prescribed for anyone who failed to extinguish his own fire – a failure usually indicated by the non-manifestation of the expected healing influence'[120]

Illustration on vase of Greek myth Prometheus having his liver pecked out

Lehrs draws our attention to the fact that, up until the scientific revolution, fire was understood to be the 'most youthful element' of the four elements. It bridged the material world (the world of the *ponderables*) with that of the spiritual world (or realm of the *imponderables*). Lighting a fire was therefore a sacred act, and tending it was a sacramental duty. Fire is referred to here (in part) in its 'outer' sense, but it is also meant more intimately, in terms of an inner fire:

> 'The spiritual significance of these fires cannot be expressed better than by the meaning of the very term needfire. This word does not derive, as was formerly believed, from the word 'need', meaning 'a fire kindled in a state of need', but, as recent etymological research has shown, from a root which appears in a German word nieten – to clinch or rivet. 'Needfire' therefore means nothing less than a fire which was kindled for 'clinching' anew the bond between earthly life and the primal spiritual order at times when for one reason or another there was a call for this.'

Now, the question arises, is not our role as teachers akin to the role of these ancient kindlers and tenders of flames? Isn't this coming closer to the meaning of Plutarch's metaphor? Are we not tasked with assisting those we teach to find their way to the sparking of their own fires, and supporting them in developing the insight and skills for tending them? At a time when one-sided materialistic and mechanistic modes of thinking dominate both our educational landscape and our view of the human being, do we not need once again to engage with the act and imagination of 'clinching' a needfire?

I think we do.

This, ultimately, is why I think it is crucial, in our increasingly digital age, to return to the woods and to take up the earliest technology of all – the fire bow – in order to learn once again the art and craft of kindling flames. I have come to throw in my lot with the 'kindlers' rather than the 'fillers' when it comes to education. I think that we risk a very ashen result indeed if we treat education as a 'system' or tick-box program that aims or claims to control the outcome of its prescribed approach. All too often, such endeavours actually stifle the very sparks of creativity and innovation that lie at the heart of cultural creation.

I think education, deep learning, like fire-starting, cannot be contrived or controlled. It can be prepared and practised, but the ultimate knack for educators is to develop a kind of focused patience, a gentle will, which ultimately allows a spark to be kindled, a fire to light up, in those who they teach, inspiring in them an 'ardent desire' to cultivate and nurture their own unique inner flame. This act of kindling is not, and will never be, a given but our acute sense for its potential is, I think, *why* we teach.

Summary

Bernard Graves

Having considered the historical basis for art and craft in the preceding chapters and the benefits of participating in the craft gestures, we can see that, by embedding handcrafts in an educational setting, benefits may be realised that go far beyond the actual production of artefacts and the related acquisition of skills and techniques required to make them. By including handcrafting in a curriculum, we will directly engage children with the school's environment and with the potential for growing and harvesting materials that can be used practically in various craft workshops. The three kingdoms of nature, **animal**, **plant** and **mineral**, not only provide us with a rich source of crafting materials but also provide us with the means of re-establishing our increasingly tenuous connections with nature.

Basic raw materials ready for crafting

Nature & Resources Context for Crafting – Transformation of Materials and the Maker

Bernard Graves

I believe that since the 1970s, digital technologies have been partly responsible for driving an ever-deeper wedge between human beings and nature. We know that we are in a global ecological crisis and that we face urgent challenges to repair the damage inflicted upon the earth by our highly industrialised societies. By fostering active engagement with nature, by crafting her materials into items both beautiful and functional, we will engender an informed and healthy relationship with the environment. This will in turn surely help to prepare and rekindle inspiration in today's children and youth, better preparing them to be the custodians of this planet tomorrow.

The following words by the Old Lakota[121] has offered me much inspiration over the years and I believe they are indeed as much a forewarning as they are a challenge to us all to live a more sustainable life:

Fire as 'Transformational'

The old Lakota was wise:

He knew that the heart of a human being
Became hard when he is not connected to the natural world.
He knew that this lack of connection
And respect for living things results in
The lack of respect for ourselves and our fellow beings.
Therefore he made sure that his children
Were bought up living with the gentle influences of –
And in harmony with – nature.

Luther Standing Bear an Oglala Lakota Chief

SECTION FOUR

LANDSCAPES FOR LEARNING

Bernard Graves

W*hen working with schools and assisting them to develop their Practical Skills curriculum it soon becomes apparent that, to avoid activities being regarded as extra-curricular and essentially just one-off activities, we need to come up with a new paradigm, context and understanding for a sustainable, practical craft programme. What has emerged over the years is the necessity for schools to develop a sense for an integrated Outdoor Practical Skills programme, where the outdoor activities relate to aspects of the indoor lessons. For instance, geology studies can be made while digging and processing for clay. By maintaining an active connection between indoor and outdoor lessons, we can experience craft activities as being embedded in nature, where we source our materials, while they also inform other educational studies and activities.*

The next section of the book draws on the experience of a number of educators who have developed their work in the outdoor classroom. These considerations break open the walls and boundaries of traditional classroom-based learning and highlight the importance of learning in the landscape.

Children schooling in the woods

CHAPTER 13

Outdoor Learning Inspires

Part 1:
'Ways of Knowing' through Landscape, Materials and Science

Bernard Graves

Working in the school garden

Environmental psychology – biophilia

In recent years a large number of studies worldwide have been carried out that investigate the significance of contact with nature, for children's health and for building strong and sustainable relationships with the environment.

Those working in environmental education and environmental psychology often highlight the importance of contact with nature, for children and young people, for their healthy physical and emotional development. In his book *Biophilia*, Edward O Wilson[122] suggests 'that humans possess an innate tendency to seek connections with nature and other forms of life'. He defines biophilia as 'the urge to affiliate with other forms of life'. Environmental psychologists also suggest that being outside and connecting with nature is important for forming a child's identity and sense of belonging. The landscape we inhabit and our relationships to it create a cultural affinity and a reference point in the forming of identity in a child.

David Orr[123] and other like-minded authors question what is happening to so many of us now that we live our lives with a decreasing connection to nature. Their observations have led them to suggest that there is a growing fear of being outside in nature. The natural world is perceived as dangerous, dirty and full of potential infections or allergens. Due to these so-called health risks, we are now seeing instances of farm visits being closed to school parties, or heavily guarded, subject to stringent health-risk assessments and a 'look-but-don't-touch' policy in place – no more direct contact with animals!

For an increasing number of young people, nature itself is not experienced as an interesting space in itself but is rather a context for physical activities and stunts like paintballing and bike trekking. There are, however, examples of forward-looking school practices that underline the importance of pre-schools and schools working consciously from early on to create a positive attitude to being outside in nature. A number of examples of this type of school can be found in Scandinavia. Educators from such schools are well aware that the experiences and relationships established in our early years shape the way we relate to nature in our adult years.

Nature as the outdoor classroom – benefits

Children spend a significant amount of their childhood at school, and its impact and memory can be profound in informing our relationship and responsibilities towards our environment in later years. Though most school grounds have a fairly industrial feel about them, successful attempts have been made in many urban schools to redevelop the school grounds to include more green spaces. To curb disruptive behaviour in certain city schools, tarmac has been replaced with garden areas and green playing spaces, with which the children become actively involved. It has been noticed that the so-called 'greening of the school's environment' has had a very positive impact on school attendance and the overall behaviour of children.

When undertaking a school grounds redevelopment, it is perhaps expedient to look at the envisaged development from the point of view and perspective of the children using it: '*How do I feel within it? Does it stimulate me and invite me to do something?*'

Landscape and grounds site survey – audit and vision

Before entering into any development of grounds, new landscaping or constructions, it is strongly advisable for any organisation to have completed what we refer to as a *Grounds Site Survey*. A site survey is an audit of the grounds, to compile an inventory of all the resources and facilities within the site and work towards developing a *vision map* with future projects identified.
The site survey process should involve all stakeholders and can take up to a year to complete.

The word *landscape* is usually used to mean '*the overall impression of the land*'. It encompasses individual details and how all the component parts affect each other. Along with the valuable information gathered through a *School Site Survey*, an important objective of the process is to

Example of a School Site Survey Vision map – The Linden's Kindergarten, Stroud, Gloucestershire), UK
(Dilly Williams)

arrive at a sense of place. A sense of place is invited by asking the question 'Who are we as a school community and what does this landscape have to offer those who are in it?'

The techniques of surveying and mapping a site are useful skills, and students are called upon to practise and develop their observational skills, their use of measurement, geometry and triangulation, drawing and drafting, identification of geology, fauna and flora, and soil sampling. Historical and current uses of grounds and buildings are also considered to reveal the past and give an overall account of the site's landscape. An understanding of *past* and *present* forms the basis for our *future* visioning for activities and developments on the site.

Conducting a *School Site Survey* ensures that structures and/or activities are rightfully placed and ultimately sustainable. The *Site Survey* is best conducted with all stakeholders involved, including children of various age groups. Investigation of the site can be divided up into different categories; layout and topography, geology and the ground structure, fauna and flora, resources available such as natural stone, trees and wood. Once a full inventory is compiled then an annotated *Vision Map* of the site is drawn up and used for reference.

As well as the school's sitemap being a reference for ongoing developments, conducting a *Grounds Site Survey* is a beneficial and appropriate way of helping students form a meaningful relationship with their site. They soon come to realise that the outdoors is also a place for learning – an outdoor classroom. Engaging in this type of active relationship with the environment also helps to sharpen our investigative skills and practical knowledge of a site's groundscape, all of which engenders positive attitudes of appreciation, respect and care for the site. During the investigative stages of the *Grounds Site Survey*, a broad ecological, geological and historical perspective of everything that is in the site can give rise to an understanding of how that piece of the landscape has its existence.

Wendy Titman, the former Director of *Learning Through Landscapes* L.T.L.[124], brings to our attention examples of schools that have noticed a marked improvement in the emotional well-being of the children and a noticeable improvement in the academic achievements of children in schools that have actively transformed the traditional tarmac surfaces of schools into imaginative recreational and educational landscapes[125].

Once a *Grounds Site Survey* has been completed and the development plan drawn up, there is still the opportunity for classes or groups in later years to revisit the survey and carry out their own investigations as to how things have developed or moved on.

By doing this at the outset of any new project, students can realise that everything within their school grounds is there for a reason. All structures and natural deposits of materials, animals, trees and plants have come into existence interdependently in any given spot. Some, such as natural occurrences of clay, stone and gravel, specific trees and plants, may have natural origins laid down ages ago, while the human-made structures, like the buildings, have a more recent history. All these elements together manifest a context of interdependence, development and origins; they may work together or we may feel they require change and improvement.

Where this approach to grounds development in a school is carried out, students rightfully feel that they are included and have the opportunity to contribute to the ongoing transformation and development of their school grounds.

Clay bread oven build – An integrating craft and science project

After developing various craft activities and projects in the manner described throughout this book, it became apparent to me that the same set of learning principles outlined in Section Three could be applied to a number of other curriculum subjects. Science is one of the areas that is worth looking at in the light of crafts and hands-on learning.

The site survey, as is evident from the above, can be an activity to engage with a broad range of integrated science topics. These include geology, botany and topography, and can include some observations of local weather (prevailing wind, precipitation). Science is, in fact, not as removed from handcraft as we might be led to think it is.

Historically, science shared many aspects of its origins with the development of traditional handcrafts, as it did with agriculture practices. Over the course of time, once the concepts that describe the characteristics, qualities and processes in nature are analysed and systematised, there is a shift from 'something you do', which in essence describes 'crafting', to 'something you know', which describes a basis for thinking. In the course of time, knowledge is transformed from craft and practical experience into scientific knowledge from which the industrialisation of crafting arose.

Many of the materials used in craft activities (such as willow, hazels, clay, stone and wood) are eminently suited to projects that invite a practical scientific awareness, like the construction and firing of various types of clay kilns, for calcining lime, for smelting iron and for the building of clay bread ovens. We have often used these projects as the starting point for various science-related lessons – calcining lime in the lime kiln in chemistry, smelting iron ore as a lead-in to metallurgy, or the construction of a clay bread oven as a basis for nutrition studies.

These clay ovens and kiln constructions are often a good context for introducing various craft techniques, such as when weaving a willow chimney structure for a kiln. 'Wattle and daub' structures woven from willows & hazel (such as garden tool sheds and outdoor classroom shelters) are further examples of how *crafting* can inform building techniques. This type of project provides an opportunity for experiencing early construction technologies. These constructions can be further pursued and discussed as part of a historical overview of architecture and design. They can also introduce topics in chemistry and physics through a 'hands-on' approach. Experiences and insights learned in this way form a sound basis for later classroom and laboratory-based experimentation and a more abstracted approach to learning.

A project such as 'From clay to pots', described by Sue Harker in Chapter 10, has at its heart the handcraft of pottery. This project, centred on clay as the primary material sourced from nature, can be further developed to involve students in constructing the kiln and firing it with wood. As Sue describes, many sciences are touched upon in these activities, including geology, local geography, chemistry, and physics. In other crafts, different sciences come to the fore, but they are present nonetheless. Land-based projects rooted in crafting, where science and art go hand-in-hand, can be said to be examples of 'integrated learning'.

Practical project opportunities

The school's clay oven and shelter
The construction of a clay bread oven is a perfect example of a project that leads from crafting techniques into considerations of integrated learning in science. Building, and then using, a clay bread oven will involve a broad range of activities, including:

- undertaking a school site survey
- sourcing materials out of the immediate landscape
- processing materials, preparing the site
- building the oven
- first firing
- cooking

A bread-oven build is essentially a social activity that is rooted in the outdoor classroom. After undertaking a site survey and identifying the best location for a bread oven, the next step is to source materials out of the landscape.

Sourcing raw materials out of the landscape

When looking for resources in nature, raw materials for a specific project, we need to develop a particular kind of 'knowing' to be able to read the surroundings and find the raw materials required; we need to know where to look.

There may be, for instance, clay at a lower part of the property where it is usually either very wet or sometimes dry and cracked. By understanding the processes that have fashioned the landscape, we can find the right kind of materials: wood, plant, sand, soil or quality of clay, materials that we need for our specific purpose.

This type of fieldwork, incorporating geological knowledge with practice and experience, can engender a kind of *intuitive* faculty that *leads* me to the materials I need; perhaps this faculty for intuitively knowing the whereabouts of different foodstuffs and things is something that the hunter-gatherer possessed.

Landscape knowledge and intuition – biophilia

Often, various tests need to be made to determine whether a material is suitable for a project. This may well involve subjecting locally dug clays to some shrinkage and firing tests, to gauge its suitability for using in ceramic work or in the constructing of a clay oven. Sometimes we are even called upon to use our sensory faculties (seeing, tasting, smelling and feeling) as well as more scientific procedures to determine the quality and suitability of a material. In my experience it has usually been best to encourage pupils first to develop personal judgments and evaluations and then to follow up these subjective evaluations with more scientific means.

This type of investigation and personal interaction with nature can be as much a source of *self-knowledge* as it is a way towards a *knowledge* of the natural world. Working with, appreciating and understanding materials in the surrounding landscape can also evoke a quality of *empathy* for nature. To be informed about, and understand, how the natural processes have fashioned and imbued materials with specific qualities, I need to explore, appreciate and be able to imagine the potential of a material. My sensory observations and interactions will help me to obtain as full a picture as possible of the material in question. The experiences received through this empathetic way of investigating the environment and working the material also teach me something about myself. When I dig, drag, trample, saw, chop, lift, etc., I actively engage with my will. In this manner, work and empathy teach me through my body about the inner qualities and characteristics of the material I am working with. Importantly, I connect that which is nature *within me* with nature *outside of me*.

By involving myself with nature in the ways described above, I realise my participation is relevant; I am part and parcel of the meaning and context of this particular environment.

The knowledge I receive by exploring natural materials and phenomena like this arises as a result of my forming a direct relationship with the materials, recognising their context and meaning in the natural world. This is not knowledge based on assertions or models of nature. It is a skill, based on my experiences of the natural world I am investigating. When I submerge myself in nature's materials and processes and come to understand how they came into existence, and when I experience the qualities and potential of a particular material, only then can my own creativity enter in. In this manner, human creativity can be seen as a prolongation of the creative power of nature. Seen in this light, the value of conducting a *Grounds Site Survey* as a basis for the sourcing of materials is far-reaching and has the potential to inform our ethical and sustainable choices in connection with nature and the particular project in mind.

It is my experience that any educational, practical project, which gives us the skills to connect with nature, also gives us the prerequisites for ethical behaviour, instead of just conveying conceptual knowledge based on assertions about nature. Practical education instils an ethical and sustainable approach, based on our discovery and awareness of resources found or cultivated in the school's environment. The outdoor classroom lends itself well to this type of teaching methodology for sciences, where the focus is on how concepts are arrived at out of practical experience rather than theory.

A clay oven building project

As a specific example of a practical project which will incorporate multi-disciplinary activities that stretch beyond 'handcrafts', I will now describe in more detail the opportunities that can be found in the building of a clay oven and its shelter.

For the success of this project a number of things have to be carefully considered. Foremost is the need for finding a suitable location for situating the oven, where food preparation can take place and where there is sufficient space around the oven for socialising and eating. Other considerations include questions such as: How large an oven is needed? Does the shelter also have a wood store facility incorporated into it? Are food-preparation and washing-up facilities built in? Can the oven incorporate a back-boiler to supply the outdoor kitchen with hot water? What form of construction and materials will be used and what materials can we source locally?

These are some of the fundamental questions we need to discuss with students and other interested parties before embarking on the project. They highlight the importance of *considered design, preparation* and *forward planning* – all essential capacities for students (working at any scale) to learn!

Having consulted the site survey and taken steps towards sourcing the necessary materials for the clay oven build, we now need to consider the following stages:

- preparing the site, processing materials.
- constructing the oven shelter.

Twin clay ovens and outdoor kitchen – Devon Steiner School

Clay oven in construction showing brick arch

- building the plinth and constructing the oven
- first firing.
- cooking and sharing a meal.

Processing materials and preparing the site

Work starts with each person and group finding their bearings in the site grounds, collecting various materials that might be used for the project. The collected materials – clays, sand and gravel, stone and wood building materials, tools and equipment – are brought to the intended location for the oven build, to be further processed.

The clay has to be processed by a method of trampling underfoot called 'puddling'. Water and sand are added to make up the right mix – not too dry, not too wet. This prepared clay will become the thermal-mass, inner layer of the oven. Later, chopped straw will be added to a portion of the puddled mix which acts as a binder when constructing the oven and then as an insulation material in the outer layer of the completed oven. This activity is usually much enjoyed by children and adults alike, with groups usually breaking into song, helping to sustain the heavy work.

While the clay is being puddled, the plinth for the oven can be constructed using either natural stone or manufactured bricks. This requires both judgment and accuracy if the plinth is to hold the enormous weight of the clay that will be placed on top of it. A shelter of some description is essential to ward off the elements that would otherwise gradually take the clay oven back into nature. Every group will come up with very different designs depending on what materials are available; some will be very organic-looking structures while others are more conventional in their design.

Children puddling clay (Frome Steiner Academy)

Building the oven

Some activities, such as weaving the 'sacrificial' willow-basket dome, require patience and skill to construct the right size and suitable shape. Onto to this willow dome, which is placed on the plinth, the mixed clay is daubed carefully, to ensure even thickness throughout. Following a thermal layer about six inches thick, the outer layer of clay and straw mix is placed and, finally, an outer layer is fashioned with whatever decorative design the group comes up with.

When the oven is completed, a slow-burning fire is placed within the oven and, after many hours of drying out the whole mass of clay, the fire is allowed to burn up to firing temperature; this is partly achieved by using dry wood and careful control of the air draft. The firing process gives students an excellent opportunity to learn about thermal dynamics, combustion and conversion of clays to ceramic.

Over a week-long bread-oven build, the focus and tempo changes as the work progresses. What was initially a range of individual tasks, scattered around the school grounds, gradually takes on a collective focus, with everyone concentrating on processing the clay and building up the oven; here many feet and many hands do indeed make the work easier.

The bread oven is foremost a functional structure, its shape and form are based on tried and tested squat-domed, shaped structures that best achieve the right flow of heat inside the oven, while at the same time conserving energy using the thick insulated straw-and-clay outer walls.

Although design for the structure, and indeed for the shelter, have to comply with certain practical

Firing the oven for the first time

Cooking pizzas the first time

considerations, there is still plenty of scope for artistic embellishment and design. Indeed the outer layer of the oven is where a group can exercise their artistic inclinations with their own design which, if done well, results in an aesthetically pleasing, sculptural piece of work. This function-led aesthetic has its own appeal, mainly because it is practical and right for the purpose.

Of course, the project would not be complete without the first cooking in the oven. Usually the favourite is Pizza – a whole new meaning to 'fast foods', as a pizza will cook in about two minutes in a well-heated clay oven at about 450°C. Everyone involved will agree that foods cooked in a clay oven taste superior to other food, and that all the effort that has gone into making the modest earth oven has been well worth it. There have been schools that use their oven on a regular basis either to provide meals for school social events or for baking products to sell as a class fundraiser – and this has certainly been a motivating factor in ensuring the social and economic use of the school clay oven.

Turning back now to consider for a moment the integrated science learning embedded in this project we can see that many different areas of learning have been included – geology in understanding the clay building materials, physics and chemistry in understanding the principles of 'updraught' working within the oven and transformation of clay to ceramic, design and building skills in the construction of the plinth, and shelter construction and food science in cooking in the oven.

Outdoor classroom management

Before looking further into the theme of science and hands-on learning, it is important to consider the following:

For the success of a project in the outdoor classroom such as a bread-oven build, a number of things have to be carefully considered. When the classroom moves outside, teaching must be planned according to the conditions provided by the environment. Out in the school grounds or field and woodlands, the normal teaching spaces and class timetable no longer provide a clear framework by which teachers and students can orientate themselves. The usual breaks and lesson times are no longer relevant; instead, the scheme of work dictates how we manage the day and the week's timetable.

An educational project, such as a *5-day clay oven build*, contains many stages and processes, making it impossible in advance to give a clear idea of every aspect of the project. Furthermore, it is not possible to provide a detailed, step-by-step outline of the stages of the project, nor would it necessarily benefit the students' understanding of what to expect. Instead, the project starts with an overview and then delegating specific tasks to groups, like the gathering of willows and hazels and digging for clay, that do not of themselves provide a complete picture of the entire project. The project starts with 'fetch, cart and carry' materials from around the school grounds.

A degree of chaos can be expected but this is a necessary part of the process whereby the individual in a group navigates through the various stages of the project. It does eventually become clear as to why a group is doing a particular task or other. One way to aid all students to get the bigger picture of the process is by sitting together at the end of each day and getting the groups to relate to each other what they have done, what they have achieved and discovered. Through these group sharings, assisted by the project leader, terminology and concepts are instilled, entering a more detailed and deeper level of understanding when linked up with practical experiences.

In this manner, collaboration between individuals occurs as a matter of course when the situation or task requires it. In this *experiential educational* approach, order and the overview of the project are fashioned by each person all the while the work progresses, rather than given upfront by the project leader. After all, we want each student to acquire a sense of ownership and experience that their contribution matters.

Experiential science and technology learning

Science has its origins in human curiosity and the need to know more about human beings, their surroundings and achievements. In studying nature and humankind, students are given the tools to affect their own well-being, as well as contribute to sustainable development.

An anecdotal memory of science lessons at school, I believe shared by many, was that if it smelled it was biology, if it exploded it was chemistry and if it didn't work it was physics. Yet what the sciences have to offer can be fun and provide gateways into essential areas of knowledge and human achievements. Incorporating the sciences as described above in the site survey and bread oven build enables pupils to have a tangible grasp of what otherwise could be complex abstractions, not always necessarily experienced as relevant to our daily lives.

Harnessing the elements: Earth, Water, Air and Fire

As a final example of the depth of experience and practical knowledge that can be had at the hand of projects like the clay oven building, the construction and firing of a lime kiln or an iron smelt, we inevitably meet with the elements – Earth, Water, Air and Fire – in a particularly accessible manner.

Without needing to talk much about the elements beforehand, it becomes apparent that this practical work engages us qualitatively in four different ways; we have to recognise and harness the power of the elements throughout the various processes. They can be seen as our 'assistants' throughout the various stages of work.

Transformation assisted by the four Elements – Earth, Water, Air and Fire

In the case of the clay oven, the *mineral* or *earth* elements – clay sand & gravel and rocks – are the start-point of the project. In order to process the clay dirt, *water* is needed to dissolve it and to flush out matter that is not wanted.

Following the construction of the oven, the element of *air* is required to dry the oven with the wind and oxygen also having a relationship with fire.

The clay oven, with its opening and incorporated flue, is constructed so that the fire can be controlled through regulating the airflow; and finally, the element *fire* is used to harden and transform the clay into a clay bread oven that, if looked after, will be serviceable for many years.

By trial and error, one has the opportunity to harness and control the usefulness of these elements and further experience that *earth, water, air and fire* form the interface between *oneself* and *the natural world*, on several different levels. Interacting with the elements provides qualitative gateways into different areas of experience, both out in nature and of oneself as a human being.

Part 2:
Nature, Science and the Human Being

Martin Levien

My teaching profession and career – as a science and craft teacher

I came to teaching after working in social services and in a psychiatric hospital, and (prior to that) after earning my living for some years from craft work and building. I began my teaching career in 1978 as a state secondary school science teacher. Later I retrained as a Waldorf secondary school teacher specialising in the sciences and teaching and assisting with various crafts.

I trained as a teacher when it was a profession with all the skills and responsibilities associated with being 'professional'. The present generation of teachers are under pressure to tick boxes, are constantly being assessed and have lost a great deal of their responsibility over (and freedom in) what or how they teach. Teachers have been progressively deskilled and schools' funding (their life blood) has been tied into a strange, competitive GCSE league-table culture which has little to do with real education and much to do with particular political agendas. I have a huge respect for the teachers who struggle daily within their schools to deliver the often excellent lessons in such trying situations. It is time to take back the responsibility and relearn the skills needed to be a *teacher* in the fullest sense, to rescue our education from the strait jacket it is in, which might have suited society 100 years ago but sadly makes it not fit for purpose in the 21st century. We could even go so far as to say that our current approaches to education are harming our students.

I recently had a major operation for a brain tumour and have been forced to take some time out from teaching. This has given me the perspective I have needed to have a fresh look at education in England; hence some of my comments in the above paragraph. As part of my convalescence, I do a lot of cycling and walking and have been very impressed with how both these rhythmical physical activities really do aid my thinking. I noticed years ago how working on the pole-lathe (see Richard Turley's chapter on Green Woodwork) that part of my mind was focused on the task while another part worked independently, and came up with connections and creative solutions to problems that I had been pondering on for a long time. What is this connection between regular repetitive physical activity and inspiration which has so often been noted by so many people?

Before I describe my reflections on teaching, wherein we weave together science and the crafts, I must say a word on health and safety. I find doing a full risk assessment before any activity essential to identify potential risks and to find ways to ameliorate them. In most cases I have found that, done properly, a risk assessment actually allows you to proceed in a safe way with activities that you might have not felt confident about and so would have not undertaken. I have worked with health and safety issues in many schools in England, Scotland and Spain and found that the culture of fear around being sued financially is confined to some institutions in England and can often be removed by a full, realistic and open risk assessment. This fear of health and safety issues has some very damaging consequences for our students who are deprived of the opportunity to learn responsibility and to grow through integrated learning experiences (hand, heart and head).

Hands on approaches to science teaching

I had the good fortune to teach for many years in a school (the South Devon Waldorf School) where colleagues and management shared a common vision of the *purpose* of education. We all worked together to develop a hands-on, outdoor-classroom-based and cross-curricular programme for the students. Combining science and practical crafts lay at the heart of our approach. I was, furthermore, able to focus on a given subject for three weeks at a time and could have each two-hour lesson segue into the next. Occasionally we managed to combine all the class's subjects into a day-long, three-week block of cross-curricular teaching. The lessons were team taught with other subject teachers joining in.

Using the hands-on and outdoor classroom approach brought many advantages. The first gain for the students was a huge increase in their interest in the sciences. The second was that the physical outdoor craft activities enabled longer bouts of concentration, which in turn engendered greater penetration of abstract theoretical details. This was apparent across all ability levels.

As a teacher, I am concerned not only with increasing my student's knowledge base but am also keen on them developing habits and attitudes that will be helpful throughout their lives. In this, the hands-on approach was particularly successful.

If one compares this method of teaching with the all too common 'teaching to the test' approach it can at first glance appear to consume much more of the students' time to cover the same volume of subject matter. A deeper look, however, shows the opposite is true. Students are so much more engaged and capable of *deep learning,* and the teacher is not simply hitting two birds with one stone but is covering multiple subjects in the same lesson.

There are so many craft activities that can be engaged with, to link up and illustrate a variety of scientific subjects, that frequently the difficulty is choosing which craft and which area of science to bring to the students' attention. In practice, however, the choice is often limited; by the season, or the facilities, or equipment, or by the availability (or lack of) specific specialist knowledge. It is important, if you are going to get the full benefit of combining the crafts and practical activities with science, for the students to engage with the practical activity/craft before you bring the abstract scientific knowledge into the lessons. The teacher's skill lies in choosing the best example according to the available materials.

The body of knowledge that the science teacher chooses to bring to the students is always only a part of the curriculum, and that curriculum is itself only a small part of the whole body of scientific knowledge. Ultimately this is not important as the successful teacher will have kindled an interest, which will live on in the student, and which will grow and develop throughout their lives.

I cannot think of a single year in which I have had the luxury of the teaching time available to include all the activities – scientific and craft – that I would have liked to. Even if I had been able to include all these activities, the sheer volume would have overwhelmed the students. Each year I have had to sacrifice one area for another. For example, one year a class was baking bread and making soup, and so many of the activities were based around that. Another year, shirts were being made, so fabrics became the entry point. In yet another year paper-making introduced us to cellulose.

Chemistry Year 10

I have chosen Year 10 Carbon Chemistry as my example of this cross-curricular, hands-on and outdoor-classroom approach to teaching. Hopefully your school teaches cooking and crafts and, if this is the case, these lessons can be coordinated with science and each will support the other.

I often start the first lesson by asking the students to take a clipboard, paper and a graphite pencil outside for 10 minutes to do a quick sketch of almost anything they find outdoors. I then introduce the idea that what they have just drawn is exactly what the world would look like if

Leaf chemistry and photosynthesis

every element apart from carbon had been removed; a colourless, but otherwise exact, record of the carbon skeleton which forms most of the basic structure of the world. This drawing is of course done with graphite (pure carbon) and on paper (predominantly carbon). From graphite we can progress to *graphene* and on to *fullerenes* and thence to *valency* and *covalent bonding, molecular structures* and *isomers*. I usually ask the students to work their sketches up into a good picture to illustrate their written work, wherein they introduce carbon.

It is difficult to understand chemistry without an appreciation of scale. A molecule of CO_2 is smaller than the wavelength of visible light, and this has many consequences. To try and illustrate this molecular scale, I hand out a grain of sand to each student and show them a picture of a sandy beach. I then ask them to imagine how many grains of sand there are on the whole beach – from the sand dunes to the low tide mark, and from where they stand, as far as they can see. I then inform them that there will be roughly the same number of molecules in the grain of sand they are holding as there are grains of sand on the beach. This leads on to discussions about orders of magnitude, and that molecular diagrams are our best attempts at imagining how it all fits together at a molecular level. I explain that in this lesson block we will be alternating between this 'fantasy world' of energy/forces/matter that we can only imagine that there is more *nothingness in matter* than anything else in the world of actual objects that we can see and touch, and smell.

Sometime before the organic chemistry lesson, the class made wine from fruit or vegetables, recording the process and their observations over a period of four or more weeks. This was basic Goethean (phenomenological) observation – i.e. making repeated observations while withholding the urge to theorise prematurely or the tendency to leap to quick conclusions.

As many molecules as grains of sand...

Photosynthesis

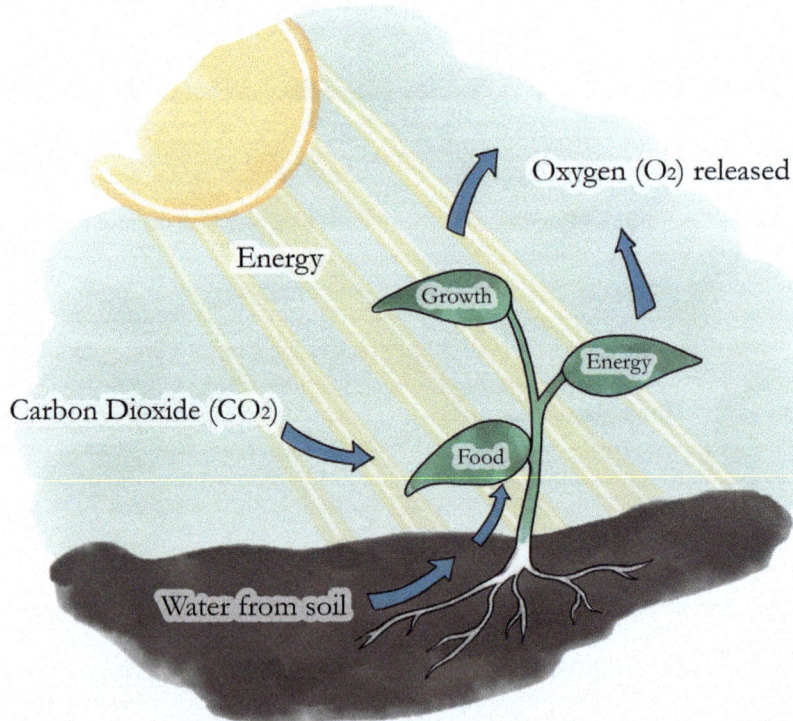

Oxygen (O_2) released

Energy

Growth

Energy

Carbon Dioxide (CO_2)

Food

Water from soil

Carbon chemistry – photosynthesis – sugars, starch & cellulose

Practical applications – cooking chemistry

Jam making

The weekend before the carbon chemistry main lesson, the students made jam at home and were asked to observe and record their observations of the sugar – focusing particularly on the behaviour of the sugar with water and with heat.

The students brought the jam and their observations to school, where we enjoyed eating the jam with bread. Discussion ensued, which was rooted in the students' actual experience and observations (the taste and the texture of the jam, what happened while they ate the bread and jam, what they observed while making the jam, the look and feel of the sugar they used, etc.). This approach led on to discussions about the use of sugar as an energy food, as a preservative, osmotic pressure, diabetes, carbohydrates food tests and so on.

Many more experiments are possible in this approach to teaching about sugars (but you have to make a choice, you can't follow them all up!). Without the practical activities introducing each subject area and continuing throughout the lessons, the intellectual detail (mono and disaccharides, alpha-glucose, beta-glucose, isomers and theoretical molecular structures) would have overwhelmed most if not all of the students.

Jam making and preserves

Bread making – from grain to bread

We then began cooking with different types of flour (pancakes, sauces, bread) and observed how it (a polysaccharide, an addition polymer of alpha-glucose) behaved with heat and water. This led on to discussions and experiments about carbohydrates in general, and details of polymerisation, which in turn was followed by harvesting stinging nettles and making string and rope from them.

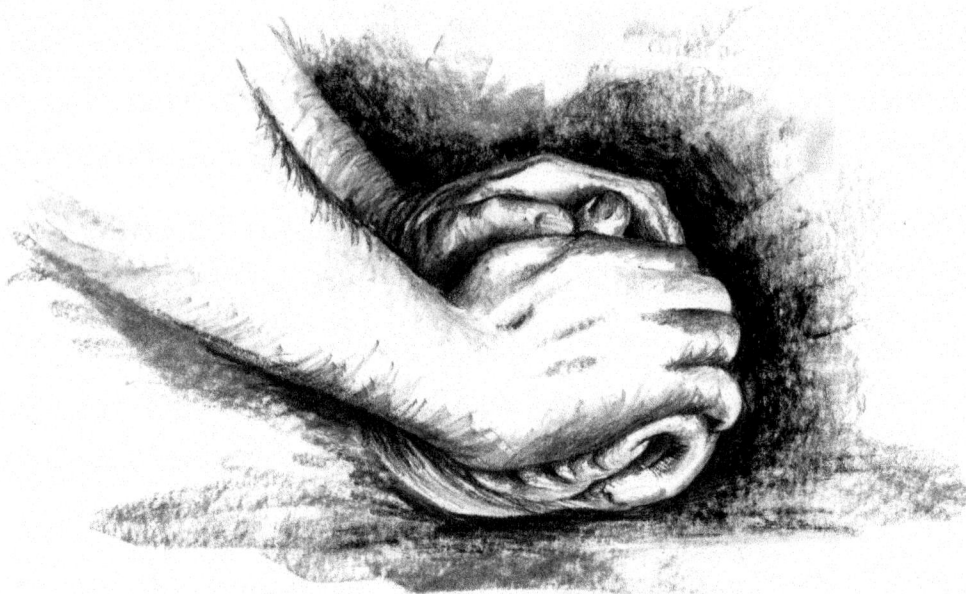

Kneading bread

From grains to bread

Cordage and fabrics

We also made rope from hemp fibres, spun hemp and played with cotton – which led to investigating fabrics of all kinds. In my best lessons this was coordinated with the students using fabrics and making garments for themselves. I even managed to have a Year 10 class, in their chemistry main lesson, use the flax that they themselves had grown in Year 8, and processed in Year 9. I have not yet had a class produce linoleum (linen impregnated with linseed oil) but I think this would be good project – even more so if the students also built a canoe, covered it with their own linoleum and then used it in a field trip.

This work with cellulose leads into a detailed look at the chemistry of cellulose (an addition polymer of Beta-glucose) and a comparison of sugars, flours and cellulose. These must still be rooted in the students' observations and experiences of the chemical differences, making connections between the detailed molecular composition of the isomer and the actual behaviour of the material (the polymer) in the world. This can lead to an extensive project on cellulose-based fabrics and cellulose acetates.

Nettle cordage

Clay insulated charcoal retort kiln – Rudolf Steiner school South Devon

Practical and industrial applications

Combustion, photosynthesis, explosives

At this point we can look into the burning of carbohydrates; making charcoal from willow, making gunpowder, and looking at the details of the energy involved in photosynthesis and combustion and the aerobic carbon cycle. In this way a fairly detailed comparison of photosynthesis and combustion, and the energy involved in each, can be undertaken.

Charcoal-making retort bin

A very good, practical project that effectively demonstrates wood combustion and reduction is for a school to construct either a charcoal making pit or charcoal retort (using a metal bin) and to make charcoal for cooking and as fuel for blacksmithing.

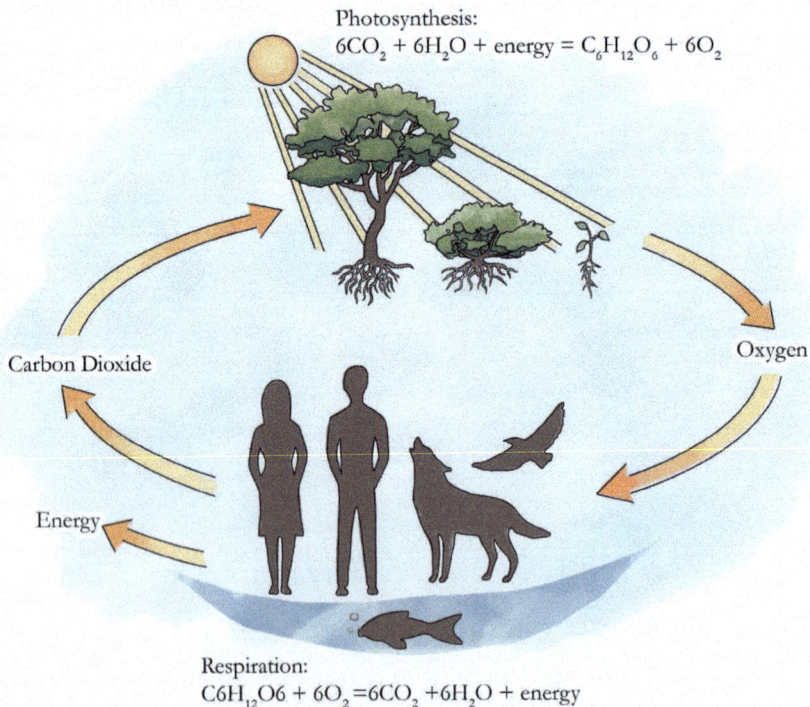

Photosynthesis:
$$6CO_2 + 6H_2O + energy = C_6H_{12}O_6 + 6O_2$$

Carbon Dioxide

Oxygen

Energy

Respiration:
$$C6H_{12}O6 + 6O_2 = 6CO_2 + 6H_2O + energy$$

The carbon and oxygen cycle – Respiration cycle

Aerobic and anaerobic respiration comes to the fore here, and we can turn to the alcohol we made previously through the anaerobic respiration of sugars and can study fermentation in depth. This leads on to the fractional distillation of our wine and on to an exploration of co-boiling points. It is also a good opportunity to address social and personal questions around alcohol, which can also be a way into drug use/abuse and addictions. The fractional distillation of the wine (making brandy) introduces the idea of changes of state and latent heat of vaporisation. We can come back to fractional distillation in the fractionating column.

Boiling and change of state of matter

We can look at the fractional distillation of alcohol and construct a graph of time and heat input, which shows the different boiling points of methyl alcohol and of water (and its co-boiling point) and clearly identifies the periods of the latent heat of vaporisation. This often leads on to an exploration of the four common states of matter (solid, liquid, gas and plasma, plasma being by far the most common and easily seen). I can recall that one year, the class became really excited about these topics and we explored the ideas on some of the other states of matter; Bose-Einstein condensates, Neutron-degenerate matter and Quark-gluon plasma. I realise that it can seem strange to be teaching fractional distillation, latent heat and change of state in a chemistry lesson but it fits here very nicely and makes sense to the students. I find that chemistry, biology and physics actually merge into each other in many of the practical processes and explorations made in this way.

Alcohol distillation & wine making

After fermentation and fractional distillation we turn our wine into vinegar, demonstrating thereby the importance of bacteria to our food industry. We have followed, in this progression,

Wine making & alcohol distillation

Indigo dye bath

the chemistry from glucose to simple alcohols (and the aliphatic series), then from alcohols to acids via acetic acid, then on to esters and lipids via tri-butyric glycerol. According to how much time was available we could do dyeing with onion skins and metal mordants. (The detailed chemistry of metals is usually taught in Year 11.)

Dying with indigo neatly introduces ideas of acids/alkalis and oxidation/reduction processes. Having previously peeled the bark from willow wands, (the willow that was used for charcoal making), we can extract the salicylic acid from it and explore the historical and chemical development of Aspirin from willow and meadowsweet.

From carbohydrates to hydrocarbons: the compost heap leading into fossil fuels and the petro-chemical industries

To give students an insight into what happens as anaerobic bacteria turn carbohydrates into hydrocarbons we can take the students out to a compost heap (one made – ideally – by the students themselves). A compost heap with the right proportion of vegetable matter (carbon), urea, (nitrogen), water and oxygen will heat up, kill all germs and return the nutrients to the soil. After looking at such a compost we can look at some vegetable matter which is rotting down anaerobically, it will be slimy and stinking! It is usually easy to find some 'rotting' organic matter near the compost heap (neat grass cuttings are a good example). This is the first stage of the anaerobic process – bacteria removing the oxygen and turning the carbohydrate into a hydrocarbon, eventually fossilising the plant into coal.

Depending on the time available, and on the interests of the class, we can sometimes spend a whole week on oil, gas and coal formation and the oil industries. This leads on to oil refining, focusing on the fractionating column and different end products, then alkanes, alkenes, and alkynes and so on to products from ethane and polymer plastics from ethane.

We end up, in this process, with making nylon 6-6 (a co-polymer) and, after a comparison of the plant products and the hydrocarbon products, finally a look at the good and bad aspects of plastics and the consequences of how we produce and use them now. I have found it very important – if you do not want to produce young cynics – to show the students how people are working with modern problems (often caused by our unthinking and over-enthusiastic application of scientific and technological advances) and to get them involved in the solutions.

School compost heap

Oil refinery

The Greenhouse Effect

Some of the infared radiation passes through the atmosphere but most is absorbed and re-emitted in all directions by greenhouse gas molecules and clouds. The effect of this is to warm the Earth's surface and the lower atmosphere.

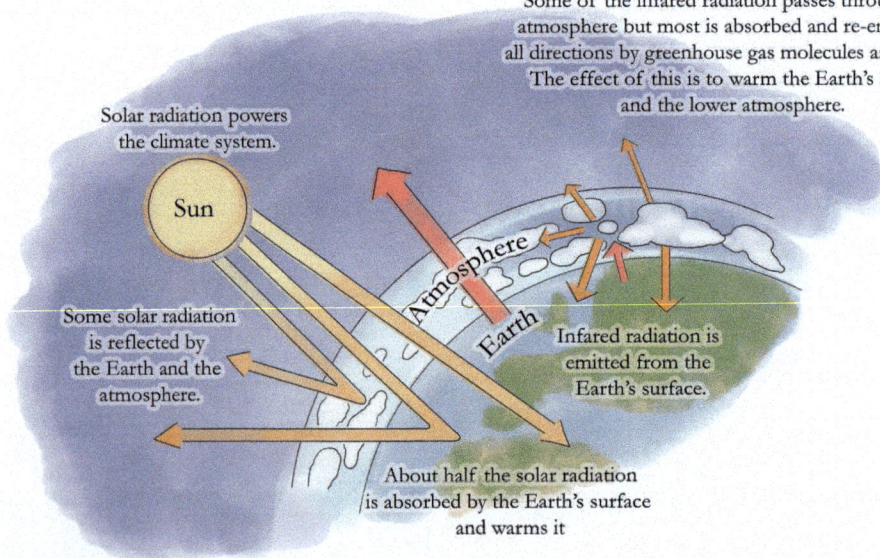

Solar radiation powers the climate system.

Sun

Some solar radiation is reflected by the Earth and the atmosphere.

Atmosphere

Earth

Infared radiation is emitted from the Earth's surface.

About half the solar radiation is absorbed by the Earth's surface and warms it

The Greenhouse Effect

One example of this approach is the following: after looking at fossil fuels, CO_2 and the greenhouse effect, the students cut and laid the hedges around the school on a rotation, producing charcoal from the trimmings. They then used the charcoal for their forge work.

Practical approaches to the study of chemistry

The diagram below summarises many of the key aspects of chemistry that the students engaged with in preceding descriptions. The diagram is presented on the last day of the lesson block. The summary diagram that I draw on the board for the students is vastly more complex than the one in this book, drawing together all the inter-relationships, and highlighting the differences and similarities of organic and inorganic chemistry. If you are a chemist you will be able to see what it is trying to illustrate in a very condensed form. If you are not a chemist it will probably be a complex jumble of symbols with some obvious and many unclear connections.

If you followed the lesson block it would remind you of all of the connections and ideas that we just explored. The students see me completing the drawing on the whiteboard with coloured pens. By witnessing the creation of the drawing in real-time (such as on a whiteboard) the students re-trace the paths of the practical and theoretical immersion in chemistry that they have just undergone. This is a further deepening of their understanding and experience.

One key point that is often obscured in standard chemistry teaching is that the real realm of chemistry is inside living organisms, which 'do chemistry' relatively smoothly and easily using enzymes. We copy these processes in laboratories using great ingenuity and intelligence, and employing a huge amount of energy, force coupled with very strong and dangerous chemicals – all corralled in hugely expensive, complex and dangerous laboratories and factories. Keep a piece of bread in your mouth for a short time and your enzymes will break the starch down to glucose using salivary amylase. Done in a laboratory this takes longer, needs strong acids and heat, special equipment and all the safety precautions that go with it.

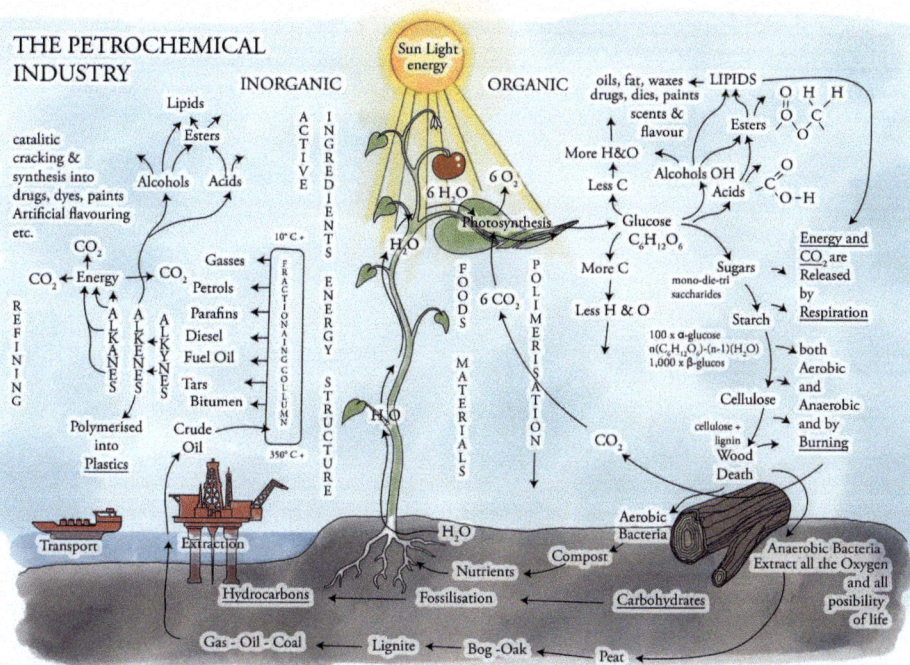

Nature & Science – Organic & Inorganic chemistry

It is important that this visual summary comes at the very end of the lesson block; if brought earlier its very abstract nature can kill the wonder and excitement of the students exploring the ideas and making their own connections and mental discoveries. My hope is that the knowledge that I bring to the students continues to grow and develop in the students themselves as they grow and develop. This knowledge should mature through their relationship with the world as their knowledge of the world grows and changes. If you bring a fixed abstract idea – say Ohms Law – too early in the teaching, it fixes the body of knowledge in the students in a rigid way so that they have difficulty continuing to change and develop their ideas on that subject as they continue to grow and develop themselves.

Any science teacher can see the myriad opportunities for illuminating science from craft activities, and any craft teacher can see the opportunities to incorporate more crafts than I have mentioned into the science teaching. The biggest challenge is making the timetable work and coordinating the different teachers required. But it also brings one of the biggest benefits.

In my experience the students take note of, and absorb, the social behaviour of their teachers. This is something that cannot be taught. When subjects such as ethics or morality – or in fact any of the social sciences – are taught as an abstract lesson they become an intellectual exercise that has little relevance to, or impact on, the students' behaviour. It is therefore very valuable for them to see the teachers working together collaboratively and striving to overcome their own difficulties and shortcomings.

I hope that this very compressed summary of Year 10 Carbon chemistry inspires you to try to incorporate aspects of the hands-on and outdoor class into your teaching. I could have used examples for Year 7 to Year 13 and it could have been physics or biology instead of chemistry. I have used this same approach in all the science main lessons.

CHAPTER 14

The Educational Landscape and Earth Citizenship

Jo Clark

Our education system

In this chapter I would like to explore how we can use our outdoor learning environments to empower the next generation so that they feel that they can be the co-creators of the future of their world.

I feel that it is, to begin with, important to give a brief critique of where we currently are in terms of our contemporary methods of teaching and growing the next generation for life.

We all have differing perspectives on what our education system is designed to achieve and, even as educators, we ask ourselves 'what is education for?' In my view, our western educational system has been constructed to educate individuals to become compliant contributors to the society that they will inherit. Schooling is therefore a protracted process of preparing children for a time when they can contribute to a society that was not created by them but by previous generations. They are, as part of this process, expected to jump through many hoops in order to get to the point when they can fully engage as young adults in this grown-up world. Inherent in this process are evaluations of their successes or failures in achieving these aims. Doris Lessing, in her preface to The Golden Notebook, wrote these words which I believe are as relevant now as when she wrote it in 1962:

'Ideally, what should be said to every child, repeatedly, throughout his or her school life is something like this: "You are in the process of being indoctrinated. We have not yet evolved a system of education that is not a system of indoctrination. We are sorry, but it is the best we can do. What you are being taught here is an amalgam of current prejudice and the choices of this particular culture. The slightest look at history will show how impermanent these must be. You are being taught by people who have been able to accommodate themselves to a regime of thought laid down by their predecessors. It is a self-perpetuating system. Those of you who are more robust and individual than others will be encouraged to leave and find ways of educating yourself — educating your own judgements. Those that stay must remember, always, and all the time, that they are being moulded and patterned to fit into the narrow and particular needs of this particular society[126]*."'*

There are reasons why many succeed: academic ability, social mobility, parental support and various other factors. There are, however, many young people that don't meet the expected standards. I was alarmed when a community governor of a local primary school said recently that they were very pleased that the school was below the national average of Special Educational Needs (SEN) children at 30%... the national average being 33%. It is important to recognise that many children who struggle, have difficult home lives or have certain disabilities, do need considerable extra support. However many of the official 33% of SEN children are deemed to have 'special educational needs' because of the assessment criteria laid down by our education system. Do not all children have special educational needs, are they not all uniquely different, on their own unique learning journey?

The criteria developed for 'success' requires children to attain certain levels of numeracy and literacy by a certain age. Alarm bells start ringing if the children fail to achieve these levels. Whilst educators recognise the importance of play, collaborative learning and outdoor experiences during the early years of education, the emphasis soon turns towards assessable (and usually quantifiable) academic achievement. Let's imagine for a moment a possible new set of essential criteria that need to be met during early childhood in order for the child to grow and develop into a well-rounded, conscious, and self-aware citizen. These new criteria would focus on the child's developing relationship with people and all things, in particular their natural and farmed world.

A relational pedagogy

Our relationship to, and our sense of being part of, the natural world varies tremendously from one individual to another. One thing we all probably agree with, however, is that as a culture we have become very disconnected from our natural and farmed environments. I believe that this

Camping on the Hill

disconnection is at the root of what seems to be western culture's apparent disregard for, and lack of sensible stewardship of, our environment.

Imagine how different our children's growing experience would be if the development and sponsoring of this environmental relationship was the first and foremost priority of any curriculum. If this was the case, it would be expected that children under ten years old would build a den in some woodland, cultivate wheat from seed and prepare it for the plate, sleep out around a fire under the stars or plant a tree and be regularly engaged in its care. The curriculum would not be based on *delivered* and *assessed* outcomes, it would be designed to enable children to have experiences that would help them to explore all of their senses and feelings in the company of their classmates. Perhaps it should be our greatest priority as educators to view the developing child as one that needs to have been offered a range of age-appropriate experiences (in the natural world) in order to develop into a well-rounded citizen of the world. This reorientation of priorities would not diminish the classroom-based academic elements of the curriculum, in fact it would inspire the children to express their experiences in the classroom. I have had very positive feedback from teachers who have brought their children on residential, land-based workshops, describing to me how motivated the children had been in the classroom for weeks afterwards. Here their teachers had the opportunity to consolidate what they had learned experientially, when back in the classroom context.

What I am proposing is a radical move from an academic, content-obsessed pedagogy to a relational pedagogy where the children's relationship with their natural and gardened environment is perceived as the most important of all. Through a growing love affair with their natural world, (yes love affair) the relationships with others (community) and with themselves can flourish. What I am suggesting is that a daily rhythm should involve children engaged in experiential activity outdoors for a substantial amount of time. When young children are offered the opportunity to really develop this relationship – knowing how plants grow, experiencing what

A child harvesting squash

animals need, interacting with mud, with water and rocks – they are meeting the world in a way that makes sense. Our natural world possesses an innate intelligence that the children will not experience in the abstract world of screens and 21st-century complexity.

I am not suggesting for one moment that it is not vital that young people grow to develop an understanding of and ability to interact with this complex and often abstract world. In order to do so, however, I am proposing that they must have developed a strong, loving relationship with – and an understanding of – the world that actually supports the life that we all experience.

I have recently had the privilege of witnessing in my grandchildren, as I did with my own children before them, those tentative explorations that a child makes during the first weeks of its life: reaching out to taste, and touch, and – as their vision becomes clearer – those wide eyes observing this new world for the first time. Good parents will facilitate these processes whilst protecting the child from harm. It is interesting to observe how the colours, textures, odours, and vibrancy of all things natural are of particular fascination to the very small child. Even unprepared and inexperienced parents naturally understand their role in facilitating their children to discover their world. Later as educators our role is to offer a continuing journey of discovery and, when their cognitive capacity has developed, we are supposed to be helping the children understand and make sense of the world in which they find themselves.

What if the world that the developing child finds itself in does not make sense? What if their educators and parents are making demands on them at a very early age that really do not appear logical or intelligent to the child? What if, by the age of six, the child finds herself in the SEN category with the rest of the 33% of children nationally because she does not understand what she is being asked to do, let alone why? The child may not have been ready to learn to read at the age of four, or understand the seven-times table by the age of six. There are groups of children that I have worked with who, if they were assessed using an environmental literacy criterion, could be classed as having very high special educational needs. I worked with a group of 18 children from a local rural school who had no idea where the flour for the pizza dough that we were making came from. I have worked with teenagers and adults, products of our national curriculum, who could not identify any of the vegetables growing in the garden.

These are two of the many examples I could share that demonstrate our young people's very tenuous understanding of where their food comes from and their knowledge of the natural and farmed environments. For these children the world is not really making sense. I have come across many groups of children who have had 100% special educational needs by my criteria.

Natural ecosystems do not waste a thing, do not have landfill sites, do not self-destruct, are not reliant on the survival of any one species but rather support and enhance all life on Earth. As 21st-century industrialised humans we increasingly find ourselves feeling alienated from nature and it is easy to ignore the fact that our survival is dependent on the well-being of all other living things as well as on healthy soil, air and water. Many of us can remember experiences in childhood and sometimes in adulthood when we have felt truly at one with, or part of, the natural world. It may have been lying in a meadow on a summer's day, alone up a tree, dreaming by a sparkling stream or sleeping out under the stars.

During discussions with adults, I have learned that for many people these early formative experiences in nature have helped them to develop the connected, intimate and loving relationship with the natural world that they say they have. Many of these discussions have been with individuals who are engaged in one way or another in work for a more sustainable world and they often attribute this calling, this motivating force, to the peak experiences in nature of early childhood. In a paper titled *Nature and Life Course* by Wells and Lekies 2006, a direct correlation between positive experience in nature during childhood and adults who choose to work as environmentalists is presented[127]. 'The results of the current study suggest that while involvement with "wild" and "domesticated" natural environments both play a role,

Preparing holes for tree planting

participation with "wild" nature before age 11 is a particularly potent pathway toward shaping both environmental attitudes and behaviours in adulthood.'

For myself, and for many people who share a profound appreciation of our natural world, it is and has been a lifelong love affair with the beauty, truth, and goodness of the wild, and the wild that we tame by farming and gardening. I had the privilege to be brought up in a rural environment where I developed my loving relationship to all things natural by being engaged in meaningful farm work as well as having space and time to play, wander and dream. I wish for all children the opportunity to be offered that depth of relationship; I believe this is possible if the priorities of any curricula are re-orientated towards the children having meaningful connections with nature.

Making sense of the world

A heartfelt connection with nature helps us to make sense of the world and I believe that, as with all healthy functional relationships, it helps us to lead happy, fulfilled and joyous lives. Secondly, a strong connection to nature throughout childhood offers a solid foundation for all the learning and the growing that needs to take place. Thirdly, all life on this Earth is in peril due to the disconnection and dysfunctional relationship that western civilisation has with our natural world. We therefore need to heal this dysfunctional relationship by re-establishing a healthy relationship with nature for the next and future generations.

Through my many years of teaching land-based education, I believe a good foundation depends on the correct recipe. If we can offer young children an experience of *the truth* and of the intelligence of nature by offering daily outdoor activities, they will develop healthy thinking. If we offer the opportunity for them to experience the full beauty of their world, their capacity to *feel that beauty* offers an opening into the inner life of emotion. A child that becomes aware of the innate goodness of the natural world that supports all life will be moved to act to care for it. We naturally do not destroy the things or people that we love; on the contrary, we act to defend them if they are in danger.

The Department of Education's directives on Citizenship for Key Stages One and Two make interesting reading. By and large they contain good advice for the growing child. It is a shame that they are non-statutory, leaving the application to the discretion of teachers. There is a mention of caring for the built and natural environment[128] and a culture of care is what we need to engender in our schools but can this be imposed only by making rules about how we treat things, environments or people?

The Educational Landscape

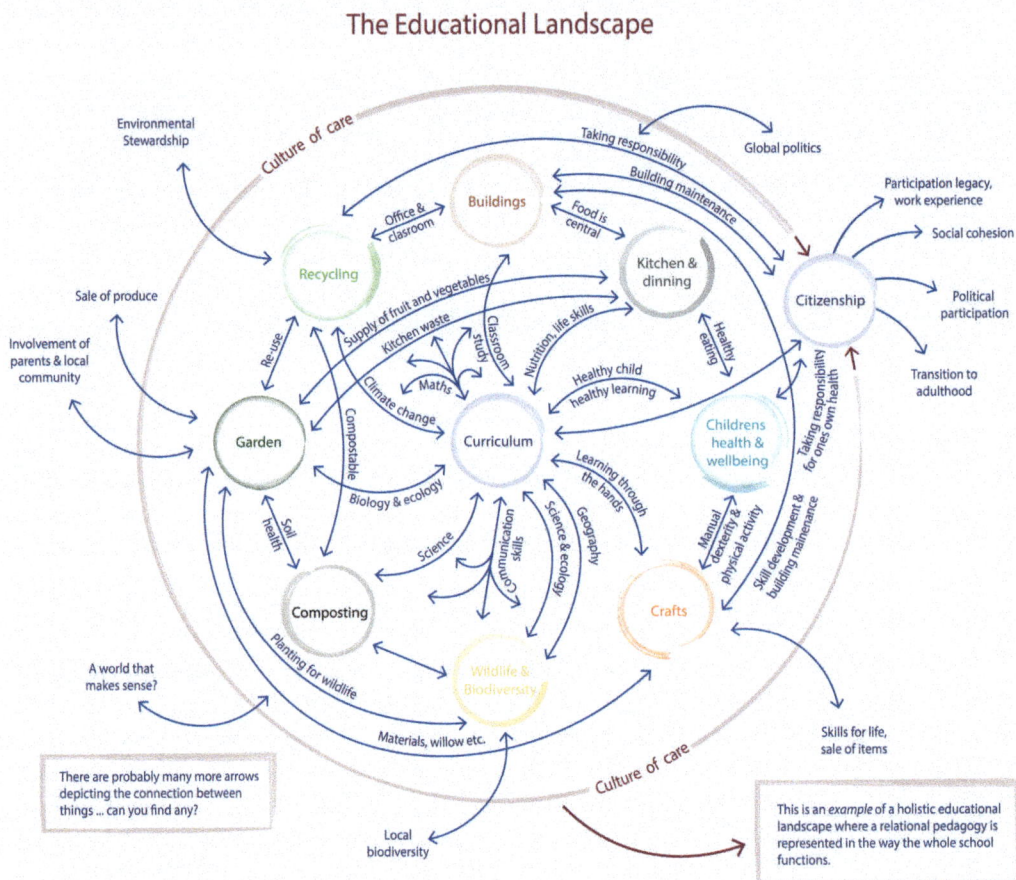

There are probably many more arrows depicting the connection between things ... can you find any?

This is an *example* of a holistic educational landscape where a relational pedagogy is represented in the way the whole school functions.

'Litter picking'

I was working in a large comprehensive school recently, complete with expansive tree-covered grounds, and I noticed two men litter picking. I questioned them about their task and they told me that they worked every day and usually collected six or seven black bin bags of rubbish daily! I reflected on the relationship the children and staff of that school had developed with their environment. Cleaners come and clean the dirt and detritus from the buildings and two men continuously litter pick. That school is just a microcosm of the global situation, mankind constantly causing damage whilst having to deal with the consequences daily and in the global context, the catastrophic consequences are becoming irreversible. I asked the men if there were rules about dropping litter and they informed me that there are rules, of course. Rules without relationship simply do not work, they are ignored and are unenforceable.

It is imperative that we work to help children to build a very different relationship with their school environment because the educational landscape is a large part of the growing child's world. How would it be if everything that needed to be done within the boundary of your school was perceived as a learning opportunity? The walls need painting, the broken window mending, the classrooms need cleaning and most of all the food needs growing, cooking and preparing for lunch. One of the greatest missed opportunities in our schools is the provision of food. There are developing obesity and diabetes epidemics, yet most schools continue to provide very poor quality food, high in sugar, fat, carbohydrates and salt. Often the children have had no conscious relationship whatsoever with what they are eating.

A school for the future

Imagine a school possessing a large garden, a polytunnel and child-friendly kitchen – where different classes take on certain responsibilities in the grounds, garden, and with food preparation. Imagine a school where elements of experiential learning in all subjects is valued and recognised as a powerful catalyst to the classroom-based lessons, and children are engaged in all aspects of the running and care of their school. In this school, there are no children seen as SEN because every child is recognised for their own unique gifts and the potential for diverse differentiation in ways of learning through the offering of many opportunities of learning-by-doing. In this school, the teacher's judgement and intuition will be valued and the children's development will not only be assessed through their academic achievements but also through their ability to solve problems by engaging in practical tasks. Included in this approach to assessment will be communication skills – with peers and with adults – and the ability to function and serve as part of their community.

Currently, our education systems are strongly focused on stimulating and measuring our cognitive abilities, to the detriment of much of our incredible potentiality. One thing I believe we can all agree on about the human condition, regardless of our view, spiritually or otherwise, is that we are hard-wired to be communal beings. It helps me to imagine this aspect of our humanity as a muscle and, like any other muscle that we don't use, it will atrophy and become redundant if it is not fostered and developed.

After the early years of education, a high proportion of a child's learning is individualised, focused very much on their own academic achievements with an emphasis on meeting certain targets. In fact, some would argue that much of the learning of social skills, emotional literacy and communication skills takes place in the playground. Our innate desire to be part of something beyond ourselves is also cultivated in the playground. Without sufficient monitoring, however, bullying can take place and an ugly 'lord of the flies' unnatural order can ensue.

When we involve children with the day to day management of a school's facilities, grounds, gardens and kitchen, we are offering the children the opportunity to exercise their 'in-service muscle' – we offer them the chance to participate more fully in the running of their lives. School then becomes *their* school and their education becomes something that is in part carried out *with them*, it is not *done to* them. When I have experienced and been part of this process I have been moved by how empowered the children feel to be trusted, and to be able to prove themselves worthy of that trust. To be actively participating in, rather than to be merely consumers of, their education brings about a tremendous change in attitude towards it.

Harvest

I was working with a group of teachers recently in a primary school in Exeter where the children were working and playing in the garden during their lunchtime. They were harvesting carrots and beans to be displayed on the stall for sale after school. What ensued was an interesting conversation amongst the visiting teachers about the extent that the children could be trusted without supervision. It became clear to everyone that these children had been permitted to develop a sense of ownership as well as a collective responsibility for their outdoor environment. In this particular school there was freedom for the children to spend their lunch time inside or out; I noticed that they all chose to spend their time outdoors.

I found this experience in Exeter to be a perfect example of where children can develop a sense of ownership for their school: 'this is our school', 'this is our garden'. Relationships change dramatically, and endless lists of rules become unnecessary, when children are imbued with a new-found pride, even feeling protective towards their school environment. If it is possible – as it has been in schools that I have visited and worked in – for the school to keep some animals, such as chickens or sheep, then there is yet another entity beyond themselves that needs looking after. As we develop our educational landscape, both in the built environment and outdoors, we are creating something that isn't all about *me* and it isn't all about *now*. The ten-year-old children who are involved in the planting of a tree in their school grounds will never consume the apples, they are planting for those who come after them, maybe even for their own children. The child that harvests some apples from a tree planted ten years ago should be told the story of those who came before, who took the trouble to plant it. Sponsoring and facilitating a relationship between the children and their school environment can only result in a culture of care in the microcosm that is their school.

Where children are given the opportunity to participate and comprehend the past, present and future, they can develop a sense of their part in the continuum of things. When age-appropriate, this can extend into the local community and the children can be encouraged to participate in activities that are of service beyond the boundaries of their school fence. All of this

Collecting eggs

experiential participation in growing a sense of community and belonging must be continually reinforced in the classroom, where their experiences can be related to every aspect of the curriculum. Much of this message is often communicated in the classroom context but when the children are engaged daily in the exercise of their 'in service' muscle the message from the classroom becomes more than information, it becomes embodied understanding. Children's relationship to their education as participants and co-designers represents a profound change in emphasis, particularly when translated into the global context as citizens of the world. We use the term *citizenship* in relation to the growing child; I feel we need to constantly inquire of ourselves and colleagues what we really mean by this, what constitutes a 'good citizen' and how this is achieved.

Child planting garlic

Immersive experiences

A teacher is often presented with a dilemma when it comes to choosing if, when and where to take a child for a school trip. Since teaching, I am fortunate that, along with my wife and colleagues, I could set up a land-based educational initiative called *On the Hill* in rural Devon that can host visiting classes of children. One local school send their Year 6 every year at the beginning of the autumn term for a five-day residential. The themes that they ask to explore are *food* and *community*. The activities they engage with include cooking for themselves and for others, gardening and undertaking a building project. They participate in other hands-on activities that contribute to the wider community who live and work at the centre. As with many school groups that I have hosted over the years, I am always amazed at the enthusiasm the children bring to these tasks; it feels as if a latent hunger within them is being satiated, that they are being given a potent means of expression for them to become truly human.

I have witnessed while on these residential programs that profound transformations take place in the children's relationship with food. We sometimes have children who will not eat anything at all. One such boy last year would not eat and was fearful of trying any new experience; we had a sense that he was afraid of life itself. On the third day of a five-day residential, the children were offered the opportunity to skin and prepare a rabbit for the cooking pot. The rabbits had been killed by a local gamekeeper who controls the rabbit population for farmers and he presented the workshop explaining the whole context, method and biology. This boy could not resist being involved even though the activity was optional and he really got stuck in. That evening he ate rabbit pie, mashed potato and carrots – and had seconds!

For the remainder of his stay his whole demeanour changed. He became curious, he took risks, he had very open conversations with staff regarding the future he wanted for himself. This child went through a transformation. His teachers were astonished; the vehicle or key was his relationship with food, which then opened up to him a whole realm of other possibilities.

Child cutting greens

Transformative relationship with nature

I have seen this sort of transformation many times and the vehicle has been food, the woods, farm animals, the garden, sleeping out and many other land-based experiences offered during a residential.

The point I am making here is that it is often the *forming of a relationship with an activity*, an *environment*, an *experience* or a *fellow human being* that is the key to enabling children to grow and to discover a deeper sense of themselves that in turn is a catalyst for their ability to learn.

To conclude, I feel it is important to define what some of the prerequisites are for our educational landscape to be an effective and appropriate environment for children to grow and learn. Firstly let us establish that the educational landscape is not just the 'outdoors', it is the whole of the school environment, the whole school organism, and even, potentially, elements of the local community.

What these environments contain may vary. It is hoped there is a garden, materials for creative play, a fire pit and other outdoor cooking facilities. Any other facilities that will provide a catalyst for all learning are welcome, but the most important element is the *relationship*. The sponsoring and nurturing of this relationship offers an opportunity to create a dynamic where the children can feel that they are participants in, and co-creators of, their education and indeed their future world.

CHAPTER 15

The Woodland Classroom

Hattie Duke

Gated school or woodland classroom!?

The gate to the primary school where I work once a week in rural Herefordshire is locked with a keypad. Recently they were told they had to invest in this expensive gate and device in order to meet Ofsted requirements. The fear is of 'stranger danger'. Teachers and parents who have forgotten the code to the keypad, frustrated by this unnecessary eight-foot-tall obstacle, climb over the traditional stone wall that runs at a height of around four foot either side of the gate. The children and staff here are lucky; in most other schools the eight-foot-tall fence extends all the way around their school.

Our task, as educators, is to prepare the inner as well as the outer landscape – to prepare the ground in which the seeds of inspiration can grow. The essence of this preparation is trust in those around us, not fear of them. As Maslow explained in his pyramid of learning needs[129], at the bottom of the pyramid there must be safety, we must feel safe in order to be able to learn. Safety and trust therefore create the fertile ground for education.

Gated community

Open woodland classroom

Woodland school – den building

Children playing in nature

At the centre of a healthy educational landscape there must be a warm centre. This is a place where the day, session or class begins and ends. Ideally there would be a hearth fire in this place, perhaps a circle of logs to sit on, but if not, a symbolic candle, or simply a stone or another natural object to gather around. This hearth creates and provides a safe, calm 'container'. It becomes a container ready to be filled with creativity.

The hearth is not only, or exclusively, a physical place. To encourage a feeling of safety there is a need to create a sense of connection. This connection ultimately needs to function on three levels: connection to self, connection to others and connection to the natural world – both around and within us.

The renewal of these connections can take time. The outdoor educational landscape provides many of the qualities required to rebuild them. The journey can be begun simply by a verse or a song. A pause at the beginning and at the end of a lesson can bring time to reconnect with ourselves, internally.

A brief word from each participant, and from facilitators, can bring hearts and minds together to facilitate cooperative learning. A moment to listen can remind us of our senses and the gateway to connection with the natural world. Alternatively, an introductory game can be used as long as it leaves everybody feeling seen and heard: valued. This vital element of building self-esteem and thus *allowing* learning to emerge has long been overlooked in our society: the knowledge that we all have a unique part to play in the creation of a world in which we want to live. The word 'hearth' includes the words 'earth' and 'heart': two words whose value is often overlooked in our modern world.

An established outdoor educational landscape may have more than one hearth. Or a main hearth might be established and then satellite points of stillness identified around the site. If there are different craft workshops on the site it may be that each workshop takes a moment to create a metaphorical centre before beginning work by using a verse or a song.

The central hearth

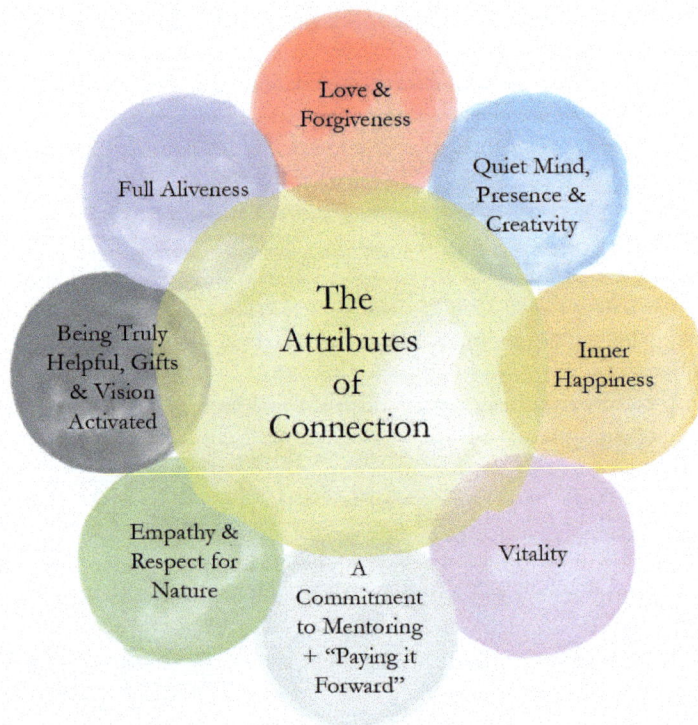

The Attributes of Connection

Gathering round the hearth

Rustic cooking on the wild side

The word 'hearth' also conjures up an image of elders around a central hearth fire, be it in an old stone cottage in the British Isles or around a fire in the desert on the other side of the world. The elders help to create a calm, safe place. Their presence emanates wisdom and experience, and whilst they may or may not contribute practically, their knowledge is always ready to be shared. Sometimes it is not possible to find a human elder willing to be part of a modern educational landscape. In the absence of human elders the 'other-than-human' world can be acknowledged and called upon. An introduction to ancient rocks and trees on the site may be appropriate. Or we may need to call on the elder within each of us, or on our knowledge of our ancestors to support our work. The important thing is to create a feeling of support, a feeling that someone, something, some entity, has 'got our back' and is encouraging the work we do in a broader context.

Change and flexibility are of paramount importance for human development; however, young people also need an anchor, a rhythm on which to balance a healthy ability to develop. Without this there is more pressure on the nervous system. More stress is created by needing to re-adjust to new situations every day, or every 40 minutes (the length of an average school lesson).

Adrenal fatigue has become an epidemic in our modern world (Dr Peatfield research)[130]. Young people and adults are in a state of alert, constantly activating the 'fight or flight' response. This puts pressure on the nervous system, drains the immune system, results in widespread insomnia, depression and lack of motivation when the body is only occasionally allowed to relax fully.

Today, many people grow up without a sense of place and home. Families do not pay much attention to moving house, moving areas, moving away from friends and relations. With fewer stable families, school is often the one constant in a young person's life. Within school very

Child whittling

Experience nature throughout the seasons

little consideration is given to ensuring pupils are in a relaxed place where they can learn. The emphasis is on delivering the lesson rather than noticing the underlying causes of pupils' ability or inability to pay attention.

The content is often superficial and without a meaningful context. I was recently asked by a parent to help her find a way to deliver some Forest School sessions as part of flexi-schooling. She felt that the sessions had become little more than duty; her son was bored and disengaged. The tasks given for one three-hour session such as 'identify some local trees in the area' could have been made meaningful if they had been 'allowed' to cover ten sessions. If there was time for her son to learn to make something from wood or learn about which wood burns well on a fire, practically using his own hands, gaining his own experience, no doubt he would have felt invigorated, inspired and confident instead of just bored.

Over a longer period of time, a natural rhythm can be found in which there is time to 'be' instead of to just 'do'. Natural rhythms are inherent to creating with our hands, especially if the whole process can be incorporated. For example, if children are set the task of carving a butter knife from hazel, the following can be experienced: a breathing-out time is spent whilst they look around the woodland to find an appropriate branch. Sawing the branch is an activity which engages the whole body's rhythmic system. While sitting and whittling to create the shape, absolute focus is required, which calms the 'monkey mind' and allows the breathing to settle into a more regular rhythm. After their initial haste, the children learn how to take off less and less wood at a time, how to gain more control to give a subtler finish. How desperately our modern world needs speed to be replaced with subtlety and sensitivity!

Working with the seasons provides a natural rhythm for learning. For younger children especially, and increasingly for children of all ages, seasonal activities are extremely beneficial. Just the practicality of teaching young children to dress themselves for the different seasons all year round provides a whole range of learning opportunities. This is so, not just for the children but for their parents as well, many of whom do not venture outdoors for any amount of time if the weather is cold.

Out in all weathers

The weather, especially with its unpredictable nature in this country, ensures that any outdoor learning environment teaches flexibility and resilience. Very young children are masterful teachers at making the most of any weather: muddy puddles turn to skating rinks in winter, dancing autumn leaves fall to form a soft winter bed, sleeping bulbs bring colour and joy in spring.

Spaces that can be warmed by a fire (always a wood-burning fire/stove, for which the children can be involved in the gathering and preparing of the wood) and have some separation from the wind and cold, are perfect as they allow the rhythm of outdoor activity to be balanced with calm slowing down, even during the colder months.

The key to rich and meaningful learning is to ensure, as part of the educational landscape, that the pupils are consistently exposed to the elements. Through this immersion they can come to know and love the variety of rhythmical changes inherent in the dynamic interplay of the elements. This builds physical strength and stamina, of course, but also, emotional intelligence.

The weather changes in this country can be helpful as a backdrop to the language of emotions. The weather can change here as often as our moods do. Being active in all kinds of weather allows children to acknowledge and experience their full range of emotions, and then to begin to step back and watch the waves ebb and flow. Children do not really need their elders to pass on the knowledge of facts and figures; all these can be obtained from the internet with ease. What they do need is guidance in building relationships (with themselves and others), in true, face to face communication and honesty.

The rhythm of the day and the night can also be extremely beneficial if one is able to incorporate it into the educational landscape. The evening offers a gentler time to share stories and face truths with the shadows of the night and without the need to show all hidden places of the soul on faces lit with sunlight. The moon and stars offer perspective on many human problems. The warmth of a campfire draws people together, without the need of social norms or rules that can be complicated and threatening for many. People gather together to keep warm in the forgiving light of a fire that is forever transforming and burning away what is no longer needed.

From my own experience of living off-grid in small spaces I know the benefits of incorporating regular exposure to the elements as a necessary part of living. I know how I will delay chopping and sawing wood, or taking a trip to the outdoor kitchen, or going outdoors to check the ropes holding a tarpaulin in place on a windy night, or even walking the dog on a day of cold, driving rain… and I know, that every time I notice the resistance and complete what needs to be done, my sense of well-being returns. My belly softens, I breathe more easily, smile gently and find my place more easily in the community of life. To find a way to include these practical daily tasks in an educational landscape is essential. One small step outside the box of comfort and incipient negative perspectives brings boundless rewards. This small step often requires creative thinking in order to resolve a practical challenge.

It may be part of our challenge as educators to prove that we are achieving numerous aims and objectives, to be able to meet our learning outcomes. However, surely the more vital challenge is to equip the children with creative minds that can solve future problems we cannot yet imagine.

I had the pleasure of spending time with the Bushmen of the Kalahari recently. In an environment that looks positively sparse compared to our own lush, fertile country these peaceful people gather and hunt, no longer to survive, but to create. As part of The Living Culture Foundation, they are creating an educational landscape for those of us who have forgotten the opportunities of living with very few belongings.

Their tools consist of a simple knife, an adze, a bow and arrow and a set of sticks to make fire. The women make jewellery from ostrich egg shells, shaping them with a hard flint like stone and rounding them by sanding a whole necklace of beads on sandstone. A leather cape serves as a baby sling, a pouch for gathering plants and a mat to sort the beads. Fewer material possessions nurture our creativity.

San bushmen Kalahari gathering around a fire

Kalahari desert people lighting a fire

In the Kalahari, the children play games with balls of earth and whatever scraps are left behind by careless tourists. They are opportunists. They sing and clap and dance and smile and laugh a lot. Many thousands of years ago, despite the hardship of surviving in the desert, they spent time finding and processing pigments to paint pictures about the life they lived. It seems that they know that humans cannot live without creative expression – a fact that many in the Western world seem to have forgotten at a great price. A lack of creativity leads to increasing levels of stress-related disorders, depression, violence against fellow humans and suicide.

If the outdoor educational landscape is developed Nature 'does the work', she absorbs excess tension, calms heightened energy, relieves tired teachers, parents, children, allowing for more facilitation and less stockpiling of facts. Natural beauty is soothing to the senses: it calms tired eyes, lightly brushes the hardened touch, provides delicate smells and a symphony of sounds.

The outdoor educational landscape is rich in any natural setting and enhanced by the presence of running water in which to play and learn and cleanse, clay and mud to model, sand to sift, trees to climb, gardens to grow, willow to craft. The presence of animals to nurture and the construction of craft workshop spaces are, of course, part of the ideal educational landscape. These have been discussed in detail in previous chapters.

The shift towards a truly educational landscape – within and without – is more urgent than ever. Without it, attempts to encourage lifelong learning and the learning of 'life skills', the realisation of 'a positive contribution from every child' (Ofsted guidelines, *Every Child Matters*[131]) fall on barren ground.

I was recently offered the use of a 22-acre woodland for my work. The site had been lived in and cherished some years ago. Walking around the woods I had an overwhelming sense of sadness. I really felt that the woodland was lonely without the interaction of a family and meaningful

Woodland grove with oak

human activity that had previously been part of its life. Around the same time, I visited a grove of trees in a field with a central old oak. This site has been used as a site of celebration four times a year for the last fifteen years. The positive feeling of vibrancy and nourishment was tangible. The natural educational landscape not only offers an opportunity for us to learn and grow; it also offers us a chance to notice that whatever we do actually matters, affects the world around us. The ripples of our actions give new meaning to the idea that we must 'leave no trace' in any natural environment.

CHAPTER 16

The Outdoor Classroom: Practical Wisdom

John Lawry

An initiative in holistic learning

How do we, as human beings, learn? Is there more than one way? What is meant by the term 'holistic learning'? An implied meaning of the term 'holistic' is that it is 'healthier', somehow better for us. If so, how do we know this to be true?

'Unity of things' – John Lawry

If there is a variety of ways to learn and some are more successful, or better for us, than others, how do we determine what 'successful' or 'healthy' learning is? What does it look like? And how is learning of this kind evidenced?

An inherent theme in the above questions is that of *methodology*. The study of holistic learning includes observations of method, of learning *how* we learn, but it is not confined to these. Questions concerning content, *what* we learn, are also important and nestled neatly within these are questions of timing; *when* do we introduce or work with different substances and processes?

There are also any number of questions related to the roles taken in the educational relationship, such as: Are the roles of teacher/student like that of the apprentice/master relationship? *Who* does what? *Who* learns? Many ancient traditions (such as the Maori Tikanga of New Zealand) have reciprocal learning at their core.

Other questions hover around those already posed. In holistic learning, does anything go? Do students just do what they want to when they want? What roles do the student and teacher share when it comes to direction and structure?

A very interesting question in addition to those posed thus far is that of how environmental contexts influence learning, i.e. *where* learning takes place. The contemporary convention of formal learning being classroom-based would suggest that the optimum context for learning is indoors. If high value is placed on there being consistency in the assessment of students' learning, especially in academic subjects, and a key strategy to achieve these outcomes is to make learning a highly-structured affair where learning behaviours are optimised in a controlled environment, then perhaps learning is best contained indoors.

If this is the case, then it follows that the more the focus of learning is on its measurable outcomes, the more attention needs to be given to controlling the variables which influence learning behaviours connected with those outcomes. Education developed in this way becomes an increasingly mechanistic process, and it is just this approach that has come to dominate in a disproportionate number of educational contexts globally. It is the antithesis of holistic education.

So how do we move beyond education as mechanistic behaviour management? George Monbiot[132] comments: 'In the future, if you want a job, you must be as unlike a machine as possible: creative, critical and socially skilled. So why are children being taught to behave like machines?"

For a beginning teacher, gaining control of the classroom behaviour is often a prime focus, a necessary strategy for the teacher's survival. Establishing patterns of behaviour which embody vital human values such as respect, and cultivating a culture of reciprocal learning that supports learning for the future, are also primary tasks for an educator. The management of classroom behaviour is, however, just one element of learning behaviour and learning is by no means guaranteed using mechanistic methods. This being the case, if a more holistic approach to education is to be developed, then the important consideration of *context*, being indoors, needs to be reconsidered.

Ends, of necessity, have beginnings: to quote an old Maori proverb, 'as the sapling is bent, so grows the tree'. If we want to have confidence in there being consistency of outcome, especially outcomes which are legitimate and characterised by well-being, then a more holistic view needs to be established: a view that grasps the entwined and reciprocal nature of whole and part. This way, the 'narrative' of learning has integrity – it has a 'beginning, middle, end'; it is coherent. As any experienced teacher knows, although students may be bodily in the room and 'physically present' as a prerequisite for learning, this presence it is no guarantee that learning will occur – whether the students are well behaved or not. A teacher may have the best plans and learning programmes in the world, a perfectly controlled environment, quiet and obedient students, but if the student is not engaged then what is it that they are learning? Is it something real, something tangible, and something that will make a positive difference to their lives?

This leads us to the very pithy question: where does 'real' learning occur? Surely it begins within the student: when the student is interested and engaged, where she displays a natural curiosity for the world. If learning is grounded in developing *interest*, if a student's love for it, knowledge about it and desire to master the skills associated with it takes root and grows, then it is a manifest reality – it has a legitimate existence. Holistic learning is essentially a human event. The relationship to learning that we have with the young human beings who stand before us, our understanding of *who* these people are and our connection with them, is the foundation of our work.

To summarise thus far: to build a living picture of the phenomena of *holistic learning*, not only does *how*, *what*, *when* and *where* need to be considered but so, too, do *why* and *who*. In reverse order these give a ready checklist of the questions that need to be considered and answered when constructing a *holistic learning approach to* learning.

Practical wisdom

I would like to explore the term *practical wisdom* in the light of the above. The etymology of these words is interesting and important to consider. *Practical* means 'fit for action' and wisdom, 'the property of being wise, a skilful seer'. By way of coming close to what practical wisdom might mean, I would like to share three meetings I recently had on a trip to Thailand, which flesh-out these initial definitions.

The umbrella maker

The first of these meetings was in a craft village, where two of the craftswomen involved took me through the process of creating an umbrella from bamboo and paper. The quiet confidence and the effortless skill with which they worked was both breath-taking and deceiving in its apparent simplicity. I watched one craftswoman shape the radial umbrella spokes using a long-handled, razor-sharp knife. With two or three strokes of the knife she had shaped the spoke and with a deft flick, affected a joint split through the spoke at its narrowest edge (approx. 5 mm thick). She then drilled a hole through a bundle of these using a push-pull drill, with just two strokes. She allowed me to try out this process. It was not as simple as it looked! She did all the above while sitting cross-legged on a raised platform. This allowed her to use her whole body as needed: her thigh, forearm, palm, fingers and thumb to work the knife and her toes to hold and steady the spoke; her hip, forearm and hands to hold and operate the drill. She employed clean, smooth movements: no more, no less than what was required to affect the task. It took her, including the time it took to show me how to use the drill, about five minutes to shape, split and drill the set of spokes needed to make one umbrella: such nimble cleverness!

Spiritual foundations of culture & work

The second meeting during which I felt that practical wisdom shone through was with Chatchawan Thongdeelert. He is the Founder and Director of the Lanna Wisdom School located in the northern cultural centre of Thailand, Chaingmai. The Lanna are the indigenous people of this region, renowned throughout Thailand for their proud traditions as craftspeople. The school he has created ensures the continuance of these craft traditions, acting as a process of cultural renewal, by connecting the young students of Chaingmai with local master craftspeople. Students in the state schools in Chaingmai get to work alongside master craftspeople of a comprehensive range of local craft traditions, in a series of structured programmes. In recent years, these relationships have blossomed into apprenticeship schemes.

Chatchawan's explanation of how they are achieving cultural renewal and the task of the teacher in this process was very interesting. Here I quote from notes of my conversation with him:

'There is an essential unity of the spiritual life of the school and the understanding of our intimate connection with all living things: the birds, animals, plants and the raw elements of our world, and the way we use them in our work. How we play music, sing, and move as we weave, beat, carve, etc., is infused with this understanding of the spiritual foundation of life: it transforms the work done.'

The role of the teacher and the person of the teacher are to be upheld and respected when the teacher is understood to be the repository of the skills and conduit of the tradition of the craft they are imbued with. Each generation 'hands it on' or 'passes it forward' to ensure not only the continuance of the tradition of the skill but also the opportunity for its refinement and development in the lines of succeeding generations. If the skills are just copied the tradition becomes mechanistic. The skill tradition requires the living reality of the life of the person to be nurtured, to grow and develop as a tradition of skill, and the person needs the discipline of the craft tradition to be nurtured, to grow and develop as a person.

The blacksmith – a forgotten art

The third meeting that I would like to describe was with a blacksmith in a small village in Kanchanaburi district, in the south-west Thailand. I was taken there by my host to use his workshop facilities, to make equipment for the Pizza oven my host and I were constructing for his wedding. My meeting with this venerable master craftsman poignantly brought home to me the pathos many of these old craftsmen are now experiencing. It was such a privilege to work together, using our common understanding of craft to 'converse'. When we left, my host informed me that the frail, serene, gentle man I had just met had no one to whom to pass on the tradition of his skills. He had had a son, whom he had trained, but his son had died and there was no one else who was interested in learning his craft.

Criteria for teaching and programmes of work in the outdoor classroom

The outdoor classroom is a context as well as a methodology for developing practical wisdom using holistic approaches. These approaches to learning adopt a 'whole human being' and 'whole of life' perspective. They are built upon some key understandings. We learn best:

- when we engage 'Hands, Heart, Head'
- when we 'Do, Reflect, Apply'

Our growth and development, from infant to adult, unfolds in developmental phases and these phases have common characteristics. For them to be the foundation of health and well-being, certain fundamental conditions need to exist. The following is an overview of one way to identify and delineate early foundational phases in human development.

The first phase (roughly between the ages of 0 – 7 or up until the change of teeth) is when we form a relationship to the physical world and to our own body. Playful exploration and fantasy, the integration of the senses, the absorption/imprinting of fundamental patterns of perception, movement and work in an atmosphere of trust and confidence are indicative of the optimum formative conditions of this phase of early childhood.

In the next phase (between the ages of 7-9 years), the foundations of healthy habits with rhythm and time predominate. Fantasy strengthens into imagination and play, especially when all the elements (Earth, Water, Fire and Air) are included, is highly interactive, and learning by doing, by making, is the predominant mode of learning.

From 9–12 years, our emotional life, our moods and feelings and our capacity for empathy predominate. Building on the healthy habits with rhythm and time, our experience of space can develop, and with this a more mature capacity for reflective thought and observation can develop. Whereas up and until now it could be said that the quality of Goodness has held reign as the fundamental experience of the world, the need for the experience of Beauty now emerges.

From 12–18 years (broadly the time of entering adolescence and moving through to the earliest stages of adulthood) the formation of one's own identity and that of others predominates. Closely associated and intertwined with this phase is the need for Truth and ethical resilience. The mastery of skills gained through practice, and refinement in the pursuit of excellence, is a core capacity to be developed in this phase.

The phases of early development briefly outlined above provide a foundation for grasping the potential for developing the outdoor classroom. These are not necessarily easy concepts to grasp; they grow with time. However, it seems to me that the nature of problems associated with contemporary educational methods is such that a new way of perceiving, thinking and acting is required and a developmental understanding of the human being is required.

By way of building a picture for the potential scope of the outdoor classroom consider the following:

Imagine a circle. A circle stands, in many cultural contexts, for the round of the year, the unity of all things, form and formlessness, all in one.

At the base of the circle let us imagine the Earth, on which we stand, the Mother of all things, the realm of growth and plenty. Here we can place the activity of GARDENING. Above the ground of the Earth – in the human realm – we have the deeply imbued wisdom of the

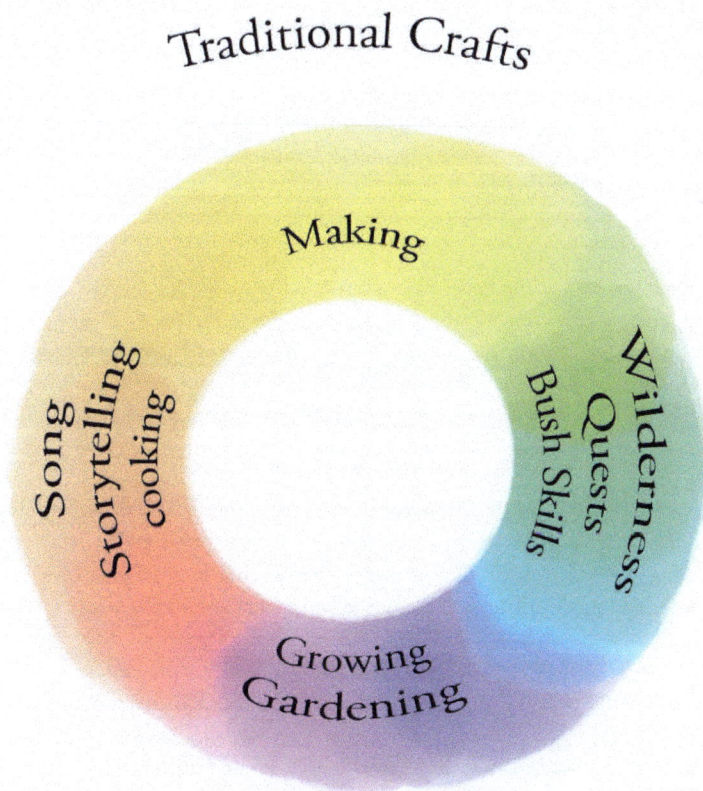

Traditional Crafts

Making

Wilderness
Quests
Bush Skills

Song
Storytelling
cooking

Growing
Gardening

Outdoor classroom concept –John Lawry

TRADITIONAL CRAFTS. To the left, gathered-in, is the meeting of Gardens and Craft: COOKING and the place of fire where food, storytelling, songs and chants emerge. To the right, reaching out, is the realm of adventure where the skills that travel with us have necessary realism as BUSHCRAFT in the wilderness of new discovery.

Spirit of place

There is also the literal ground on which we stand, the *locus genii* that needs to be lived into and connected with, the organic reality of this work. Here is where the real work begins and how one goes about doing this, identifying resources, useful orientation processes, etc., and how these perceptions/experiences are developed into craft-based learning programmes which are sustainable and location-based is the vital and necessary first step in developing the outdoor classroom.

The necessity for 'hands-on' learning

In many schools around the globe we can witness a contemporary fixation on literacy and numeracy as core skills to be taught at school. There is often even a legal necessity that achievements by students in these skills are publicly reported. It is worthwhile examining how robust a definition of 'core skills' these, in fact, are.

The three Rs (Reading, 'Riting and 'Rithmetic) are popularly stated as the core focus for teachers. In contemporary parlance the title has been condensed even further becoming 'Literacy' and 'Numeracy'.

Where does technology fit into this picture? Being literate and numerate is of course vital, and these skills are fundamentally connected to our identity as human beings. However, when given prominence as subjects, and a certain degree of 'special' status, they seem to hold a ranking of importance which places them superior to all else. If this is what schooling is emphasising and it happens that you struggle to acquire these skills (and one could list a multitude of 'conditions' and 'special needs' that evidence the growing number of students for whom this is the case) and are deemed to be 'failing' in your efforts then *what do you do?*

Consider the following quote from *Will-Developed Intelligence* by David Mitchell & Patricia Livingston:

> *'Bruce Archer, a professor at the Royal College of Art, had an old great-aunt who, in the early 19th century, first wrote the catchy educational phrase that has come to be known as the three R's (reading, 'riting and 'rithmetic). This, his aunt maintained, was a misquotation of an earlier aphorism: 'reading (and writing), reckoning (and figuring), and wroughting (and wrighting)'. A young person's experience with wroughting, or blacksmithing, was considered to be an important foundation in the development of thinking[133].'*

There is a certain irony in the fact that literacy and numeracy, the use of symbols (script and numerals) to record, calculate and convey meaning is, in fact, a primary technology. When we learn to read and write and figure we are, indeed, replicating a core technology. In his Rhone-Poulenc Science Prize-winning book *Guns, germs and steel*, Jared Diamond[134] argues this case convincingly.

'The etymology of "*Technology*" = "*the systematic treating of... an art, craft or technique*". This being the case then most of schooling is "technology" based. Simply put, it is "the way we go about doing something".'

But there is another condition which can intrude, an associative meaning of technique we need be wary of: 'tedium'.

Systematic treatment is an essential part of mastering a technique or skill. However, repetition devoid of meaning is tedium. The fusion of practice and meaning is more readily established when the process of learning approximates the generic sequence of development, the pathway, by which that technique or skill came into being. In my experience, students become 'hooked' by this approach: it's like solving a mystery or entering into a grand story (which of course it is). It's very hard to 'put down'.

Under these circumstances, learning isn't just copying something for it to be regurgitated. It follows the more organic pathway (think food); it is assimilated, digested, reconstituted (made one's own), the unnecessary or harmful eliminated: the good maintained, practised and practised to the point of reflex, and then it is worthy of reproduction.

Summary

The outdoor classroom is predicated upon the idea that 'making' is a fundamental literacy; the necessary companion to language, literacy and numeracy. The programmes developed (experiences made possible) engender intrinsic rather than extrinsic motivational capacities. The student's experience of this relationship is made evident as their skills develop. Intellectual rigor, emotional maturity, cohesive social skills and physical nimbleness are mutually developed.

Those students injured by schooling that is focused on disability gain tremendous confidence when their skill development is objectified. Not only is the physical evidence of skill improvement before them, in their hands, but also the 'inner' experience of previously unknown capacities is waking up; 'problems' associated with making, especially in a traditional craft context or experimental archaeology inquiry, are not new problems. Knowing this they can come to trust their instincts and develop confidences which are subjectively and objectively 'right and true'.

Accordingly, their senior school years have a foundation, both wide and deep, for them to draw upon as they enter the workshops, studios, laboratories, theatres and halls of higher learning. Not only are they prepared to do well in formal study and examination but also, and perhaps more importantly, (in a student's own words), 'the skills I have learned this way are "life skills"'; like riding a bike, it is something they will never forget… a life bespoke.

Landscapes for Learning: some concluding thoughts

Bernard Graves

Alliance for childhood

It is significant to note that The Alliance for Childhood, an internationally agreed UNICEF charter safeguarding the rights of Children, has stated within its document that children '… need a relationship with the earth: to animals and nature'[135]. Surely we would concur with this right; that everyone needs to have direct experience in nature, to touch and smell the earth, to see things growing and to wonder at the marvel of it all.

When deprived of the opportunity of being in and engaging with nature, potential nourishing and educational opportunities are missed. With a lack of physical and sensory engagement in the real world through play, education and work, there is the danger that children, young people and adults may well lose their connection with the real world – replacing it with an alluring Virtual Reality experience!

On the other hand, by crafting natural materials, and working in the school garden or local woodlands, valuable learning opportunities arise, as well as beneficial personal experiences. These experiences provide a sense of meaningfulness, purpose and connectedness with what we are doing. Activities like digging and processing clay, making an artefact, constructing a bread oven and firing it, all help to integrate experience and to learn when sensory experiences have been fragmented.

Children playing in nature

Recent research has substantiated that much can be gained in our early years of maturation for our healthy development – neurologically, emotionally and intellectually – by immersion in nature.

The crisis that we can witness today, in growing numbers of children and arising from our separation from the natural environment, has given rise to the 'Nature Nurture' therapeutic activity groups in America and the UK. The often-disruptive behaviour and learning difficulties evident in many young children are increasingly being seen as a result of our 'overprotection' from the natural environment. The prevalence of these learning and behavioural difficulties has resulted in what is now referred to as Nature Deficit Disorder, a relatively recently documented condition[136] (Louv, 2005).

The remedy for such children consists in an immersion in a managed natural environment, for instance a small woodland, where the child is allowed to interact with nature playfully. Positive results in children's behaviour from such initiatives are encouraging, but it could be considered that the very fact that we now need such remedial approaches is, in itself, quite alarming.

Schools for the 21st century

'Students in the next century will need to know how to create a civilisation that runs on sunlight, conserves energy, preserves biodiversity, protects soils and forests, develops sustainable local economies and restores the damage inflicted on the earth. In order to achieve such ecological education, we need to transform our schools and universities.' Prof David Orr[137]

Over the years, I have been fortunate to work as a consultant with a number of schools that have had measurable successes in providing hands-on opportunities for children. These schools have integrated rich and meaningful experiences of the natural world throughout their curriculum, either through encouraging play in nature or by providing more formal activities like gardening, farming or traditional land and handcraft activities. Many schools have made exemplary inroads into developing themselves as traditional establishments of academic learning, while also providing a whole environment of contemporary, sustainable learning opportunities in a variety of outdoor classroom settings. To do this satisfactorily always requires that the school grounds be developed with a vision for a variety of resources and facilities such as:

- *a garden area that supplies seasonal foods for the kitchen*
- *grounds maintained with compost heaps*
- *a tree nursery*
- *creative play areas with natural materials*
- *an outdoor classroom and a variety of craft workshop spaces*
- *a withy bed for basketry*
- *a dye plant bed for dyeing of wool, etc.*

In such ecologically developed schools, the children's engagement in activities in the outdoor classroom is not experienced as just 'time out of class' but as opportunities to participate in 'real life' affairs. Children often show good motivation and willingness to take effective responsibility in such activities.

Such developments require vision, resources and commitment by the whole school community – but they are well worth it. The rewards are beneficial to all who work in and share the school grounds – the school becomes a school to be proud of and one that supports the well-being of the whole community.

SECTION FIVE:

TRANSFORMING PLACE

CHAPTER 17

Reimagining that which had potential: a tale of three mills

Aonghus Gordon

A s a potter – in my youth – I shaped a material that was drawn, extracted and refined directly from the Earth – clay. In the process of working with clay, I unconsciously developed certain skills for shaping those 'mundane' materials provided by nature. Awakening to the transformation of potential offered by the clay, however, took much longer than acquiring the skill to make a teapot. Through the process of shaping and refining porcelain for the quintessential British tea ceremony, I was brought closer to discovering a hidden *social* law. This is the social law of the *community*, the actual commissioner and designer of the pot. A social need called forth the pot, whereas I was merely its maker! This realisation changed the way I looked upon the world of *making*. The obsession with the figure of the designer-maker was, for me, nothing more than a distraction. What intrigued me instead was how willingly makers submit themselves to the consensus of the community, the true commissioners and designers of the craft item, about its purpose and use.

The internalisation of this discreet social law, which is woven into the process of making (particularly as a potter) helped me develop a new muscle: one of reflective practice about what was being made and who I was ultimately working for. As a maker, I had to submit my will and my design intention to what is socially established as a teapot – one that does not drip but rather pours with elegance, is held in gratitude and performs with simplicity. This was a subtle discovery but one which did not go unnoticed. In observing how the 'inner life' of the maker is subject to a form of re-shaping. this insight into the process gave way to a new, transformational understanding of the nature of work and service. In short, the clay did more towards reshaping *me* than I could possibly exercise in shaping the clay to my own will.

This inner dialogue between clay, community and potter involved both a reflection on action and a feedback loop to the maker. The process contributed to discovering a whole new awareness of *craft work as personal transformation*. The maker is forever being renewed by the commissioner, the community. The commissioner extends a gesture of personal entrepreneurship, an invitation to take on a 'new risk' in each act of making. The commissioner enables a new fluidity of response, in which this sense of shaping according to a 'social law' generates a new realisation that there is a personal task to accomplish. The material is a resister, a responder – and it is also a mirror.

In the case of clay, the material is a skin. It gives boundaries, it communicates the existence of an inside and an outside world. The clay, as skin, lives in the realm of the potter's touch. It brings together 'I' and 'you'. The material is unforgiving because of its 'lawful' nature – but also deeply personal. It does not – and cannot – lie. The clay in the potter's hand encompasses thoughtfulness, concealment and skill all in one. If it is unforgiving – sometimes to the point of ruthlessness – when its transformation is accomplished, it offers catharsis to the maker and the recipient. A maker may be said to live in the perpetual tension of what might be described, psychologically, as the *depressive position*, of never knowing fully what has been created, or what has lived as a picture in the imagination of the commissioner. The risk of rejection is ever present when undertaking the transformation of clay.

Re-shaping spaces

To transfer these insights from the process of transforming clay into one of reimagining industrial iconic buildings throughout the industrial core of England, required another transformation of skill, that of imagination. Out of the centres of *making* in England (Stroud, Stourbridge, Sheffield and later Birmingham) the world had once been provided with hundreds and thousands of items of excellence: finely crafted textiles, glassware and cutlery to adorn the infantry, shipping lines and the silver service of millions of households. These items flowed from these remarkable centres and from the hands of skilful craft makers. By the late 20th century these centres were in decline, their craft makers dispersed, their buildings unwanted.

What was now brought into these industrial buildings was an emotional, practical and social aesthetic found particularly in John Ruskin's and William Morris's transformative ideas on labour, material and function. 'The Mill' in Nailsworth, a derelict wool mill, was renewed and re-founded as Ruskin Mill. The old Royal Doulton Glassworks in Stourbridge was renewed as Glasshouse College. The Sterling works in Sheffield found new life as Freeman College. This process of renewal required reimagining that which had once had potential.

In each site, finding the specific context for this *reimagining* involved a triangulation which included understanding its particular Genius Loci (the biography of place) and applying Ruskin Mill Trust's spiritual scientific method, informed by Rudolf Steiner. These elements were woven together to serve young people between 16 and 25 with needs and challenges that include autism spectrum conditions, oppositional defiance, ADHD and mental health issues.

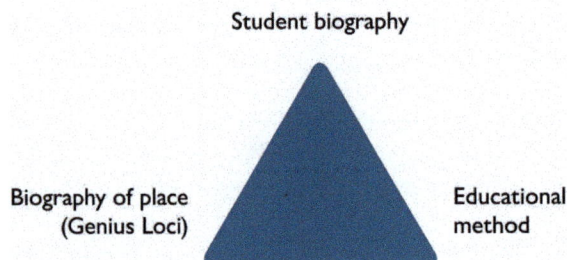

Student biography

Biography of place
(Genius Loci)

Educational
method

Historical legacies

The materials and craft legacies from previous centuries very often became, through this process of reimagination, the 'medicine cabinet' for the recovery of both place and people. It is a paradox that in the industrial past the very processes, materials and industrial conditions gave rise to the subjugation of those who worked in them – while through this new lens the same processes and buildings offered centres of renewal and recovery. In each industrial centre, an exploration using the Genius Loci method discovered a history of remarkable achievements, but also the shadow that accompanied these achievements. The human bruising that arose through the industrial division of labour, the conveyor belt methods of production and the potential toxicity of the process itself, all contributed to this shadow.

This shadow lived in the physical, social and imaginative life of highly skilful working people, whose employment had invariably continued across generations and spread out into large surrounding areas of the community around the production of cloth, glass and silverware. We should not misunderstand this shadow, however, as millions of people received the benefits of the highest grade cloth, world-class glass and world-class silverware. It may be argued that these three mills contributed to developing the highest degree of human consciousness in crafted material, in which civility was celebrated and new light generated out of a production process which invariably held a quality of darkness. At the same time, the recipients of the items produced in these centres of craft rose to new levels of civility and social decorum.

Ruskin Mill

If we consider the origins of Ruskin Mill, the building itself provided a place in which cooperation was essential, both upstream in terms of the flow of water and downstream in terms of its products. Each mill applied its specific skill to the ultimate goal of producing the finest cloth in Europe. There was synergy between the materials: the sheep on the hill, the teasels harvested from the valleys for carding, the fuller's earth for cleansing, the flow of the water creating power for production, the spring line, the limestone and the quintessential nature of Stroud's five valleys. These all coalesced in a cooperation of human imagination, social cohesion, timely cooperation

Ruskin Mill North Side Renovation 1983 (original)

Ruskin Mill 2000

Weaving – the signature craft of the Stroud valleys – A Ruskin Mill Trust student learning to weave on a frame loom, developing the power of focus.

and physical resource to create a new economy for the district. The buildings at Ruskin Mill arose in 1812 during the Regency period, and represented one of the period's quintessential high points of architectural aesthetics. During this period the mills – built of oolitic limestone with clean frontal edifices – gave an impression of manorial splendour rather than one of factories.

By the late 20th century, however, this splendour was no longer obvious. It was only later, through an exploration of the Genius Loci, that we discovered that the spaces to the North and South of the building had originally held a Regency pediment, forming a cruciform shape with a lantern bell tower. Restoration required forces and qualities of reimagination, meticulous research and strenuous arguments with the listed buildings inspectorate to accomplish.

Stourbridge and Sheffield

To rediscover this external collaboration in each industrial centre, we had to undertake a comparable internal audit and evaluation of their respective industrial processes: textile production at The Mill, glass cutting and blowing at Royal Doulton Glassworks and the hand forging of tableware at Sterling Works. Evaluating the movements of weavers, glassblowers and silver spoon forgers through observation and deep participation in each of the processes enabled further insight into their therapeutic potential. This potential needed to be experienced first-hand, re-sounded in the researcher's own interior in order to know how to apply the relationship between the craftsperson's movement, the choreography with the material, and the specific conditions of the young people undertaking craft apprenticeships. Hence the emerging term Practical Skills Therapeutic Education.

Glasshouse College Renovation 2000

Renovation of the Glasshouse is ongoing 2018

This meant that a further relationship arose between the building in its location, the biography and condition of the student, and the method, together enabling an overcoming of barriers to learning. From this perspective the buildings themselves are none other than vessels. They are the containers and providers of an external membrane, within which transformative movements can be performed and reimagined.

In this method, the young adult with special needs encounters the lawfulness of the materials and the master craftsperson. Each one is enabled to enter the slipstream of the master, as the lawful movements of craft work reshape the interior of these young, challenged students. In the case of glassblowing, the nature of the molten material requires a series of movements, which then flow from the glass back into the muscle memory of the young person. Miraculously, the young person submits to the flow of molten glass and the movements needed to manage it. The glass is moving the young adult; it is not the young adult who moves the glass!

In biographies which have been marked by many obstructions to learning, this submission to an external but non-arbitrary authority provides significant and accelerated opportunities for learning. In this re-embodiment of movement, I relinquish my previous habits – habits that are not entirely free but are rather habituated and culturally inflicted. This enables a whole new arena of neurological processing, cognitively, emotionally and practically. The student is befriended by the master craftsperson and held within the authority of movement, in a reimagined building, where there is coherence between communities of practice and the biographies of students, and where 'progress' is expected.

If we enter into the movement choreography of master glassblowers and their apprentices over the last hundred years, we can sense a patterning process not only in the place but in the community. There is a potential for skill; it is encoded, it is subconscious, it is latent. This latent genius in the hands of the community is easily liberated in the Practical Skills Therapeutic Education programme at the Glasshouse College, whose signature and iconic craft is hot glass blowing and glass cutting. The task of the contemporary craft practitioner or maker is thus to

Glasswork – the signature craft of Glasshouse College

Blacksmithing at Clervaux College

The Sterling Works renovation for Freeman College, Sheffield 2006

release those preordained movements that build human capacity. A key example is in offering a reintegration of the planes of space (left–right, front–back and up–down), which our students often struggle with. These in turn generate our prized human capacities that facilitate learning (the focus, grasp and step of the craftsperson), to be reanimated through the eyes, hands and feet of the student.

It is the same in the communities of practice further north, in Sheffield, in the work of cutlery making and spoon forging. The skill set and intensity of focus that requires the hands to strike the silver spoon, time after time after time, elicits, just as in glass, a new interior of resonance: knowing how the movements of craft making are subject to the law of the material and to the community as commissioner. In the case of silver spoon forging, the attention moves from the emotional

Freeman College 2008

domain to the cognitive. In the formation of glass, the students enter a highly refined domain of feeling for the fluidity of the material; the body is required to move within seconds, or else the molten glass is on the floor. By contrast, in the convex shaping of the silver spoon, the result of each hammer strike remains static until removed by another strike. Both the material itself and the student's power of reflection drive each hammer strike, to slowly build a reflective concave mirror which we call a spoon.

Above all, in these world-standard industrial processes of crafting excellence, the maker is required to submit him or herself. The craftsperson therefore gifts his or her movement to the shaping of vessels that perform services of function and social civility. With these young adults who for whatever reason have missed crucial stages in their own development, craftwork offers a change to restep these capacities for movement which bring together thought, emotional and practical movement into one. These

Spoon forging – the signature craft of Sheffield – A Freeman College student with a copper billet learning to forge a spoon as a prototype for a silver spoon, an intensification of focus and grasp

---

The imperative in focus, grasp and step for our executive function and ego experience

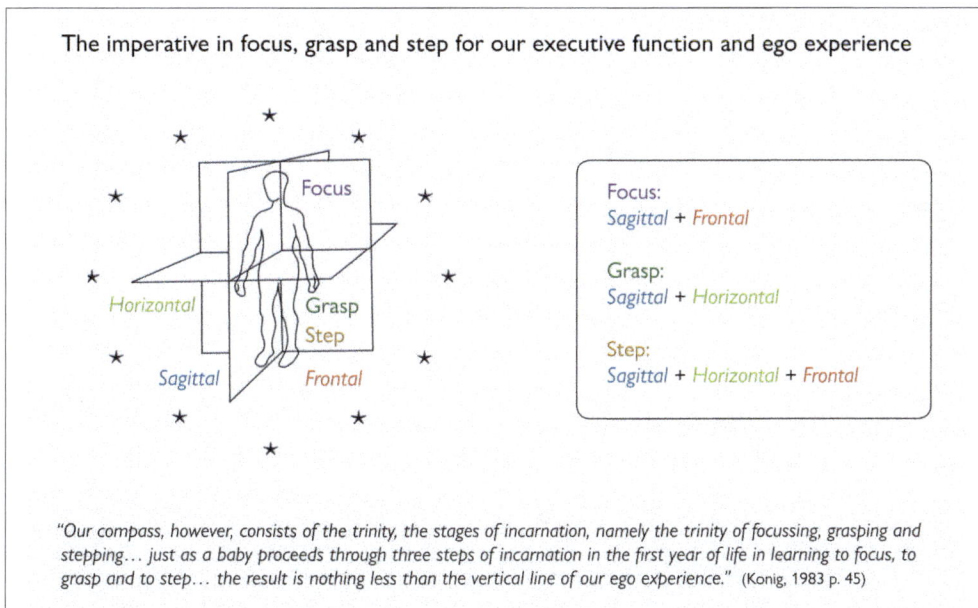

Focus:
Sagittal + Frontal

Grasp:
Sagittal + Horizontal

Step:
Sagittal + Horizontal + Frontal

"Our compass, however, consists of the trinity, the stages of incarnation, namely the trinity of focussing, grasping and stepping… just as a baby proceeds through three steps of incarnation in the first year of life in learning to focus, to grasp and to step… the result is nothing less than the vertical line of our ego experience." (Konig, 1983 p. 45)

The imperative in focus, grasp and step for weaving, blowing glass and forging

industrial processes and many others can be reimagined and reshaped through a new pedagogical paradigm. They can be measured as having significant impact on the destiny and learning journey of young people with needs – and they also benefit others. The reimagined industrial buildings themselves hold significant interest for the cultural and historical communities around them. These communities have given significant funds towards their renewal, from their initial condition of once having had potential to their current one of giving potential.

We can relearn through making. According to the founder of the Camphill movement Dr Karl König[138], focus, grasp and step are the prerequisites for further development that should be laid as foundations before the age of two. However, many of us – whether challenged or not – need to undertake some catch-up in various areas. Within craft making, a curriculum involving re-stepping back to those missed early developmental stages often provides what is needed to move on to the next level. The previous illustration shows the integration of the physical planes of space and action. These form the foundations of what we prize most of all in later life, namely executive functioning. Behind this executive functioning lies the capacity to move: to move thoughts, emotions and skill.

Epilogue

Bernard Graves

The power and potential of hands-on learning

Along with the replacement of the hands of the craftsman by the machine and the electronic circuit, and with the loss of traditional craft skills through an increasingly automated culture, we have, today, little opportunity for *hands-on learning* with natural materials.

It is today common for the processes of making and designing to unfold using designer software programmes. Once, when working for the charity *Tools for Self-Reliance*, I had the opportunity to collect from a secondary school an entire set of hand tools for woodworking. I believe the school was upgrading this department's equipment; hence, all older tools were now surplus to requirements. On arrival at the school, the nearly retired woodwork master – wearing the traditional brown overall coat of the tradesman – took me to the school's technical department and assisted me in carrying the many boxes of tools already packed for removal. I could see immediately from the empty state of the workshop that it was not fitted with any new woodworking tools. Somewhat perplexed, I asked the teacher what was happening to his department. When we finished packing a large van-load of boxes, he invited me to follow him to the school's new technological department.

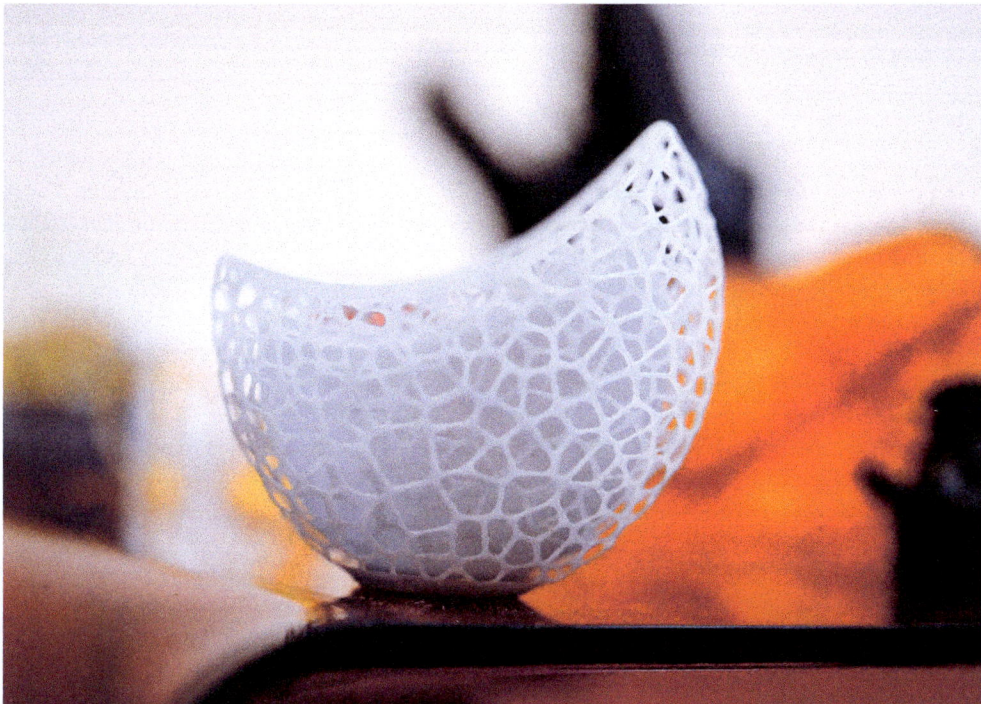

New technologies are changing the face of materials

The new technology department was fitted out with an array of computer consoles and other paraphernalia suited to the new designer technologies. Around each console were seated small groups of children, all engaged in looking at the screens and busily typing away. I approached one group to see what exactly they were doing.

They had the task to design a table – a boy explained that they were satisfied with the table top and were now trying to find appropriate legs. By pressing but one key the design of the leg could be changed in an instant from the baroque style to that of a Mackintosh. No saws and carpentry tools were needed any more. In the same room, a group of girls had the task to create a design for pizza packaging that would help sell the pizza. Clearly, advertising and marketing skills were now deemed more important than the traditional cookery lessons of old.

In this climate, both at school and in the home life, there are diminished opportunities for children and adults to be creative in their play or work through *hands-on* engagement.

Technological richness but skill poverty

Living in a de-skilled society we sadly forgo the joy and sense of achievement that creativity can give us. We stunt critical formative opportunities that handwork provides the growing child as well as transformative possibilities for the adult. Craftwork is *formative* in many more ways than is usually assumed. Crafting is not just about the skills acquired and what is made from the materials used but it is also about *the crafting of the maker* – the effects that the materials and process of working them have on the maker.

In the activity of *crafting*, head, heart and hands are brought into a very particular relationship. The *mind and imagination* are activated, *feelings and aesthetics* are awoken and the *hand and body* enlivened through an engagement with tools and materials. Craft activities also serve to convey a more hidden, transformative and therapeutic aspect to the maker when practising craft.

The very nature of handwork is to *bring order* and to *bestow order*; to bring order to the materials used and to bestow order upon the maker, the creator. In the practising of crafts, we have the potential to rise above our created state, to nurture and cultivate our creative capacities.

Dual action of the craft gesture

The vehicle for this dual action is what I have called (in Chapter Four) the *craft gesture*, which is evident and experienced at the hand of well executed and skilled movements of craftsmen and women. When these movements are acquired, they play upon the soul of the human being, providing *musicality*; a *beat* in the sphere of will, *rhythm* in the realm of the heart and feelings and *melody* in the field of thinking and ideas.

Perhaps as a child it was just this musicality of the blacksmith at work that I experienced and which captivated me from that moment onwards. It was as if the blacksmith – in his dancing and rhythmic striking on the anvil – had been transformed by some invisible being of movement, having the power to both transfix my gaze and transport my childlike soul.

In essence, the movements that the maker enters into in handwork and craft activities do not just develop motor skills. In executing working gestures the creative will of the maker is made subject to a greater governing order. It is in the very nature of this process that the character of the gesture works inwardly to foster the unfolding and harmonious development of cognition, aesthetic sensibility and practical know-how.

This book has hopefully outlined the case for *crafting* and *experiential learning* by encouraging the development of activities in the outdoor classroom setting. Throughout the school, this involves a renewal of the craft and associated practical skills curriculum related to the school grounds and environment. We believe that this approach fosters an ethos of *education for sustainability*. But more than this, it is a *regenerative education* and an education for *future-building*.

'The musicality of smithing'

Young people today live in times of rapid technological and societal change. Working in the outdoor classroom, wherever that may be in the manner described throughout this book, offers learners of all ages an opportunity to discover *real values* and many skills – both social and practical. These personal and social skills will help in shaping their lives and prepare them for their role as active participants in a society where we can live a more sustainable future.

Engaging young people in a conscious and meaningful way with their environment will help them learn to appreciate it and to care for it. Experience and current research by such organisations as Learning through Landscapes strongly suggest that well-cultivated school grounds do a great deal to support the moral development and well-being of the child. As we have described in several chapters of this book, another important potential engagement with the school grounds and its environs is to source raw materials for various traditional handcraft activities, for example digging clay from the school grounds for pottery and for kiln building.

Crafting: Transforming Materials & the Maker advocates an educational process that develops real powers of perception and judgement in relation to life and living. This, we believe, can be achieved by working cooperatively and collaboratively with teaching staff, parents and pupils together, across the school, on projects on the school grounds and in craft activities. Crafting develops an appreciation for beauty combined with functionality. Connecting to the various natural materials used across the curriculum will afford pupils a sense for the intrinsic moral nature of the materials and the natural world from which they come and will, in turn, provided pupils with a sense for their value.

From the authors

We have the privilege of living in extraordinary times, times that pose both existential and concrete threats to our civilisation as a whole. On one side we have the enormous environmental and social questions posed by global climate change, which our leaders appear unable to address. On the other hand, there are major concerns regarding employment and social stability posed by the adoption of an unregulated artificial intelligence that is 'unaligned' with human values, and which is already stripping away jobs, from both the bottom and middle of the labour market. Combined with resource exhaustion – from metals and minerals to water, from soil to oil – the ground beneath the feet of society, and of the individuals within it, is shifting in unknown and unpredictable ways.

It seems to us that a crucial response to such huge issues is to find ways to develop and express our true humanity. This response encompasses the social imperative of meeting the needs of the displaced, unemployed or oppressed, but it also calls upon us individually to develop our *creativity* – a unique facet of our species. History shows us that our *hands* are the key to the expression of creativity, of bringing into form the culture and values of each successive human civilisation.

We leave you with the thought that this ancient relationship of *working with our hands to transform materials,* a process which in turn shapes and transforms us, is a profound and fundamental part of our evolving humanity; nothing could be more significant in the times in which we live.

For readers that are interested in reading more about specific crafts and practical projects, Hands on Press will be publishing a series of booklets to follow on from this publication on crafting. Booklets will go into detail about crafting processes such as making traditional willow baskets, constructing wattle-and-daub lime kilns and calcining limestone.

I would like to extend heartfelt thanks the co-authors, illustrators and editor for working so diligently in the production of this book and all those teachers, parents and children that work, enjoy living and learning in the outdoor classroom, wherever that may be.

This end is but your beginning – Bernard Graves

Authors' Biographies

Bernard Graves

Consultant, Practitioner & tutor for experiential education & teacher training

Bernard is an experienced traditional craft practitioner and tutor, both with children and with adults, and he facilitates workshops in practical skills and activities combining ancient and contemporary technologies as a means to access vital areas of experience and learning. Bernard's decades of dedication to initiating and enabling practical craftwork in education informed his impulse to convene and oversee this co-authored book on the significance of *crafting* in education.

Bernard is the founder of *Pyrites: Living & Learning with Nature* (www.pyrites.org), an educational initiative that promotes and facilitates practical skills education in schools and practical skills teacher training courses throughout the UK and around the world.

Bernard founded Hands on Press to be able to co-ordinate the writing of this craft book and intends to follow this publication with a series of How to Make booklets in the various crafts and practical skills projects referred to in this publication.

Simon Gillman BA, MA(Education)

Outdoor educator and craft teacher

Simon worked extensively in the conservation movement in his early career. He ran volunteer work camps, then worked as a forester in Yorkshire, moving on to become an estate worker with the Nature Conservancy Council in Derbyshire and subsequently a contractor in Snowdonia National Park.

For the last 20 years Simon has taught gardening, forestry and green woodwork to adolescents in a Steiner school, as well as helping class teachers to integrate outdoor and practical work into their frontline teaching.

He has contributed to Steiner teacher training and led workshops in Germany, France and China, and recently completed a training in permaculture.

Johannes Steuck, BA, MSc.

Artist, teacher and author

Johannes is an art, craft and humanities teacher and regularly runs courses and workshops in stained glass and sculpture (www.johannesart.co.uk). As a practicing artist his major commissions include the Mourne Grange Chapel Windows (1996/97), Morton in the Marsh Lamps (2001), Life Processes Windows, Freeman College (2008).

Johannes has contributed to several books featuring the work of artist Greg Tricker (The Catacombs, Vox Humana Press 2002; Francis of Assisi, Paintings For Our Time, Green Books 2005; Kaspar Hauser, The Holy Fool and the Path of Sacrifice, Mill Wheel Art Press 2006). Johannes is the author of The Fire in the Snow, Anastasi (2008); White Sand and Grey Sand, Autobiography Vol.1 (2016).

Frances Graves

Teacher, teacher trainer & tutor for experiential education

Frances grew up on a farm on the island of Mull in Scotland. These early years spent on the farm fostered her practical side and her love for making things. Frances raised four children and worked as a Steiner Kindergarten teacher. She taught handwork classes in a Steiner School and, since learning about felting and natural plant dyeing of fleece, she has facilitated many adult teacher training workshops on felting. These workshops have included introductions to plant dyeing of fleece.

Frances is very interested in both the educational and therapeutic aspects of wool crafts and she has many years of first-hand experience in the great benefits of this craft for learners of all ages.

Jeannie Ireland, BSc.

Leatherworker, teacher trainer & tutor for experiential education

Jeannie's primary craft is leatherwork, including tanning the leather itself. Jeannie spent five years as an apprentice to a Native American Medicine teacher, during which time she learned to make rawhide and buckskin and to craft the tools of the Shamans' trade: rattles and drums.

Jeannie has worked in education both as a teacher and an educational administrator, working with learners of all ages, abilities and dispositions. Jeannie has taught at craft camps and delivered 'Animal skins to leather' workshops as part of Practical Skills Teacher Development courses. In 2017 Jeannie contributed to the development of 'Craft at the Centre', a Community Interest Company based in Stroud, which offers craft courses and bench space for local craftsmen and women.

Lucy Meikle

Basket maker, teacher trainer & tutor for experiential education

Lucy has been a basket making tutor at Ruskin Mill College, Nailsworth, for over 27 years. She is also a Senior Tutor at the College, working with a team of craft and land tutors engaged with the Practical Skills and Therapeutic Education programme that the College provides.

Lucy has been a key contributor to the holistic education provided by the College in the areas of craft, agriculture, nutrition, living skills, environment and commerce and has first-hand experience of how the crafts allow learners to break down their 'barriers to learning' and to realise their potential for making meaningful contributions to society.

Lucy runs workshops for both children and adults and has been a member of the Basket Making Association for 26 years.

Richard Turley, BSc. MSc.

Woodwork teacher, teacher trainer & tutor for experiential education

Richard was born north of Leeds between city and dales and spent much of his childhood outdoors. He studied Geology and developed a fascination for the wonderful geological history of his home land. Richard gained a PGCE in secondary school science. Life led him not into the classroom, however, but to the Cotswolds where he began teaching out on the land at Ruskin Mill College. He continues to teach young adults how to manage the woods, the craft of green woodwork, and shares with them his passion for storytelling.

Richard studied green woodwork with Gudrun Leitz and Mike Abbott. He recently completed a master's degree in Practical and Therapeutic Education and he continues to undertake research alongside his teaching, crafting and family life.

Sue Harker

Potter, teacher trainer and tutor for experiential education

Sue has been a teacher of pottery, art and gardening for over 25 years. Over the years she has become interested and engaged in dissolving subject boundaries and integrating craftwork, land work and practical skills throughout the school curriculum. She is very enthusiastic and committed to taking the experience of learning back to its source in the 'outdoor classroom'.

Sue is passionate about the value of craft as an educational medium and its power to foster a deep connection to the natural world. Sue has many years of experience in how the crafts enable and empower young people to develop the skills, resourcefulness and knowledge to become responsible stewards of the earth and to become well-rounded human beings. Sue co-directs a community craft centre in Stroud, Gloucestershire.

Arian Leljak

Professional blacksmith tutor and educator.

After arriving in the UK in 1989, Arian initially trained in Biodynamic agriculture and Art (Sculpture) and Waldorf education at Emerson College, Sussex.

He worked at Ruskin Mill College for young people with Special Educational Needs for 20 years. There he was involved with setting up blacksmithing as part of the outdoor craft curriculum.

Arian is a trained teacher and has worked with adults and children in public and school settings, and in craft camps, and has contributed to professional training and conferences on experiential education in the UK, Sweden and USA. He has trained with famous Swedish axe makers at Gransfors Bruks, and is inspired by the indigenous Scandinavian Sami craft and knife-making.

Currently Arian is a Director and tutor at Nailsworth Community Workshop and runs his own blacksmithing and knife-making workshops for the Home Education movement, the general public and schools.

Jonathan Code, BA, MEd.

Soap maker, teacher trainer and educational researcher

Jonathan was able to deepen a long-standing interest in the crafts and outdoor education when he was invited to teach soap making at Ruskin Mill College and to develop a 'practical chemistry' curriculum for the Hiram Trust. While developing a soap making workshop on the edge of a biodynamic farm, the integrative nature of the crafts became ever more apparent to Jonathan and his students. The transformative nature of crafting continues to be a 'touchstone' for Jonathan's ongoing work as an adult educator, a researcher and an author.

Jonathan is a co-director and core faculty member of Crossfields Learning, a higher education provider based in Stroud, UK (www.crossfieldslearninghub.com). His book Muck and Mind: Encountering Biodynamic Agriculture is published by Lindisfarne Books (2014).

Jo Clark

Land-based educator, tutor for experiential education

Jo grew up on a traditional farm in Devon where he learned many practical skills, including animal and plant husbandry as well as his deep love and appreciation of nature. Joe completed an Education Studies Degree in Steiner Education at Plymouth University and went on to teach science, games and crafts at Bristol Waldorf School, where he became inspired by an experiential approach to science. Jo took a full-time teaching post as a gardening teacher at the South Devon Steiner School where he designed an outdoor learning environment that supported and catalysed the classroom-based content of the Waldorf curriculum.

Jo developed a land-based education programme at Embercombe in Devon (www.embercombe) and ran it with colleagues for over ten years. He is currently one of the directors of On the Hill (www.onthehill.camp) where he and his colleague continue to offer land-based learning opportunities for schools and families.

Martin Levien
Craft practitioner, science teacher and tutor

Martin has worked in secondary schools, both state and Waldorf, as a science, outdoor activities and craft teacher for 36 years. Before that he worked as builder, carpenter and leather worker and had a smallholding. Martin has also worked in a psychiatric hospital and in social services. This wealth of experience informed his teaching in both the state sector and in Waldorf schools.

In his teaching career, Martin has had the good fortune to be able to take the science laboratory out into the outdoor classroom and – where appropriate – to develop an experiential and hands-on approach to science teaching, successfully incorporating landscape observations and practical skills and techniques in the process.

Hattie Duke
Outdoor education tutor and teacher trainer

Hattie Duke is the creator of 'Firelight: Hearth Centred Education, Adventures in Nature'. www.firelight.org.uk

She is currently based in Herefordshire but her life's journey over the years has taken her to work on practical projects in all the continents.

Hattie trained as a Waldorf Teacher, having worked as a class and subject teacher for a number of years. Trained by Bernard Graves in the Pyrites Practical Skills for Teachers training course, she is also a Forest School leader and an mentor, running woodland groups and facilitating nature connection work for children and adults of all ages throughout the seasons.

She is passionate about guiding children in the outdoor Classroom.

John Lawry, BA

Craft practitioner, outdoor educator and trainer
John trained and qualified as a teacher but after graduation he chose to take a year in solitary retreat to focus on sculpture, poetry and Zen practice.

After some years occupied with learning and practising crafts, John moved into teaching, beginning with a two-year, in-depth, in-service training as a Steiner teacher. he was a class teacher for 16 years, and also taught fine arts and hard materials technology in the high school.

In 2010, John began the process of establishing and developing a comprehensive outdoor classroom curriculum at Michael Park Steiner School New Zealand. Inevitably his skills and passion for craft and outdoor learning has involved him in running teacher training courses, consulting, presenting workshops and papers and organising conferences. John lives in Auckland, New Zealand.

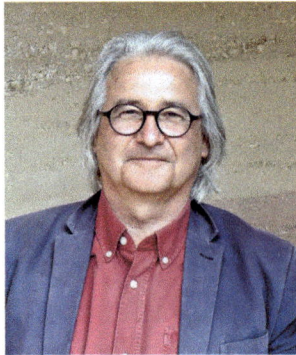

Aonghus Gordon, BA, PGCE, MEd

Founder and Executive Chair of Ruskin Mill Trust
In 1983, Aonghus founded Ruskin Mill Centre for Cultural Development. Through this he pioneered the Living Earth Training course for special needs education. In 1996, Ruskin Mill Trust was founded. In 2005, Aonghus was awarded Social Entrepreneur of the Year by Ernst and Young and *The Times* newspaper.

Ruskin Mill Trust currently delivers a unique specialist method, Practical Skills Therapeutic Education, across its five colleges and three schools. The inspiration is drawn from the work of Rudolf Steiner, John Ruskin and William Morris and is applied through a Goethean scientific method.

The Trust's research centre, the Field Centre, currently runs a Masters in Practical Skills Transformative Education in collaboration with Lillehammer Inland University, Norway. The Field Centre sponsors extensive research and currently supports four PhDs in craft pedagogy, biodynamic ecology and Rudolf Steiner's sensory integration, including research into the Trust's method itself. www.rmt.org

Ruskin Mill Trust currently works with initiatives in the US, China, Hungary and Norway.

Further reading

Abbott, M. *Green Woodwork*, Guild of Master Craftsmen Publications, 1989.

– Living Wood, *From Buying a Wood to Making a Chair,* Living Wood Books, 2004.

– Going with the Grain, *Making Chairs in the 21st Century,* Living Woods Books, 2011.

Alexander, John, actual name Jennie Alexander (1930–2018) *Make a Chair from a Tree: An Introduction to Working Green Wood,* 2nd edition, Taunton Press Inc. (1985).

Alexander, JD. *Make a Chair From a Tree: An Introduction to Working Green Wood.* The Taunton Press, 2011.

Auer, Arthur (1949– 2015), *Learning about the world through Modelling Sculptural ideas for School and home,*

Barn the Spoon. Spoon, *A Guide to Wood Carving and the New Wood Culture*, Virgin Books, 2017.

Bergström, Matti. *Sunrise Magazine,* Theosophical University Press, June/July 1991.

Brown, J. *Welsh Stick Chairs*, Stobart Davies Ammanford, 2009.

Burkett, ME. *The Art of the Felt Maker*, Titus Wilson and Son, 1979.

Coperthwaite, B. *A Handmade Life: In Search of Simplicity*, Chelsea Green, 2003.

Coperthwaite, William S. (1930–2013) A native of Maine, U.S.; pioneered yurt building in the United States. *A Handmade Life: In Search of Simplicity*, Chelsea Green Publishing Co (2007).

Crawford, Matthew, *The Case for Working with your Hands*, Penguin (2010)

Durrant-Peatfield, Dr Barry, MB BS LRCP MRCS: *Your Thyroid and How to Keep it Healthy: The Great Thyroid Scandal and How to Survive it*, Hammersmith Press, London (2006).

Gaudier-Brzeska, Henri, (1891–1915) French artist and sculptor who developed a rough-hewn, primitive style of direct carving.

Heaney, Seamus, *Door into the dark*, a collection of poems, Faber and Faber (1969)

Herrigel, Eugen , German philosophy professor, *Zen in the Art of Archery* (*Zen in der Kunst deBogenschießens*), Vingate (1999), (first published in1948).

Hill, Jack *Country Chair Making*, David & Charles (1998) ISBN-10: 0715303139

Korn, P. *Why We Make Things and Why it Matters*, David R Godine, 2014.

Langlands, A. *Craeft: How Traditional Crafts Are About More Than Just Making,* Faber and Faber, 2017. ISBN 9780571324408

Langsner, D. *Green Woodworking: A Hands on Approach*, Lark Books, 1995.

Law, B. *Woodland Craft*, Guild of Master Craftsmen, 2015.

Lehr, Ernst, PhD, *Man or Matter*, Aeterna publishing (2010).

Louv, Richard, *Last Child in the Woods: Saving our Children from Nature-Deficit Disorder*, Atlantic Books (2005) ISBN 978 1 84887 083 3

Mitchell, David and Livingston, Patricia, *Will-Developed Intelligence*, Association of Waldorf Schools in North America (1999),

Orr, David, *Developing the Global Teacher – Theory and Practice in initial Teacher Training*, edited by Miriam Steiner, Trentham Books Ltd. (1996)

Plotkin, B. *Nature and the Human Soul*, New World Library, 2008.

Pyne, Stephen, *Burning Bush: A Fire History of Australia*, University of Washington Press (1998).

Salomon, OA. *The Theory of Educational Sloyd*, Reprinted Nabu, 1898.

Schama, S. *Landscape and Memory*, Fontana, 1996.

Sennett, R. *The Craftsman*, Allen Lane, Penguin Books, 2008.

Sennett, Richard, OBE, FBA, FRSL (b.1943) *The Craftsman*, Penguin (2009) ISBN 9780300119091.

Smith, Sheila and Walker, Freda. *Feltmaking: The Whys and Wherefores*, Dalefelt Publications, York, 1995.

Steiner, Rudolf, 'Man, Hieroglyph of the Universe', 16 lectures given in Dornach, Switzerland, between 9th April and 16th May 1920.

Titman, Wendy, *Special Places, Special People: The Hidden Curriculum of School Grounds*, Southgate Publishers (1994).

Steiner, Rudolf, *The Foundations of Human Experience*, 14 lectures previously titled *Study of Man,* Anthroposophic Press (1996), (first published 1918).

Turnau, Irena. *Hand-Felting in Europe and Asia from the Middle Ages to the 20th Century*, Warsaw, 1997.

Vogel, J. *The Artful Wooden Spoon*, Chronicle Books, 2015.

Williams, F. *The Nature Fix*, W.W. Norton & Company, 2017.

Wilson, Edward O, *Biophilia*, Harvard University Press (1984).

Waldorf Publications (2001).

Wilson, Frank R, MD, Stanford University. *The hand, how its use shapes the brain, language and human culture*. New York, Vintage Books (1998).

Wilson, Frank R, MD, Clinical professor of Neurology, Stanford University. *The hand, how its use shapes the brain, language and human culture*. New York, Vintage Books (1998).

Winnicott, DW. *Playing and Reality*, Routledge Books, 2005.

Wymer, N. *English Country Crafts*, Batsford, 1946.

Whymer, Norman, *English Country Crafts*, B.T. Batsford Ltd (1946).

Endnotes

1. Dr Matti Bergström (1922–2014) Finnish professor of neurology and researcher at University of Helsinki.

2. Steiner Waldorf education: Rudolf Steiner & Steiner Schools: The first Steiner school opened in Stuttgart in 1919 for children of workers at the Waldorf–Astoria cigarette factory. The school's benefactor was Managing Director Emil Molt, who asked Dr Rudolf Steiner to found and lead the school in its early stages.

   This philosopher and scientist's insights inspired what has become a worldwide movement of schools that espouse and promote universal human values, educational pluralism and meaningful teaching and learning opportunities. This progressive, international schools movement is noted by educationalists, doctors, policy-makers and parents for the effective education that it offers children. The ideas and principles which inform the education provide a credible and thoughtful perspective to the debate on education and human development. Steiner schools are always co-educational, fully comprehensive, and take pupils from 3 to (ideally) 18. They welcome children of all abilities from all faiths and backgrounds.

3. 'Man, Hieroglyph of the Universe', 16 lectures Given in Dornach, Switzerland, between 9th April and 16th May 1920 by Rudolf Steiner.

4. Frank R Wilson MD, Clinical professor of Neurology, Stanford University. *The hand, how its use shapes the brain, language and human culture*. New York, Vintage Books (1998).

5. Dr Matti Bergström (1922–2014), Finnish professor of neurology and researcher.

6. David Orr is the Paul Sears Distinguished Professor of Environmental Studies and Politics at Oberlin College and a James Mars Professor at the University of Vermont.

7. Wilfred Wellock (1879–1972), socialist Gandhian and sometime Labour politician and MP.

8. Suzi Leather, 'RSA Focus on Food Campaign', *Teaching and Learning Design and Technology*. edited by John Eggleston. Continuum, London and New York (2000). Further reading: Craft Council Publication, 'Learning through making: an executive summary' – UK Craft Council (1998), endorsed by Sheffield, Manchester & Reading universities.

9. M Voříšková, *Gypsy Folk Tales*, Hamlyn (1966)

10. Vusamazulu Credo Mutwa, *Indaba My Children: African Folk Tales*, Blue Crane Books (1964)

11. Georg Kuhlewind, *From Normal to Healthy* Lindisfarne Press (1988)

12. David Orr, *Developing the Global Teacher – Theory and Practice in initial Teacher Training*, edited by Miriam Steiner, Trentham Books Ltd. (1996)

13. Ken Robinson: TED talks, TED2006: "Do Schools Kill Creativity?" at 10.44

    https://www.ted.com/talks/ken_robinson_says_schools_kill_creativity?referrer=playlist-the_most_popular_talks_of_all#t-504458 https://www.unicef.org/media/files/ChildPovertyReport.pdf

14. Mary Bousted, general secretary of the Association of Teachers and Lecturers (ATL), says, 'We know 50,000 teachers left last year, that's 11% of the workforce, and we will have 300,000 more pupils in our schools by 2020. It's largely due to the toxic mix of accountability pressures, curriculum and qualification reform, compounded by mixed messages from the government.' The article also suggests 50% of state school teachers intend to leave in the next 5 years.

15. 'Primary School Children lose marks in SATS tests for misshapen commas' *Guardian*, 10.7.2017

16. Cambridge Review, p.32.

17. *The hand, how its use shapes the brain, language and human culture*. New York, Vintage Books (1998).

18. see www.pestalozzi.org.uk

19. Celestin Freinet (1896–1966).

20. J Dewey, *Democracy and Education*, Simon and Brown (2011).

21. www.la-ferme-des-enfants.com

22. Rudolf Steiner, Austrian philosopher (1861–1925). www.rudolfsteinerweb.com/Rudolf_Steiner_Biography.php

23. Christopher Clouder and Martin Rawson, *Waldorf Education*, Floris Books (2003).

24. Hans van der Stock, Founding member of the Camphill Community, Thornbury. 'The Spiritual Origin of Everyday Things' (1986).

25. Mark Cartwright *Aztec Art – Definition*. https://www.ancient.eu/Aztec_Art/

    Further reading: The Met- Heilbrunn Timeline of Art History Aztec Stone Sculpture https://www.metmuseum.org/toah/

26. 'Ceramic and Glass Materials: Role in Civilization', *A Brief History of Ceramics and Glass*. https://ceramics.org/about/what-are-engineered-ceramics-and-glass/brief-history-of-ceramics-and-glass

27. The Venus from Hohle Fels is actually the oldest figurine of a woman made by human kind. The statuette is around 40,000 to 35,000 years old and was carved from mammoth ivory. The Venus broke to pieces during the time she laid in the sediment.

28. Endnotes

29. Mircea Eliade, *The Forge and the Crucible*, 'Masters of Fire' p.79 The University of Chicago Press, Chicago and London (1978).

30. The earliest evidence for controlled use of fire outside of Africa is at the Lower Paleolithic site of **Gesher Benot Ya'aqov** in Israel, where charred wood and seeds were recovered from a site dated 790,000 years ago. The next oldest site is at **Zhoukoudian**, a Lower Paleolithic site in China dated to about 400,000 BP, Beeches Pit in the UK at about 400,000 years ago, and at **Qesem Cave** (Israel), between about 200,000–400,000 years ago. https://www.thoughtco.com/qesem-cave-in-israel-172282

31. Further Reference: Stephen Pyne *Burning Bush: A Fire History of Australia*, University of Washington Press (1998). Further reading: Ernst Lehr PhD, *Man or Matter*, Aeterna publishing (2010).

32. *History and Development of Pottery* https://en.wikipedia.org/wiki/Pottery Note the following approximate time periods: **Stone Age Art** (40,000–2500BC) **Bronze Age Art** (3000–1100BC) **Iron Age Art** (1100–200BC).

Paleolithic Pottery

Up until the 1990s, most archaeologists and anthropologists believed that pottery was first made during the period of **Neolithic art** (c.8000–2500BC), after the Ice Age ended, when humans turned from hunter-gathering to farming and animal husbandry. However, the discoveries at Xianrendong and Yuchanyan, together with the cache of Jomon pottery discovered at Odaiyamamoto I site (14540BC) at Aomori Prefecture, Japan, prove beyond doubt that ceramic pottery was being made ten thousand years earlier, during the European era of **Solutrean art** (20000–15000BC) – a surprising development given the relative absence of Chinese **cave art** during this period. Moreover, with better dating techniques being developed, it is probable that we will find even older sites from the Middle period of the Upper Paleolithic. For primitive Stone Age cooking pots, all that was needed was a supply of clay and a source of heat.

Thus, most Chinese pottery of the Upper Paleolithic (until about 10000BC) was roughly made earthenware, fired in bonfires for a short time at temperatures up to 900°C. Vessels were made with round bottoms, thus avoiding any sharp angles or rims that would be more prone to cracking. Glazes were not used, while decoration was limited to the use of coiled ropes and basketry. (In Japan, from about 14000BC, the Jomon culture was named after the decorative technique of leaving impressions on the outside of the pot, by pressing rope into the clay before firing it.)

33. The Venus of Dolní Věstonice (**Czech:** Věstonická venuše) is a **Venus figurine**, a **ceramic statuette** of a nude female figure dated to 29000–25000bc (**Gravettian industry**). It was found at the **Paleolithic** site **Dolní Věstonice** in the **Moravian basin** south of **Brno**, in the base of **Děvín Mountain**, 549 m (1,801 ft). This **figurine** and a few others from locations nearby are the oldest known **ceramic** articles in the world. Wikipedia.

34. Medieval Guilds and Craft Production http://employees.oneonta.edu/farberas/arth/ARTH200/artist/guilds.html

    'The development of guilds during the later Middle Ages was a crucial stage in the professional development of artists. The power of the artists during this period was not based on their individual capacities as we will see being developed during the Renaissance, but their willingness to join together and act as a collective. Within towns and cities during the later Middle Ages the different practitioners of a particular craft, whether it be the cloth makers, shoemakers, apothecaries, masons, painters, sculptors, joined together to form guilds that were able to gain control of the production, standards, and marketing of the particular craft. As individuals, the craftsman had little power, but as a group they were able to have extraordinary power. Through the development of guilds, artisans were able to pull themselves out of the ranks of serfs on the estates of members of the nobility and day laborers, much like migrant workers today, to establish associations that could protect their social and economic autonomy'

35. *Learning through making: a national enquiry into the value of creative practical education in Britain*, The Craft Council (1998)

36. Jos Verhulsts, *Developmental Dynamics in Humans and Other Primates: Discovering Evolutionary Principles through Comparative Morphology*, Floris (2003)

37. Immanuel Kant, German philosopher (1724–1804).

38. Basle Course, 1920.

39. David Papineau, *Get a Grip* https://archive.nytimes.com/www.nytimes.com/books/98/07/19/reviews/980719.19 papinet.html

40. Fight-or-flight response: https://en.wikipedia.org/wiki/Fight-or-flight_response

41. Matti Bergström (1922 – 2014) Finnish professor of neurology and researcher at University of Helsinki.

42. Matti Bergström article on 'Finger Blindness':

    'The brain discovers what the fingers explore. The density of nerve endings in our fingertips is enormous. Their discrimination is almost as good as that of our eyes. If we don't use our fingers, if in childhood and youth we become 'finger-blind', this rich network of nerves is impoverished – which represents a huge loss to the brain and thwarts the individual's all-round development. Such damage may be likened to blindness itself. Perhaps worse, while a blind person may simply not be able to find this or that object, the finger-blind cannot understand its inner meaning and value. If we neglect to develop and train our children's fingers and the creative form-building capacities of their hand muscles, then we neglect to develop their understanding of the unity of things; we thwart their aesthetic and creative powers.

    Those who shaped our age-old traditions always understood this. But today Western civilisation, an information-obsessed society that overvalues science and undervalues true worth, has forgotten it all. We are 'value-damaged'. The philosophy of our upbringing is science-centred and our schools are programmed toward that end. These schools have no time for the creative potential of the nimble fingers and hand and that arrests the all-round development of our children – and of the whole community.'

43. Arthur Auer (1949– 2015), Arts teacher and educator in the USA. *Learning about the world through Modelling Sculptural ideas for School and home*, Waldorf Publications (2001).

44. Arvia MacKaye Ege (1902–1989), former Waldorf School handwork teacher, daughter of the playwright Percy MacKaye, founded the Rudolph Steiner Association in Ghent, New York, which became the umbrella organization for the Hawthorne Valley Farm at the Hawthorne Valley School,

the Hawthorne Valley Visiting Students Program, an environmental centre, and the Hawthorne Valley Artists and Artisans. She was the author of *The Secret Iron of the Heart, The Battle for the Sunlight: A Modern Legend* and *The Power of the Impossible*.

45. Prof. Suzanne Kemmer, 'The Origin and Evolution of Human Language' https://www.ruf.rice.edu/~kemmer/Evol/opposablethumb.html

46. Bart Blankenship, *Earth Knack: Stone Age Skills for the 21st Century*, Gibbs Smith (1996)

47. Frank R Wilson MD, Clinical professor of Neurology, Stanford University. *The hand, how its use shapes the brain, language and human culture*. New York, Vintage Books (1998).

    The human hand is a miracle of biomechanics, one of the most remarkable adaptations in the history of evolution. The hands of a concert pianist can elicit glorious sound and stir emotion; those of a surgeon can perform the most delicate operations; those of a rock climber allow him to scale a vertical mountain wall. Neurologist Frank R. Wilson makes the striking claim that it is because of the unique structure of the hand and its evolution in cooperation with the brain that Homo sapiens became the most intelligent, preeminent animal on the earth. In this fascinating book, Wilson moves from a discussion of the hand's evolution – and how its intimate communication with the brain affects such areas as neurology, psychology, and linguistics – to provocative new ideas about human creativity and how best to nurture it. Like Oliver Sacks and Stephen Jay Gould, Wilson handles a daunting range of scientific knowledge with a surprising deftness and a profound curiosity about human possibility. Provocative, illuminating, and delightful to read, The Hand encourages us to think in new ways about one of our most taken-for-granted assets.

    'A mark of the book's excellence [is that] it makes the reader aware of the wonder in trivial, everyday acts, and reveals the complexity behind the simplest manipulation.' *Washington Post*

48. http://www.visual-arts-cork.com/prehistoric-art-timeline.htm Prehistoric Art Timeline (2.5 Million–500BC). Further reading: Jo Marchan, 'A Journey to the Oldest Cave Paintings in the World', Smithsonian Magazine. The discovery in a remote part of Indonesia has scholars rethinking the origins of art – and of humanity. https://www.smithsonianmag.com/history/journey-oldest-cave-paintings-world-180957685/#3o7sv1AHSGvgLlBg.99

49. Rudolf Steiner, *The Foundations of Human Experience*, 14 lectures previously titled *Study of Man,* Anthroposophic Press (1996), (first published 1918).

50. ibid.

51. Eugen Herrigel, German philosophy professor, *Zen in the Art of Archery* (*Zen in der Kunst des Bogenschießens*), Vingate (1999), (first published in1948).

52. 'When with our limbs we carry out Repetitive, Regular Movements the Cosmic Heavenly Bodies echo in our movements'. Rudolf Steiner, *The Foundations of Human Experience*, 14 lectures previously titled *Study of Man,* Anthroposophic Press (1996), (first published 1918).

53. Mel Robin *Muscle Memory: A Handbook for Yogasana Teachers – The incorporation of Neuroscience, Physiology, and Anatomy into the Practice,* Wheatmark (2009)

54. David Mitchell and Patricia Livingston: *Will-Developed Intelligence*, Association of Waldorf Schools in North America (1999), p. 9.

55. 'Overview of Learning Styles', *The 7 styles of learning*, www.learning-styles-online.com/overview/

56. Seymour M. Berger and Suzanne W. Hadley 'Some Effects of a Model's Performance on an Observer's Electromyographic Activity', *American Journal of Psychology*, 88, 2, 263-76, Jun 75.

57. Why Teach Knit & Crochet: Craft yarn Council https://www.craftyarncouncil.com/classbenefits.html

58. Scientific research thus confirms what Rudolf Steiner described in 1920: our finger movements are significant teachers of elasticity in our thinking. A person with very clumsy hands will also not be a very subtle thinker. He or she will tend to think in less subtle terms and will tend to be more suited to materialism. This is because in order to be able to grasp a spiritual world-view, we require fine-meshed thoughts. Rudolf Steiner then went on to speak of Waldorf education in which, for

such very reasons, the boys as well as the girls learn to crochet and knit. Waldorf teachers need to know the significance of being able to move our fingers skilfully. Briefly said: our finger movements influence our brain and ability to think – which has now been proved scientifically. Rudolf Steiner, 'Man, Hieroglyph of the Universe' 25th April 1920.

59. Hella Krause- Zimmer. 'The Brain and Finger Dexterity', *Das Goetheanum*, 14th Jan 1996

60. King Thrushbeard, tale no.52, Grimm brothers (1812).
http://rspb.royalsocietypublishing.org/content/early/2011/07/12/rspb.2011.1024.short

61. Frank R Wilson MD, Clinical professor of Neurology, Stanford University. The hand, how its use shapes the brain, language and human culture. New York, Vintage Books (1998).

62. Berthold Laufer, The Early History of Felt, http://www.marisadobiash.com/uploads/1/0/8/7/10876720/american_anthropologist_history_of_felt.pdf
https://www.freunde-waldorf.de/en/the-friends/publications/catalogue-waldorf-education/nimble-fingers-make-nimble-minds/

63. Immanuel Kant, German (1724–1804), German philosopher, a central figure in modern philosophy.

64. Dr Matti Bergström (1922–2014) Finnish professor of neurology and researcher at University of Helsinki.

65. Frank R. Wilson is the medical director of the Peter F. Ostwald Health Program for Performing Artists at the University of California School of Medicine, San Francisco.

66. B. B. McBride, C. A. Brewer, A. R. Berkowitz, W. T. Borrie, 'Environmental literacy, ecological literacy, Eco literacy: What do we mean and how did we get here?' First published: 31 May 2013
https://doi.org/10.1890/ES13-00075.1

Abstract: Numerous scholars have argued that the terms environmental literacy, ecological literacy, and ecoliteracy have been used in so many different ways and/or are so all-encompassing that they have very little useful meaning. However, despite the seemingly arbitrary and, at times, indiscriminate use of these terms, tremendous efforts have in fact been made to explicitly define and delineate the essential components of environmental literacy, ecological literacy, and ecoliteracy, and to firmly anchor their characterizations in deep theoretical and philosophical foundations. A driving purpose behind these ongoing conversations has been to advance complete, pedagogy-guiding, and broadly applicable frameworks for these ideals, allowing for standards and assessments of educational achievement to be set. In this manuscript, we review a diversity of perspectives related to the often nuanced differences and similarities of these terms. A classification of the numerous proposed frameworks for environmental literacy, ecological literacy, and ecoliteracy (advanced within the fields of environmental education, ecology, and the broader humanities, respectively) is presented, and used to compare and contrast frameworks across multiple dimensions of affect, knowledge, skills, and behavior. This analysis facilitates close examination of where we have been, where we are, and where we might be headed with respect to these vital conversations. This work also offers points of reference for continued critical discourse, and illuminates a diversity of inspiration sources for developing and/or enriching programs aimed at cultivating these types of literacies.

What is Literacy?

Until the late 1800s, the word literacy did not exist. In fact, according to the Oxford English Dictionary, the word literacy was predated by the word illiteracy by several hundred years (Venezky et al. 1987). Although the original term literacy referred only to the ability to read and write, its usage has si nce been extended greatly in scope, beginning during the Industrial Revolution. Emerging in Britain in the late 18th century and then spreading throughout Western Europe and North America, the Industrial Revolution was a period of rapid industrial growth via the introduction and advancement of machinery, with far-reaching social and economic consequences. During this era, mandatory and widespread elementary public education grew to resemble its present magnitude. Although the precise relationship between industrialization and the rise of public education is difficult to establish, there are nevertheless strong correspondences between the two (Carl 2009). Gains in income and wealth during the industrial age made possible larger public expenditures for the welfare of the general population, in the form of schools and teaching resources. A focus on the three Rs, reading, writing, arithmetic, was seen as essential for preparing a work force that could understand basic instructions, engage in rudimentary written communication, and perform simple office functions, thereby creating the most skilled mass workforce in the world. Additionally, through the cultivation of the western cultural perspective emphasizing rational individuals and egalitarianism, public education promoted a sense of national unity and success (Carl 2009). In the years following the Civil War, the ability to read and write was used to determine whether one had the right to vote. Thus, like other abstract nouns such as freedom, justice, and equality, literacy came to denote a value that was promoted throughout the population of the United States. Government officials, industrial leaders, and educators all began to see illiteracy as a social ill and literacy as something to be advanced for the benefit of society as a whole (Michaels and O'Connor 1990, Carl 2009).

Current dictionaries (e.g., Merriam Webster, Oxford English Dictionary) generally provide two definitions of literacy: (1) the ability to read and write, and (2) knowledge or capability in a particular field or fields. Today's broader understanding and application of literacy has essentially arisen from the latter interpretation (Roth 1992). Within the field of cognitive science, literacy has been reconceptualized as a tool for knowledge construction (i.e., using reasoning or problem solving to obtain new knowledge) (Michaels and O'Connor 1990). This work set the stage for the extended scope of the term used today. As defined by the United Nations Educational, Scientific, and Cultural Organization (UNESCO Education Sector 2004:13), "[l]iteracy involves a continuum of learning in enabling individuals to achieve their goals, to develop their knowledge and potential, and to participate fully in their community and wider society".

Clearly, the concept of literacy has evolved considerably from its origin in the ability to read and write. Especially over the last 50 years, expectations for a literate citizenry have been extended to include the ability to understand, make informed decisions, and act with respect to complex topics and issues facing society today. The term literacy also has been extended to refer to such knowledge and capabilities in many different discourses (e.g., computer literacy, mathematics literacy, cultural literacy, arts literacy). Additional notions of literacy that have emerged are environmental literacy, ecological literacy, and ecoliteracy.

Environmental Literacy, Ecological Literacy, Ecoliteracy

Numerous scholars have argued that the terms environmental literacy or ecological literacy have been used in so many different ways and/or are so all-encompassing that they have very little useful meaning (e.g., Disinger and Roth 1992, Roth 1992, Stables and Bishop 2001, Payne 2005, 2006). The introduction of the term ecoliteracy has further complicated the conversation. Disinger and Roth (1992) contended that the almost arbitrary application of the term environmental literacy has resulted in nearly as many different perceptions of the term as there are people who use it, and that while various groups often use the term to solidify or demonstrate correctness of either themselves or their clients, they give little or no indication of what they actually mean. Similarly, Stables and Bishop (2001) argued that the meaning of environmental literacy has been greatly muddled as a result of its indiscriminate application. Recently, Payne (2005, 2006) also dismissed the notions of environmental or ecological literacy as vague and messy, arguing instead for a "critical ecological ontology," a curriculum theory focusing on the learner's experience of being in the world. Given the multitude of literacies now being promoted, and the widespread and seemingly arbitrary use of the terms environmental-, ecological-, and eco-literacy in particular, it is easy to see how these authors made these assessments.

Despite the widespread, and at times, indiscriminate, use of these terms, efforts have been made to establish a definition and identify key components of environmental literacy, ecological literacy, and ecoliteracy, and to firmly anchor their characterizations in broad theoretical and philosophical frameworks. A driving purpose behind this work has been to advance complete, pedagogy-guiding, and broadly applicable frameworks allowing for standards and assessments of educational achievement to be set. Widely varying discourses on the nature and essential components of environmental literacy, ecological literacy, and ecoliteracy have arisen primarily within the fields of environmental education, ecology, and the broader humanities, respectively.

The term environmental literacy was first used 45 years ago in an issue of the Massachusetts Audubon by Roth (1968) who inquired "How shall we know the environmentally literate citizen?" Since then, the meaning of the term has evolved and been extensively reviewed (e.g., Roth 1992, Simmons 1995, Morrone et al. 2001, Weiser 2001, North American Association for Environmental Education (NAAEE) 2004, O'Brien 2007). The notion of environmental literacy has been and continues to be promoted through creative and intensive discourse from a diversity of perspectives. The most widely accepted meaning of environmental literacy is that it comprises an awareness of and concern about the environment and its associated problems, as well as the knowledge, skills, and motivations to work toward solutions of current problems and the prevention of new ones (NAAEE 2004).

More recently, the term ecological literacy was first publicly used 27 years ago by Risser (1986) in his Address of the Past President to the Ecological Society of America. Risser (1986) urged ecologists to ponder, debate, and arrive at consensus as to what comprises basic ecological literacy, adopt a vigorous stance, and embrace their responsibilities as promoters of ecological literacy in their students and the general public. Since then, characterization of ecological literacy within the field of ecology has evolved considerably (Cherrett 1989, Klemow 1991, Odum 1992, Berkowitz 1997, Berkowitz et al. 2005, Jordan et al. 2009, Powers 2010), focusing on the key ecological knowledge necessary for informed decision-making, acquired through scientific inquiry and systems thinking.

The term ecoliteracy was first published 16 years ago by Capra (1997), who founded the Center for Ecoliteracy, a nonprofit organization dedicated to education for sustainable living (Center for Ecoliteracy 2013a). Drawing heavily on the work of Orr (1992), Capra and others in the broader humanities have advanced ecoliteracy, with a focus on the creation of sustainable human communities and society (e.g., Capra 1997, 2002, Cutter-Mackenzie and Smith 2003, Wooltorton 2006, Center for Ecoliteracy 2013b).

Despite a shared concern for the environment and recognition of the central role of education in enhancing human-environment relationships, researchers have adopted widely differing discourses on what it mean for a person to be environmentally literate, ecologically literate, or ecoliterate. We approached the multiplicity of theoretical and practical perspectives by developing a classification of the literacy conversation. This involved considering similar propositions within groups (i.e., within the fields of environmental education, ecology, and the humanities), describing each of these groupings and distinguishing it from the others, and highlighting areas of similarity and divergence.

We focused on comparing definitional treatments of environmental, ecological, and ecoliteracy. That is, we focused on contributions that explicitly used one of these terms and attempted to provide or refine a precise definition or framework to describe it. A definition attests to and presents as a description "… a statement of the exact meaning of a word …" or "… the nature, scope, or meaning of something … ," attributing to a term a commonly understood precise meaning (Oxford Dictionaries 2013). Such an approach characterizes a phenomenon as embodying a compendium of key attributes, defined a priori (see Davis and Ruddle 2010). We focused on contributions that took this approach to (re)defining environmental, ecological, or ecoliteracy. As it was impossible to consider all relevant contributions to our collective understanding of human-environment relationships, our focus on definitions and frameworks served to set practical limits on the scope of our study.

In contrast to a definitional approach, a conceptual approach regards phenomena as abstract ideas, whose attributes arise from a particular and identifiable theoretical framework concerning the factors that organize human relationships and affect the human condition (Davis and Ruddle 2010). Stable and Bishop's (2001) and Payne's (2005, 2006) aforementioned critiques of efforts to characterize these types of literacies are based on the argument that these approaches are definitional rather than conceptual/theoretical. Indeed, these are entirely different ways of understanding and explaining phenomena, but they are both valid (Davis and Ruddle 2010). We recognize that innumerable other contributions, on a global scale and throughout history, have directly or indirectly led to broader theoretical conceptualizations related to these types of literacies, often without even naming them as such. However, it was beyond the scope of our study to consider all of these contributions.

In this manuscript, we trace the evolution of the term environmental literacy within the field of environmental education. We also examine the development of the more recent terms ecological literacy and ecoliteracy, and explore how and why they evolved from environmental literacy. We present a classification of the numerous proposed frameworks for environmental literacy, ecological literacy, and ecoliteracy, and compare and contrast these frameworks across multiple dimensions of affect, knowledge, skills, and behavior. This analysis facilitates close examination of where we have been, where we are, and where we might be headed with respect to these vital conversations. This work also offers points of reference for continuing critical discourse and illuminates a diversity of inspiration sources for developing and/or enriching programs aimed at cultivating these types of literacies.

Table 1. Components of environmental literacy, adapted from Simmons (1995).

Component	Description
Affect	• Environmental sensitivity or appreciation, in terms of responsible attitudes toward pollution, technology, economics, conservation, and environmental action, and a willingness to recognize and choose among differing value perspectives associated with problems and issues. Motivation to actively participate in environmental improvement and protection, desire to clarify one's own values, and confidence to make decisions and judgments about environmental issues according to one's sense of morality.
Ecological knowledge	• An ability to communicate and apply major ecological concepts including those focusing on individuals, species, populations, communities, ecosystems, and biogeochemical cycles. An understanding of energy production and transfer, and the concepts of interdependence, niche, adaptation, succession, homeostasis, limiting factors, and humans as ecological variables. An understanding of how natural systems work, as well as how social systems interface with natural systems.
Socio-political knowledge	• A clear awareness of economic, social, political and ecological interdependence in urban and rural areas; i.e., how human cultural activity influences the environment from an ecological perspective. An understanding of the basic structure and scale of societal systems and of the relationships between beliefs, political structures, and environmental values of various cultures. Geographic understanding at local, regional, and global levels and recognition of patterns of change in society and culture.
Knowledge of environmental issues	• An understanding of various environmentally-related problems and issues and how they are influenced by political, educational, economic, and governmental institutions. Understandings of air quality, water quality and quantity, soil quality and quantity, land use and management for wildlife habitat, and human population, health, and waste.
Cognitive skills	• Identification and definition of environmental problems/issues, and the analysis, synthesis, and evaluation of information about these issues using both primary and secondary sources and one's personal values. Abilities for selecting appropriate action strategies and creating, evaluating, and implementing action plans. Abilities to conduct scientific inquiry and basic risk analysis, think in terms of systems, and to forecast, think ahead, and plan.
Environmentally responsible behaviors (ERB)	• Active participation aimed at problem solving and issues resolution. Action through selected lifestyle activities, including environmentally sound consumer purchasing, using methods for conserving resources; assisting with the enforcement of environmental regulations; using personal and interpersonal means to encourage environmentally sound practices; and supporting environmentally sound policies and legislative initiatives.
Additional determinants of ERB	• A locus of control and assumption of personal responsibility. Locus of control is an individual's perception of his or her ability to bring about change because of his or her behavior; individuals possessing an internal locus of control believe their actions are likely to advance change (see Hines et al. 1986, Newhouse 1990).

67. William S. Coperthwaite (1930–2013) A native of Maine, U.S.; pioneered yurt building in the United States. *A Handmade Life: In Search of Simplicity*, Chelsea Green Publishing Co (2007).

68. Richard Sennett OBE, FBA, FRSL (b.1943) Centennial Professor of Sociology at the London School of Economics and former University Professor of the Humanities at New York University. He is currently a Senior Fellow of the Center on Capitalism and Society at Columbia University. *The Craftsman*, Penguin (2009) ISBN 9780300119091.

69. Henri Gaudier-Brzeska (1891–1915) French artist and sculptor who developed a rough-hewn, primitive style of direct carving.

70. Constantin Brâncuși (Romanian: [konstanˈtin brɨŋˈkuʃ]; (1876–1957) Romanian sculptor, painter and photographer who made his career in France. Considered a pioneer of modernism, one of the

most influential sculptors of the 20th century, Brâncuși is called the patriarch of modern sculpture. As a child he displayed an aptitude for carving wooden farm tools. Formal studies took him first to Bucharest, then to Munich, then to the École des Beaux-Arts in Paris from 1905 to 1907. His art emphasises clean geometrical lines that balance forms inherent in his materials with the symbolic allusions of representational art. Brâncuși sought inspiration in non-European cultures as a source of primitive exoticism, as did Paul Gauguin, Pablo Picasso, André Derain and others. However, other influences emerge from Romanian folk art traceable through Byzantine and Dionysian traditions.

71. Benjamin Lauder Nicholson (1894–1982) English painter of abstract compositions (sometimes in low relief), landscape and still life.

72. Valentin Louis Georges Eugène Marcel Proust (1871–1922) French novelist, critic, and essayist best known for his monumental novel *À la recherche du temps* perdu (*In Search of Lost Time*, earlier rendered as *Remembrance of Things Past*), published in seven parts between 1913 and 1927. He is considered by critics and writers to be one of the most influential authors of the 20th century.

73. Rudolf Steiner, *The Study of Man* (1918), Chapter 4.

74. Richard Sennett, *The Craftsman*, Penguin (2009) ISBN 9780300119091.

75. John Dewey (1859–1952) American philosopher, psychologist, and educational reformer whose ideas have been influential in education and social reform. Dewey is one of the primary figures associated with the philosophy of pragmatism and is considered one of the fathers of functional psychology. A Review of General Psychology survey, published in 2002, ranked Dewey as the 93rd most cited psychologist of the 20th century. A well-known public intellectual, he was also a major voice of progressive education and liberalism. Although Dewey is known best for his publications about education, he also wrote about many other topics, including epistemology, metaphysics, aesthetics, art, logic, social theory, and ethics. He was a major educational reformer for the 20th century. The overriding theme of Dewey's works was his profound belief in democracy, be it in politics, education, or communication and journalism. As Dewey himself stated in 1888, while still at the University of Michigan, 'Democracy and the one, ultimate, ethical ideal of humanity are to my mind synonymous.' Known for his advocacy of democracy, Dewey considered two fundamental elements–schools and civil society–to be major topics needing attention and reconstruction to encourage experimental intelligence and plurality. Dewey asserted that complete democracy was to be obtained not just by extending voting rights but also by ensuring that there exists a fully formed public opinion, accomplished by communication among citizens, experts and politicians, with the latter being accountable for the policies they adopt.

76. JW von Goethe (1749–1832), German writer and statesman. His works include four novels; epic and lyric poetry; prose and verse dramas; memoirs; an autobiography; literary and aesthetic criticism; and treatises on botany, anatomy, and colour.

77. John Alexander: actual name Jennie Alexander (1930–2018) of Baltimore, Maryland. Considered a pioneer in the woodworking world, 'Instrumental in designing the now iconic two-slat post-and-rung shaving chair'. She also coined the term 'greenwoodworking' as a single word in her book, *Make a Chair from a Tree: An Introduction to Working Green Wood*, 2nd edition, Taunton Press Inc. (1985).

78. Drew Langsner (b.1942), Los Angeles. Has practised traditional woodworking for over 25 years. He started Country Workshops in 1978 in Western North Carolina, where he teaches traditional woodworking with hand tools. He is the author of several books on woodworking.

79. Peter Korn, *Why we make things and why it matters*, David R Godine (2014).

80. Ben Law lives and works at Prickly Nut Wood in West Sussex. Apart from making a living from coppicing, he trains apprentices and runs courses on sustainable woodland management, eco-building and permaculture design. Ben also runs a few ticketed open days each year, to experience Prickly Nut Wood and visit the Woodland House. Ben specialises in Roundwood Timber Framing and has developed specialist jointing techniques for the architectural style of building he creates. These he passes on through his flagship Roundwood Timber Framing course. The building of his house was filmed for Channel 4's Grand Designs programme and was voted the most popular

Grand Design ever by viewers. Ben is also a prolific author, having written seven books. His latest book *Woodland Workshop* is a practical construction book of traditional and modern woodland devices. Translations of Ben's book *Woodland Craft* are available in French and German. Roundwood Timber Framing is also available in French.

81. Barnaby Alexander Carder, known as Barn the Spoon (b.1982), is a British artisan spoon carver, teacher, author and co-founder of Spoonfest, the annual international festival of spoon carving in Edale in Derbyshire, UK. He is also founder of the Green Wood Guild, a collective of green wood carvers who run carving workshops, and owns a spoon shop and woodworking venue in Hackney in London's East End. Carder also teaches spoon carving, woodworking and bladesmithing (with master smith Nic Westermann).

82. Sir Simon Michael Schama CBE FRSL FBA (b.1945) is an English historian specialising in art history, Dutch history, Jewish history and French history. He is a University Professor of History and Art History at Columbia University, New York.

83. *A History of Britain* is a three volume work written by Simon Schama to accompany a series of documentaries he presented for the BBC. The volumes are: *Volume I: At the Edge of the World 3000BC–AD1603*; *Volume 2 The British Wars 1603–1776*; *Volume 3 The Fate of Empire 1776–2000* (BBC Books 2003).

84. Alexander Langlands is a British archaeologist and historian, also known for his work as a presenter of the educational documentary series 'Digging up Britain's Past' on British television. *Craeft: How traditional Crafts are more than just making*, Faber & Faber (2017) ISBN 9780571324408

85. Jack Hill *Country Chair Making*, David & Charles (1998) ISBN-10: 0715303139

86. Norman Whymer *English Country Crafts*, B.T. Batsford Ltd (1946).

87. Philip Clissett (1817–1913) Victorian country chairmaker who influenced and inspired the English Arts and Crafts Movement through various architects and designers.

88. Ernest William Gimson (1864–1919) English furniture designer and architect. Gimson was described by the art critic Nikolaus Pevsner as 'the greatest of the English architect-designers'.

89. Peter Korn, *Why we make things and why it matters*, David R Godine (2014).

90. David William Pye OBE (1914–1993) Professor of Furniture Design at The Royal College of Art, 1964–1974. Among his pupils were David Colwell, Richard la Trobe Bateman, Charles Dillon, Jane Dillon, Floris van den Broecke and Roger Dean.

91. Donald Woods Winnicott FRCP (1896–1971) English paediatrician and psychoanalyst who was especially influential in the field of object relations theory and developmental psychology.

92. Otto Aron Solomon (1849–1907) Swedish educator and both a noted writer and proponent of educational sloyd. Born in Gothenburg, Sweden, Salomon studied at the Institute of Technology in Stockholm but left after a year to accept a position as Director of the Sloyd Teachers Seminary in Naas, Sweden.

93. David Ballantyne 'Renaissance Man of Clay' *Ceramic Review* 128 (1991) davidballantyne.net

94. John Ruskin (1819–1900) Leading English art critic of the Victorian era, as well as an art patron, draughtsman, watercolourist, prominent social thinker and philanthropist. He wrote on subjects as varied as geology, architecture, myth, ornithology, literature, education, botany and political economy.

95. Mohandas Karamchand Ghandi (1869–1948) Indian activist who was the leader of the Indian independence movement against British colonial rule. Employing nonviolent civil disobedience, Gandhi led India to independence and inspired movements for civil rights and freedom across the world.

96. John Ruskin (1819–1900) was a leading art critic in the Victorian era as well as an art patron, draughtsman, watercolourist, a prominent social thinker and philanthropist.

97. R. Sennett, The Craftsman, Allen Lane (2008).

98. Matthew Crawford, The Case for Working with your Hands, Penguin (2010)

99. Seamus Heaney, Door into the dark, a collection of poems, Faber and Faber (1969)

100. Alan Evans (b.1952) leading artist blacksmith, brought up in an Arts and Crafts Movement household in the Whiteway colony. On leaving Shoreditch Teacher Training college he was offered workshop space in exchange for 'help with heavy work' by Alan Knight, the blacksmith from Worcestershire. He set up his own forge in 1978 and began working almost exclusively in iron, he was one of the few makers at the time designing and making original/site-specific architectural ironwork rather than the (still prevalent) sub-18th-century style. In 1980 he was selected for the Crafts Council Index and shortly after won the design competition for the Saint Paul's Cathedral treasury gates sponsored by the Crafts Council.

101. Henry Wadsworth Longfellow (1807–1882) American poet and educator whose works include 'Paul Revere's Ride', The Song of Hiawatha, and Evangeline. He was also the first American to translate Dante Alighieri's Divine Comedy and was one of the Fireside Poets from New England.

102. Aonghus Gordon (b.1955) Founder & Director of Ruskin Mill Education Trust and Executive Chair: MEd BA PGCE Born in Gloucester; formative years spent in Venice. Attended Rudolf Steiner schools. Completed BA in Ceramics and Art History followed by teacher training, gaining a Post Graduate Certificate in Education at Breton Hall, Leeds in 1981. Travelled extensively before settling down in 1982 to renovate what is now called Ruskin Mill Art & Crafts Centre, Gloucestershire. Founded the Living Earth Training Course in 1984, co-founded Waldorf College, Stroud, Gloucestershire in 1999, established Glasshouse College, Stourbridge in 2000, co-founded Makhad Trust for endangered nomadic tribes particularly in Sinai and Tibet, in 2003, established Freeman College, Sheffield in 2005 and Brantwood Specialist School, Sheffield in 2011. In 2012 co-founded the MSc in Practical Skills Therapeutic Education, the method of Ruskin Mill Trust, with Crossfields Institute and the University of the West of England (UWE).

103. Edward Raymond Payne (1907–1991) Renowned stained glass artist who spent most of his working life in Box living in the house known as the 'Triangle'. He was born in 1906 in Birmingham. His father Henry, a teacher at the Municipal School of Art in Birmingham, married Edith Gere in 1901. They were both members of the Birmingham Group of artists and had close links with the Arts & Crafts Movement. In 1909 they moved to Amberley in Gloucestershire.

104. William Morris (1834–1896) British textile designer, poet, novelist, translator and socialist activist associated with the British Arts and Crafts Movement. He was a major contributor to the revival of traditional British textile arts and methods of production.

105. John Ruskin (1819–1900) Leading English art critic of the Victorian era, as well as an art patron, draughtsman, watercolourist, prominent social thinker and philanthropist. He wrote on subjects as varied as geology, architecture, myth, ornithology, literature, education, botany and political economy.

106. Christopher Whitworth Whall (1849–1924) British stained-glass artist widely recognised as a leader in the Arts and Crafts Movement and a key figure in the modern history of stained glass.

107. El Greco (1541–1614) Doménikos Theotokópoulos, most widely known as El Greco. Greek Renaissance painter, sculptor and architect of the Spanish Renaissance.

108. Fact of Fiction? Glass is a (supercooled) Liquid – Scientific American – 22 February 2007

109. Pliny the Elder (AD23–AD79) Naturalist, author, philosopher, naval and military commander, friend of the Emperor Vaspasian.

110. Johann Wolfgang von Goethe (1748–1832) German writer and statesman. His works include four novels; epic and lyric poetry; prose and verse dramas; memoirs; an autobiography; literary and aesthetic criticism; and treatises on botany, anatomy, and colour. *Theory of Colours* (German: Zur Farbenlehre), John Murray (1810), about the poet's views on the nature of colours and how these are perceived by humans ... Unlike Newton, Goethe's concern was not so much with the analytic treatment of colour, as with the qualities of how phenomena are perceived.

111. Wilhelm Pelikan, *The Secrets of Metals*, Steiner Books Inc (1973).

112. Plutarch, Moralia (c.AD100). The passage quoted continues as follows: 'Imagine, then, that a man

should need to get fire from a neighbour, and, upon finding a big bright fire there, should stay there continually warming himself; just so it is if a man comes to another to share the benefit of a discourse, and does not think it necessary to kindle from it some illumination for himself and some thinking of his own, but, delighting in the discourse, sits enchanted; he gets, as it were, a bright and ruddy glow in the form of opinion imparted to him by what is said, but the mouldiness and darkness of his inner mind he has not dissipated nor banished by the warm glow of philosophy.'

113. William Butler Yeats (1865–1939) Irish poet and one of the foremost figures of 20th-century literature. A pillar of the Irish literary establishment, he helped to found the Abbey Theatre, and in his later years served as a Senator of the Irish Free State for two terms.

114. Plutarch (c. AD46–AD120), born in Greece, later named, upon becoming a Roman citizen, Lucius Mestrius Plutarchus. Greek biographer and essayist, known primarily for his *Parallel Lives* and *Moralia*. He is classified as a Middle Platonist. Plutarch's surviving works were written in Greek, but intended for both Greek and Roman readers.

115. Gert Biesta uses this reference at the outset of his book *The Beautiful Risk of Education*, Routledge (2016).

116. A commonly used fungus for its ability to smoulder slowly over a long period of time – and thus prolong the life of an ember – is *Fomes fomentarius*, also known as the Hoof Fungus.

117. A common name for *Clematis vitalba*, also known as Traveller's Joy or the wild clematis. The dried, 'silky appendages' of the seeds are used as tinder by some fire-lighters in climates where this plant grows.

118. Many websites provide in-depth instruction into how to source and prepare fire-lighting tools and what types of tinder are suitable. It is not the intention of this chapter to duplicate material that is so readily available and easily accessible. These very informative sources for learning the fire-lighting craft will, however, need to be worked with in the kindler's own context in order to contextualise the instructions given.

119. Johann Wolfgang von Goethe (1748–1832) German writer and statesman. His works include four novels; epic and lyric poetry; prose and verse dramas; memoirs; an autobiography; literary and aesthetic criticism; and treatises on botany, anatomy, and colour. Quote: 'Knowing is not enough; we must apply. Willing is not enough; we must do.'

120. Ernst Lehrs (1894–1979) German anthroposophist, Waldorf teacher, lecturer and writer.

121. The Old Lakota By Wisdom Pills / wisdompills.com / Mar 3, 2015.

Luther Standing Bear was an Oglala Lakota Sioux Chief who, among a few rare others such as Charles Eastman, Black Elk and Gertrude Bonnin occupied the rift between the way of life of the Indigenous people of the Great Plains before, and during, the arrival and subsequent spread of the European pioneers. Raised in the traditions of his people until the age of eleven, he was then educated at the Carlisle Indian Industrial Boarding School of Pennsylvania, where he learned the English language and way of life. (Though a National Historical Landmark, Carlisle remains a place of controversy in Native circles.)

Like his above mentioned contemporaries, however, his native roots were deep, leaving him in the unique position of being a conduit between cultures. Though his movement through the white man's world was not without 'success" – he had numerous movie roles in Hollywood – his enduring legacy was the protection of the way of life of his people. By the time of his death he had published four books and had become a leader at the forefront of the progressive movement aimed at preserving Native American heritage and sovereignty, coming to be known as a strong voice in the education of the white man as to the Native American way of life.

122. Edward O Wilson, *Biophilia*, Harvard University Press (1984).

123. Professor David Orr is the Paul Sears Distinguished Professor of Environmental Studies and Politics at Oberlin College and a James Mars Professor at the University of Vermont.

124. Wendy Titman, *Special Places, Special People: The Hidden Curriculum of School Grounds*, Southgate Publishers (1994). The research project 'Special Places; Special People' is designed to provide insight

and advice in the management of schools and their grounds for the benefit of children. This document describes the project's research methodology and findings, explores some of the wider implications arising from the study, and suggests ways in which schools might embark upon effecting change. Research findings are discussed on how children read the external environment and school grounds. Issues arising from these findings examine the importance of school grounds to children in a modern society, the messages school grounds convey about the ethos of schools, and children's attitudes and behaviour that are determined by the school grounds and the way they are managed. The report's concluding section contains an alphabetical listing of references and resource information on school grounds development, play theory, children and the environment, children's games, and lunchtime supervision and management. (GR) https://files.eric.ed.gov/fulltext/ED430384.pdf

125. 'Environmental psychology' https://www.englishoutdoorcouncil.org/research.in.outdoor.learning. html

This section provides summaries of key findings from reviews of research and major studies in Outdoor Learning. Each review asks different questions about a different kinds of Outdoor Learning. The overall impact of these collections of research studies is impressive. They demonstrate what can be achieved through Outdoor Learning. The outdoors provides a wide array of opportunities for achieving a whole range of outcomes. Some outcomes require careful design and facilitation, whereas other outcomes simply arise from being outdoors.

126. Doris Lessing CH OMG (1919–2013) British-Zimbabwean novelist, born to British parents in Iran, where she lived until 1925. Her family then moved to Southern Rhodesia, where she remained until moving in 1949 to London, England. Awarded Nobel Prize in Literature.

127. Nancy M. Wells and Kristi S. Lekies, 'Nature and the Life Course: Pathways from Childhood Nature Experiences to Adult Environmentalism.' Children, Youth and Environments 16(1): 1-24 (2006). Retrieved from http://www.colorado.edu/journals/cye/.

128. Guidance about teaching citizenship in England, Department of Education, 16th Feb 2015.

129. Abraham Harold Maslow (1908–1970) American psychologist who was best known for creating Maslow's hierarchy of needs, a theory of psychological health predicated on fulfilling innate human needs in priority, culminating in self-actualisation.

130. Dr Barry Durrant-Peatfield MB BS LRCP MRCS: Your Thyroid and How to Keep it Healthy: The Great Thyroid Scandal and How to Survive it, Hammersmith Press, London (2006).

131. Every Child Matters. Statutory guidance to UK Border Agency on making arrangements to safeguard and promote the welfare of children: UK Home Office, Issued under Section 55 Borders, Citizenship and Immigration Act 2009.

132. George Joshua Richard Monbiot (b.1963) is a British writer known for his environmental political activism. He writes a weekly column for *The Guardian* newspaper and is the author of a number of books, including *Captive State: The Corporate Takeover of Britain*, Macmillan (2000) and *Feral: Searching for Enchantment on the Frontiers of Rewilding*, Allen Lane (2013). He is the founder of The

Land is Ours, a peaceful campaign for the right of access to the countryside and its resources in the United Kingdom www.monbiot.com/

133. David Mitchell and Patricia Livingston: *Will-Developed Intelligence*, Association of Waldorf Schools in North America (1999).

134. Jared Diamond, *Guns, germs and steel: A short history of everybody for the last 13,000 years*, (Chapter 12, 'Blueprints and Borrowed Letters' p 195, 295), Rhone-Poulenc Science prize-winning book, Vintage (1998).

135. The Alliance for Childhood is a tax-exempt non-profit research and advocacy organisation founded in February 1999, incorporated in the US state of Maryland, and based in College Park, Maryland. A partnership of educators, health professionals, researchers and other advocates for children, some of whom are supporters of Waldorf education, its stated mission is to 'promote policies and practices that support children's healthy development, love of learning, and joy in living. Our public education campaigns bring to light both the promise and the vulnerability of childhood. We act for the sake of the children themselves and for a more just, democratic, and ecologically responsible future.'

The Alliance's work in its first ten years has focused on the following issues:

- Defending and restoring child-initiated, open-ended play in and out of school.
- Challenging the overuse of computers in education and the proliferation of electronic entertainment in children's lives.
- Questioning the misuse of standardized high-stakes testing in education.
- Working with other groups, especially the Campaign for a Commercial-Free Childhood, to end marketing to children.
- Raising public awareness of the childhood obesity problem.
- Promoting education for peace.

The Alliance's reports and position statements have inspired hundreds of news reports. The publication of 'Fool's Gold: A Critical Look at Computers in Childhood in 2000' ignited a national conversation about technology and children, as reported in The New York Times by Katie Hafner. A follow-up report, 'Tech Tonic: Towards a New Literacy of Technology', was published by the Alliance in 2004.

In March 2009 the Alliance published 'Crisis in the Kindergarten: Why Children Need to Play in School', written by Edward Miller and Joan Almon, two founders of the organisation. Its findings – that children in all-day public kindergartens in New York and Los Angeles were spending most of their time being instructed and tested on literacy and maths, with almost no time for free play – provoked a flurry of reactions, including a column by Peggy Orenstein in The New York Times Magazine.

136. Richard Louv, Last Child in the Woods: Saving our Children from Nature-Deficit Disorder, Atlantic Books (2005).

137. David W. Orr is the Paul Sears Distinguished Professor of Environmental Studies and Politics at Oberlin College and a James Marsh Professor at the University of Vermont.